THE STARLIT DOME

by the same Author

*

THE STARLIT DOME

Studies in the Poetry of Vision

by

G. WILSON KNIGHT

with an Introduction by
W. F. JACKSON KNIGHT
and an Appendix on
Spiritualism and Poetry

A starlit or a moonlit dome disdains
All that man is,
All mere complexities,
The fury and the mire of human veins.

W. B. YEATS

Methuen & Co Ltd
11 NEW FETTER LANE · EC4

ORIGINALLY PUBLISHED BY THE OXFORD UNIVERSITY PRESS IN 1941
REPRINTED IN 1943
FIRST PUBLISHED BY METHUEN, 1959
REPRINTED IN 1964
CAT. NO. 2/6150/10

1·2

PRINTED BY LUND HUMPHRIES
LONDON AND BRADFORD

TO MY BROTHER

W. F. JACKSON KNIGHT

CONTENTS

PREFACE

THIS reprint follows the original edition with only a very few corrections. I have remedied the misunderstanding of Wordsworth's 'bell-bird' on pages 78–9, to which I drew attention in the 1943 reprint after being told of it by Mr. Frank C. Nicholson. I regret certain slipshod abbreviations of titles, and there are other roughnesses. The text was hurriedly and severely compressed for publication at Cheltenham during the anxious summer of 1940. But I have attempted no proper revision, since the exigencies of offset printing preclude all but essential alterations.

My study of *Kubla Khan* was originally undertaken on a suggestion from Mr. Francis Berry that I should turn my interpretative methods to an elucidation of Coleridge's three most famous poems, and it appeared first in *Programme* (Oxford, Oct., 1935) during the early thirties. I would take this opportunity of drawing attention to the striking advance in poetic exegesis marked by Mr. Berry's *Poets' Grammar* (1958), and in particular to the importance of its commentary on Shelley and Keats.

The essay 'Spiritualism and Poetry' was first published in *Light*, March 1956. References in the following pages are to the Oxford University Press editions of the poets concerned. I record my gratitude to Dr. Patricia M. Ball for contributing a much-needed index to this new edition.

LEEDS, DECEMBER 1958   G.W.K.

My attention has been drawn by Mr. Munir Ahmad to Coleridge's interesting dramatic fragment *Diadesté*, printed by Earl Leslie Griggs in *Modern Philology*, Chicago, May 1937 (vol. 34, pp. 377–85).

INTRODUCTION
TO THE NEW IMPRESSION
by
W. F. JACKSON KNIGHT

WHEN, to our great pleasure, we heard that *The Starlit Dome* would be reprinted, my brother said that he could not quite see how to write an introduction to the new impression, reviving his interests of long ago. I told him that I thought that it would be easy to write at least something, and indeed that I could do it myself. To my surprise he took this seriously.

After his first three books of Shakespearian 'interpretation' my brother wrote a number of long notes on various English authors for the use of undergraduates. He came to think that some of these notes might make a book on two sorts of poets, different, but each sort successive to Shakespeare. They were the poets of vision, such as Shelley, and the poets of action, such as Byron. The book started, and grew; and divided into two books. *The Burning Oracle*, on the poets of action, came out in 1939. Its contents are now being dispersed and amplified, and two of the essays have been incorporated in *Laureate of Peace* and *The Sovereign Flower*. *The Starlit Dome*, on the poets of vision, came out in 1941. It went out of print; and is to reappear in 1959.

The Starlit Dome applied to Wordsworth, Coleridge, Shelley and Keats an 'interpretative' method which was already well known. Not only does this book use this method, but it clarifies it, because the examples are peculiarly fortunate and impressive, and may easily be the best introduction to such 'interpretation'. The method is a decipherment, like a decipherment of pictographs when no bilingual inscription is available and meaning can only be extracted through comparison of symbols and symbol-groups. Poets, especially these 'romantic' poets, tell strange, wild stories full of outlandish occurrences and ideas drawn from their imagination or fancy but most often their imagination. Those who read their poems like them for various reasons, which affect and condition their reaction. But the main reaction is below the level of clear consciousness. The message is felt, which is good. If it can also be understood, that is better still. To make the poetry more clearly intelligible, what is called 'the spatial approach' can be used. The time-sequence of the story is put in the background; and the people, animals and things in it are observed in their places, as if the story did not continue in time, but could all be seen at once in a single view, like a patterned carpet. The same kinds of people, animals, and things are then seen to occur, similarly grouped, in many different places. Associations suggest meanings, and, if the meanings are right, other associations elsewhere confirm them. In this way many powerful symbols are identified and interpreted. The poetry of these 'romantic' poets is very highly symbolic; and this symbolic language urgently needed to be explained. How it is worked out is very impressive.

The 'dome' itself may fairly claim the chief importance. A 'dome' had become a frequent symbol before the Romantic Period, and in that period became more frequent still. A dome is sometimes what we now understand by a dome, but the word is cognate with other words conveying other meanings, for example, 'cathedral' or merely 'house'. Now the poets regularly introduce an edifice of some sort when they are thinking about aspiration generated in human life. Human life flows onwards, but it is not content with the horizontal flow. We aspire to a reality more high, and more stable and permanent; that is, to an eternity. How neat, and how satisfying, these identifications can be is shown in this book by the interpretation of Coleridge's *Kubla Khan*, which is probably the clearest and most quickly convincing example of the method and its results so far published. In this poem the human river comes from the dark and goes to the dark, and the mere flow would have little value and little refreshment if there were not also the 'sunny pleasure-dome, with caves of ice', permanent above. When so much is noticed, every detail in the poem falls into place. Further, the poem is at last known for what it is, a well-formed and comprehensive, though concise, solution to an important, if not the most important, problem, and not at all the unintelligible fragment which it used to be considered.

Seldom has it been made more clear than it has in some passages of *The Starlit Dome* that a poem may have quite a different meaning than any intended, or even understood, by the poet who wrote it. Coleridge himself said in a modest note that he did not himself understand some lines in his poem *The Destiny of Nations*, but thought them fine lines, nevertheless. A comparison of them with *Kubla Khan* has now made them intelligible.

Kubla Khan reveals a pattern which all the four poets examined in the book followed in their life-work. Wordsworth spent about the first half of his on the visible nature in which life is lived, and the other half, approximately, on the other sphere of being which is symbolized in domes and other edifices. Shelley's aspiration towards the eternal world is so passionate that in one of his characteristic figures his rivers actually appear to flow uphill into mountains on which, finally, edifices are found. Keats' symbols are as clear as any one's, but all the way along he notably blends all the opposites together, nature and art, the temporal and the spatial, life as it is and aspiration, and indeed time and eternity. Once his 'dome' becomes a Grecian urn, with ardent living still pictured on it in eternal permanence.

It is not too soon, but I am scarcely the one, to proclaim the measure of the achievement which such 'interpretation' represents. I have watched it going on

for nearly forty years, in anxiety, in pride, and in content-
ment; and have admired this superb and sustained force
of intellectual activity with an admiration which, if it is to
be expressed, must be expressed rather on some other
occasion than on this.

W.F.J.K.

EXETER, SEPTEMBER 1958

I

THE WORDSWORTHIAN PROFUNDITY

I

THE best single key to Wordsworth's life-work is his *Recluse* fragment (as such I shall henceforward refer to it, there being no title) printed in his own preface to *The Excursion*. This may serve as a general introduction. The poet invokes Urania or some 'greater muse', since he is to

> breathe in worlds
> To which the heaven of heavens is but a veil.

No Jehovahs nor other old imaginings of chaos, hell, or utter vacancy

> can breed such fear and awe
> As fall upon us often when we look
> Into our Minds, into the Mind of Man—
> My haunt, and the main region of my song.

Yet Beauty accompanies the dark adventure. Old paradises, Elysian fields, Atlantis are all rough outlines of a truth, of some psychological possibility:

> For the discerning intellect of Man,
> When wedded to this goodly universe
> In love and holy passion, shall find these
> A simple produce of the common day.

Marriage metaphors are powerful. Wordsworth himself chants in loneliness the 'spousal verse' of this 'great consummation': he will speak, he says, in realistic terms to awake 'the sensual' (i.e. those prisoned by normal sense-perception) 'from their sleep'. He will assert (i) how 'exquisitely' the mind, with all other 'progressive powers' of the race, is 'fitted' to its 'external world', and (ii) how 'exquisitely' that world is 'fitted' to the mind. This

appears to him a 'high argument' of supreme importance.
The process and its results he explicitly asserts to deserve
the dignified title of a 'creation'. Poetry is the language
of the higher integration, and the fusion metaphorically
throws up a *sacred structure*:

> Descend, prophetic Spirit! that inspir'st
> The human Soul of universal earth,
> Dreaming on things to come; and dost possess
> A metropolitan temple in the hearts
> Of mighty Poets. . . .

Wordsworth's life-work is compacted in this fragment
It and my essay will prove therefore mutually interpreta
tive.

I shall next discuss *The Prelude*. This must be read as
both (i) a roughly true autobiographical account, and (ii)
a series of poetic meditations in maturity. Detailed theses
concerning the sincerity of Wordsworth's self-examination
lead to a morass of insoluble problems. Were it not for
Wordsworth's poetry we should not trouble about his
life: therefore his life as here reflected by his poetry exists
in its own right. However, my present purpose, concerned
primarily with attention to key-passages of importance,
need lay no emphasis on narrative sequence.

Here, as in the *Recluse* fragment, Wordsworth emphasizes the complexity of human experience involving
(i) the mind with both its emotions and laws of thought,
and (ii) the objective, normally the natural, world. These
are felt in significant interplay:

> To every natural form, rock, fruit, or flower,
> Even the loose stones that cover the high-way,
> I gave a moral life: I saw them feel,
> Or linked them to some feeling: the great mass
> Lay bedded in a quickening soul, and all
> That I beheld respired with inward meaning.
>
> (III. 127)

The passage is basic. The 'great mass' and heavy
inanimacy has a living, moral, and almost personal,

existence. Such a recognition is, indeed, active within all metaphoric speech; in poetry itself widely understood; and, finally, implied by the very nature of consciousness. Wordsworth's nature-mysticism is at once a theory of poetry and an analysis of consciousness.

He sees psychological origins in maternal terms (ii. 232–65). To the child all is coloured by its mother's personality, the flower picked for it is mother-toned, all ugly things suffused by a predominant and nurturing love. Therefore it is an inmate of an 'active universe': a universe living, because humanized, indeed strictly personal. Now this original experience need not be lost but should continue to grow as agent of the 'one great mind' and steadily 'create, creator and receiver both' from daily intercourse with objective phenomena. This greater spirit remains specifically maternal and is also called 'poetic', and may remain 'pre-eminent till death'. The statement is profound, and relates deeply to the Christian tradition, while also clarifying the mother-complex so close-rooted in literature, and sometimes almost seeming, as Wordsworth suggests, to condition poetic creation. He describes his own mother (v. 246–93) with an introduction on the 'parent hen' recalling Shakespeare's comparison in *Coriolanus* and a neat reference of maternal trust to divine care. For she left her children to natural impulse, having faith

> that He
> Who fills the mother's breast with innocent milk,
> Doth also for our nobler part provide. . . .   (v. 271)

Trust is placed in 'innocent instincts' and the 'simplicities of opening life': so 'weeds' yield 'honey' and all that is misnamed 'evil' ceases to threaten danger. You can see why mothers and children are important throughout Wordsworth. The growing child still holds 'unconscious intercourse with beauty old as creation' and drinks in 'organic pleasure' from mist and lake (i. 562–6). Being one with the creative process it 'sits upon a throne' of

more power than 'all the elements' and points equally to
pre-existence and the life to come (v. 508): the *Immortality Ode* is closely suggested. As for the mother, he can
image a happy 'mother and child' even although the latter
'sleeps in earth' (VII. 316–29). Both are archetypal figures
training our deeper understanding, while the earth itself
is the great 'grandame' of us all, designing playthings of
nature for her children (v. 337).

The transition to moral categories is easy. Human love
may be distinguished as (i) *eros*, and (ii) *agapé*; the one
usually considered instinctive, the other often directly
related to divine grace. I have elsewhere argued that
agapé is as closely rooted in parental or filial emotions as
eros in those sexual; and Wordsworth supports the contention. He is always attracted by both helpless infancy
and weak, or strongly enduring, old age. For example,
he writes of ballad-tunes,

> Food for the hungry ears of little ones
> And of old men who have survived their joys.
>
> (v. 211)

A typical figure, too, is his old man seen in London bringing
a 'sickly babe' regularly to a certain grass plot for the sunshine (VII. 608). The emotion behind and raised by such
creations is deeply Wordsworthian; and is, moreover, felt
in organic continuity with nature. He tells how nature's
'fountains' generated in him love of an unsexual sort, not
even contingent on ordinary friendship, a 'kindliness of
heart' and 'love for the human creature's absolute self'
(that is, essential personality) to be distinguished from
more spectacular, romantic, and glamorous delights
(VIII. 121–44). The sub-title of Book VIII runs: 'Love
of Nature leading to love of Man.' Wordsworth redis-
covers that conviction and selfless compulsion which in
the New Testament demands love of mankind through a
feeling for the universal parenthood of God. Yet something is lacking. His sympathy is never, as St. Paul's,
ardent: it remains somewhat cold and austere.

Indeed, *The Prelude* insists continually on nature's sterner moods, with a definite preference for winter over summer, and darkness, or, what is grimmer, cheerless gloom, over light. Wordsworth claims indeed to love the sun (II. 177–88), yet it seems to be most enjoyed if 'unfelt' (II. 93). Certain passages, as at the end of Book II, announce a healthy, pantheistic, gospel of natural life in all its obvious excellence. He describes the tingling intermixture of man, starry universe, and the divine in one 'blaze' (VIII. 476–94). But the most convincing and urgent passages are, definitely, sunless. Unless the scene be wintry or foggy he prefers night-time or, at the most, sunset. Once he admits that his dark moods lead him to these preferences (VI. 171–8). The most energetic realization of spontaneous and communal joy is the famous, but wintry, description of skating:

> So through the darkness and the cold we flew,
> And not a voice was idle; with the din
> Smitten, the precipices rang aloud;
> The leafless trees and every icy crag
> Tinkled like iron.   (I. 438)

The approach of winter is felt as a poetic inspiration in a long introductory passage of great interest (VII. 1–42). He can, certainly, express at times a more sunny spirit, but generally favours naked ridges, gaunt rocks, and dreary wastes, and seems most happy addressing those 'souls of lonely places' that 'haunt' him (I. 466–9). His is, pre-eminently, a *ghostly* apprehension. He goes for lonely night-walks in an 'elevated mood by form or image unprofaned' (II. 305), queer though the phrase may seem for a nature-poet. Such experiences touch not so much 'our purer mind and intellectual life' (that is, the daylight, rationalizing consciousness) as some obscure, darkly possible sublimity, or profundity, beyond man's normal comprehension. He then apologizes (II. 322–9), as though half-guiltily surprised, assuring us that he could find strength from happier scenes too: and the apology speaks volumes.

In his valuable study *Scepticism and Poetry* Mr. D. G.
James has already discussed *The Prelude's* more grim
apprehensions. My own choice of incidents and quotations often follows his, while both his and my treatment
might be compared with A. C. Bradley's essay on Wordsworth in *Oxford Lectures on Poetry*, to which Mr. James
refers his own readers. Wordsworth tells in Book VIII
(376–9) how, when he first attempted poetry, nature and
his fictions began a process of mutual beautifying similar
to that we have already discussed:

> From touch of this new power
> Nothing was safe: the elder-tree that grew
> Beside the well-known charnel-house had then
> A dismal look; the yew-tree had its ghost.

Hearing of a widow who died in misery he actually delights to image her as 'wetting the turf with never-ending
tears' (VIII. 384–91). The morbid pleasure makes contact
with the highly respectable fascination of horror-stories.
Even more striking is his ghastly experience (v. 426–59)
when at twilight he sees unclaimed garments by the
'breathless stillness' of a lake. The scene-description
deliberately aims to convey an other-worldly, anti-
natural, sense of eternity-apprehension. Next day follows
the business of grappling irons and recovery of the body
which

> . . . bolt upright
> Rose, with his ghastly face, a spectre shape
> Of terror. . . .

He, a child of nine years old, actually revelled in it; or
thinks afterwards that he did. He was already used to such
things, his 'inner eye' having experienced them already
in faery romances whose spirit thus 'hallowed' the spec-
tacle, giving it an 'ideal grace' and a classic, poetic, dignity.
The description is profoundly interesting, and may be
related to both the sense one sometimes experiences
after nightmare of a warm, comfortable, and thoroughly
pleasant remembrance, and to the horror-tendencies and

cathartic processes of great literature. Wordsworth is here, as so often, claiming to have experienced directly what most of us know only through dreams and artistic composition or receptivity. The incident is amazingly introduced by:

> Well do I call to mind the very week
> When I was first entrusted to the care
> Of that sweet valley.

Nature's maternal care is thus to be directly associated with deathly horrors. In Wordsworth a 'sorrow' that is 'delight' and a 'misery' not exactly painful in report directly furthers his sense of man's true being and glorious destiny (xiii. 245–9).

There is, too, his riding by chance against a gibbet in a spot supposed haunted by the murderer hanged there, and his subsequent flying in terror and seeing a girl with a pitcher battling against the wind by a 'naked' pool under a 'lone eminence': a characteristic setting. Later, at a period of young love—one of the very few such references —his pleasure is enriched, and not exactly by contrast, through treasured remembrance of that 'visionary dreariness' (xii. 225–71). The passage is introduced by a talk on the 'renovating virtue' of certain experiences that teach us how the mind is a 'lord and master' with 'outward sense' its slave, and capped by advice that we must give in order to receive. The mind in such passages receives more emphasis than objective nature; or we can say that the poet deliberately selects, or instinctively remembers, objects of a peculiar sort. In the same book (xii. 287–335) the boy Wordsworth spends an afternoon on a wild day by a 'naked well' with a 'single sheep' one way and a 'blasted hawthorn' the other way, dreaming of the coming holidays. Next, his father dies: which he accepts as a reproof of that afternoon's carefree enjoyment, yet thereafter derives a stern pleasure from remembering 'the bleak music from that old stone wall'. He is resting back, in deepest, almost filial, reliance on all deathly impressions

and their reflection in natural phenomena. He is an other-
worldly inhabitant, nourished best by all that opens out
avenues of haunting mystery and desolate horror.

The experience is both tragic and transcendent; and,
though not painful, weighted with gloom. His mountains
are thus peculiarly his own: they are gaunt symbols of
immensity, of the inhuman, of unalterable place and
eternal power. Through them, or in them, he focuses
supernal, dark yet living, existences. He describes how,
rowing by evening, he felt the live power of a great rock:

> When, from behind that craggy steep till then
> The horizon's bound, a huge peak, black and huge,
> As if with voluntary power instinct
> Upreared its head. I struck, and struck again,
> And growing still in stature the grim shape
> Towered up between me and the stars, and still,
> For so it seemed, with purpose of its own
> And measured motion like a living thing,
> Strode after me.   (I. 377)

In terms of such awful imaginations the fusion of mind
and inanimate matter is most powerfully accomplished.
Elemental giant-beings are thus envisioned, or created,
behind or beyond daylight reason and almost independent
of manifestation. For many days after his brain

> Worked with a dim and undetermined sense
> Of unknown modes of being: o'er my thoughts
> There hung a darkness, call it solitude
> Or blank desertion. No familiar shapes
> Remained, no pleasant images of trees,
> Of sea or sky, no colours of green fields;
> But huge and mighty forms, that do not live
> Like living men, moved slowly through the mind
> By day, and were a trouble to my dreams.   (I. 392)

This passage holds the key to much in Wordsworth.
Notice the 'solitude' closely related to other-worldly
intuitions. It helps us, too, towards elucidation of certain
technical problems raised by his work. In *A Midsummer*

Night's Dream the poet glances from earth to heaven, imagination next 'bodies forth the *forms* of things unknown', and the poet's pen translates these to '*shapes*': Wordsworth presents a similar contrast. Now since 'familiar shapes' and natural 'images' are clearly at least half of the poet's, especially the nature-poet's, stock-in-trade, our passage constitutes almost an attack on poetry itself. What then can a poet do with such at once abysmal and transcendental experience? Yet the experience is itself surely in some sense poetic, and the vast 'forms' indicated close or distant relations to those more precisely dramatized in Milton and Byron's *Cain*; or, to choose more colourful expositions, Shelley's *Prometheus* and Keats's *Hyperion*. Insistent questions swarm about the passage. Of course, it is itself in reality composed of symbolic 'shapes'; moreover, the experience recorded is a kind of poetry. Wordsworth is living a mythology. Therefore in another great passage he asserts that anyone properly responsive to nature will react similarly to that 'great Nature that exists in works of mighty poets', the technical process of poetic composition being analogous to that very fusion Wordsworth claims to have experienced in actuality:

> Visionary power
> Attends the motions of the viewless winds,
> Embodied in the mystery of words:
> There, darkness makes abode, and all the host
> Of shadowy things work endless changes—there,
> As in a mansion like their proper home,
> Even forms and substances are circumfused
> By that transparent veil with light divine,
> And, through the turnings intricate of verse,
> Present themselves as objects recognised,
> In flashes, and with glory not their own. (v. 595)

The passage is confusing. Invisible 'power' is 'embodied' in words; darkness and shadowy forces push up, to the surface, the ever-changing appearance; 'forms and substances', vague eternal presences, find their home here

and receive, through expression, a 'light divine'; presenting themselves as 'objects' which we can recognize (either
through their realistic projection or because we feel dimly
the deeper meanings); and finally something results
known in 'flashes' of insight and enjoying a glory beyond
itself. In a similar fashion Wordsworth reacts, for no
particular reason, to the news that he has just crossed
the Alps. Some vast, crushingly superhuman, and eternal
presence is revealed, or darkly felt:

> But to my conscious soul I now can say—
> 'I recognise thy glory': in such strength
> Of usurpation, when the light of sense
> Goes out, but with a flash that has revealed
> The invisible world, doth greatness make abode,
> There harbours.   (vi. 598)

This revelation through sense-extinction may assist the
reading of horror-passages together with Wordsworth's
continual obsession with death. There is an awful disclosure revealing heights and depths unsearchable,
clothed as a mountain-force earthed in the eternal and
darkly clouded by infinitude. An 'immeasurable height
of woods decaying, never to be decayed' symbolizes the
fusion of time and eternity; sky-born waterfalls seeming still present an identity of fluid and solid; rocks that
'mutter' express a living, sounding, inanimacy:

> Black drizzling crags that spake by the wayside
> As if a voice were in them, the sick sight
> And giddy prospect of the raving stream,
> The unfettered clouds and region of the Heavens,
> Tumult and peace, the darkness and the light—
> Were all like workings of one mind, the features
> Of the same face, blossoms upon one tree;
> Characters of the great Apocalypse,
> The types and symbols of Eternity,
> Of first, and last, and midst, and without end.
> (vi. 624-40)

The statement compresses a miniature of the creative

mystery. Movement and stillness are blended. Darkness and light, as in our recent passage on poetry, replace the more abysmal glooms and presences. The mountain, too, is itself felt as truly alive before becoming a symbol. The balances are beautifully held. It is Wordsworth's *Prelude* equivalent to Coleridge's dome in *Kubla Khan*.

These awe-inspiring revelations open abysses of the subjective consciousness:

> Caverns there were within my mind which sun
> Could never penetrate.   (III. 243)

This is the 'half-known world' Melville once wrote of as dangerous and, if submitted to, all-demanding, akin almost to madness. Nature as usually understood is scarcely here honoured at all: human choice or human associations play a dominating part. Wordsworth asserts that the mind is no 'mere pensioner on outward forms' (VI. 737). Scenes, moreover, are 'more potent' when impressed on it 'with an appropriate human centre' (IV. 354-70): the hermit in his wilderness, the votary in a vast cathedral, the watchman on some storm-lashed Atlantic lighthouse, a deserted road as the 'soul' of the 'great power', Solitude. These correspond to the pine-grove beyond the woodman's reach and the lonely house supposed a witch's home in Coleridge's *Dejection*, where the Satanic associations serve as an interesting commentary on Wordsworth. The dread power of these desolate scenes thus forces the creation of many solitary human figures of an other-worldly significance. There is the 'blind beggar' in London with a label telling his name felt as a symbol of an ultimate human destiny, his 'sightless eyes' serving as an 'admonishment' from 'another world' (VII. 639-49). In a deathly still scene setting the stage for some appalling recognition Wordsworth sees by moonlight a soldier, meagre, uncouth, pallid, and alone; a being of 'desolation', 'simplicity', and an 'awful steadiness'. When addressed he picks up his 'oaken staff' and tells his tale, walking as a 'ghostly figure':

in all he said
There was a strange half-absence, as of one
Knowing too well the importance of his theme,
But feeling it no longer.   (IV. 370–447)

The serenity resembles that induced by poetic, especially
tragic, composition. Such figures are, as Mr. D. G. James
well observes, beyond passion and grief, resembling
Keats's Moneta. There is an utterly unattached awareness of emotional stress, but no actual emotion. Wordsworth's *subject-matter* is poetry itself. Just as those
eternity-structures, his mountains, become almost personal, so his favourite, usually solitary, persons become
likewise symbols of eternity. *Resolution and Independence*,
to step out of *The Prelude* for a moment, provides our best
example. The poem penetrates far deeper than its title
and superficial didacticism indicate. A mood of 'dim sadness' and 'blind thoughts', with meditation on the tragic
destiny of man and especially of 'mighty poets in their
misery dead', frames the advent of a lonely, aged,
figure:

The oldest man he seemed that ever wore grey hairs.

He is compared to 'a huge stone' on 'the bald top of an
eminence' whose position makes it seem a 'thing endued
with sense', like some 'sea-beast crawled forth' 'to sun
itself'. He appears neither all alive, nor dead, nor asleep,
standing 'motionless as a cloud'. You see how nature's
enigmatic and awful appearances are identified with a
human figure of this lonely, enduring, unemotional, type.
The poem is more than a eulogy of endurance. It
attempts a reference of the deeps of human personality
to man's natural setting and tragic destiny. These are
all, moreover, self-exploitations; for Wordsworth too is
solitary, monastic, and prophetic in cast of mind, bearing
as best he may some awful yet mystically placid, yet again
disturbing, revelation. His simple heroic persons, he
takes care to tell you, are not literary poets; and neither,
in his main direction, is he. He is rather a lonely prophet
of the eternal.

Wordsworth sounds profundities of the individual personality not apparent to the objective reason. He would touch the 'point' within the souls of all men 'where all stand single' (III. 185). Its voice is 'imagination', the 'awful Power' rising from 'the mind's abyss' (VI. 594). These abysses, it would seem, demand expression in terms of a wild and rugged nature, dark frowning heights, terror and death, tragic experience being the readiest way to split open the two worlds of subject and object and show the subjective self in its dark abysmal nakedness. There is an all but ultimate disparity between the 'I' of personality and any objective reality whatsoever. Now it is this ultimate 'I' Wordsworth explores; what Coleridge meant by the 'eternal I am', repeating a Biblical phrase; what I have referred to as the 'I'-ness of persons revealed, though very differently, in Shakespeare. Wordsworth fascinatingly relates this mystery to a dark, almost cruel, impressionism, to sight of other-worldly powers, to death itself. We all but reach the equation: Death = individual personality. The 'caverns' of the mind which 'sun could never penetrate' (III. 243) are indeed direct analogies to those 'caverns measureless to man' leading to death's 'sunless sea' in *Kubla Khan*. There is, however, a supervening peace, such as that felt within Keats's Moneta and asserted by the Christian tradition. *The Prelude* follows Christianity in so far as it emphasizes the other-worldly and awe-inspiring. It is, however, closer to the Old Testament than the New and less pantheistic than either. Wordsworth is not unlike an Hebraic prophet, though with an emphasis on tranquillity drawing him perhaps nearer to Indian mysticism.

But what now of that balance of subjective and objective factors in experience asserted by the *Recluse* fragment? The geometric, rationalizing, and daylight intelligence is definitely slighted. Why? Wordsworth's 'mind', in the *Recluse* fragment called the 'haunt' and 'main region' of his 'song', is often best rendered by 'personality'. It includes the rationalizing intelligence, but sinks deeper into what psychologists call the 'unconscious', and is therefore dark, mysterious, and haunted. The 'exquisite' fitting of mind to object considered so wondrous in the fragment is therefore far from platitudinous. Rather the poet would celebrate the identity of deep spiritual experience with the natural order that is its birth and setting: man's deepest longings and aspirations are to be natural, while nature is to be given personality. Such an equation is extremely hard to realize. An urgent and crushing significance is always most readily felt through negative emotions, and in such terms natural powers are often most convincing, as in Coleridge's *Dejection*, the opening of *Maud*, Hardy's and J. C. Powys's novels, Eliot's *The Waste Land*. The Wordsworthian concentration is similar. Daylight nature is overwhelmed, sucked down, into the cavernous darkness, the haunting 'mind'; while our most powerful persons are actionless, passive, beyond all normal impulses and responses, and, like so many natural objects in Wordsworth, solitary.

We are therefore left poised over an abyss, a bottomless universe. The tragic mood which so often suffuses narrative here *is* the narrative. The danger is not unlike that expressed in Tennyson's *Palace of Art*, where such lonely apprehension is shown as peopling your home with ghosts: poetry turns in on itself, lacking objective nourishment. Wordsworth would isolate the poetic essence for awed inspection instead of using it. The cause lies in some rejection of the erotic instinct: for it is that instinct, and that alone, which seems to bar mankind from the full natural integration, of which it also, paradoxically, prompts the desire. Man's most obviously natural instinct is thus at once the main obstruction and highway to a naturalistic paradise. The confusion is tantalizing. Wordsworth, however, shows here a striking deficiency.

The more objective and rational intelligence is not, however, ignored; nor does Wordsworth altogether forget the rights of nature, as such. He is keenly aware of what might be called 'pure intelligence'. Like Pope, he is

impatient of a too-confident science attempting to cut
off the heart 'from all the sources of her former strength',
to 'unsoul' by 'syllogistic words' the 'mysteries of being',
and relegate the 'visible universe' to a 'microscopic view'
(xii. 75–92). Science is often merely a 'prop to our
infirmity', a 'false secondary power by which we multiply
distinctions' and then worship the 'boundaries' of our own
making (ii. 212–19). No truly organic life is susceptible
of precise analysis, and you cannot 'parcel out' your mind's
own story 'by geometric rules' (ii. 203). But elsewhere
Wordsworth guards against a final rejection of science.
Moreover, he rates pure geometry high (vi. 115–67),
meditating with 'Indian awe and wonder' on the fascinating relation of such 'abstractions' to 'Nature's laws', and
their dual application to the human mind and the outer
universe of starry systems. Indeed, they induce a peaceful
intuition of 'permanent and universal sway', pointing
'finite natures' towards the 'Supreme Existence, the surpassing life' beyond all boundaries, changeless, and with
no 'welterings of passion'. This relation of the geometrical to 'God' and 'transcendent peace' reflects
Coleridge's circular dome-symbolisms, wherein the geometrical mind is clearly at work. A man shipwrecked by
'stormy waters' solaces himself with geometry; that is,
with eternity. So will it be 'with poets ever', a way of
release from both 'images' and introspection:

> And specially delightful unto me
> Was that clear synthesis built up aloft
> So gracefully. . . .

In which Wordsworth adopts a definitely architectural
symbolism, pointing to *Kubla Khan*.

He here puts, however, slight trust in such eternity-
symbols. He considers how, if the world were disturbed
by some vast upheaval, nature would regain composure,
but man's creative achievements, whether built by
'reason' or 'passion', 'Bard' or 'Sage' (called 'twin
labourers'), would be blotted out (v. 29–45):

                    Oh! why hath not the Mind
            Some element to stamp her image on
            In nature somewhat nearer to her own?
            Why, gifted with such powers to send abroad
            Her spirit, must it lodge in shrines so frail?

                                              (v. 45)

This is a deliberate cry for some sacred structure outlast-
ing time, while also striking to the heart of all artistic
creation, architectural or poetic, to the desire to eternalize
in symbols what would else be fleeting, to impose structure,
with an attendant satisfaction in a feeling, however irrational, that something permanent has been made. Shortly
after this passage we find the twin faculties, poetic and
geometric, embodied in a neat symbolism (v. 50–140).
The poet has been musing on 'poetry and geometric
truth', and in sleep sees a Bedouin with a stone and a
shell, the latter of 'surpassing brightness'. The stone is
'Euclid's elements': it symbolizes the material and static
and the mind's study according to spatial laws. The other
is of even 'more worth': 'in an unknown tongue', which he
yet mysteriously understands, its harmonious and passionate 'ode' prophecies 'destruction to the children of the earth'.
The stone is scientific 'reason', holding 'acquaintance
with the stars' and binding 'soul to soul'; the language
of general scientific intelligence and accepted reason.
Though it ranges through universal law, it remains the
human mind, as we know it. But the shell holds the key
to an entirely new psychic order to be developed further
by Shelley and Keats. It symbolizes a hidden eternity-
music within the inanimate, and relates to and fuses both
time and space, being a melodious solid. Therefore it is a
'god', and applies to all nature and the human 'spirit' or
'heart'; and it, rather than the stone, deserves the privilege of comparison with Coleridge's 'dome'. As with
Coleridge, the whole passage is saturated in a paradoxical
dream-consciousness blending impossibilities. The objects
are themselves, yet also books; their possessor is Don
Quixote, yet also an Arab: of 'these was neither, and was

both at once'. The incident is most valuable and given a symbolic colour rare in Wordsworth: perhaps because he is in truth (as he claims) recounting an actual dream.

The Arab himself is a pictorial exotic among Wordsworth's solitaries. *The Prelude*, moreover, shows a reserve in respect of fine symbolic structures. There are, of course, examples, but mainly in slightly derogatory terms. Autobiographical poetry is once an 'unsubstantial structure' melting before the very sun that 'brightens' it (i. 225). The poet writes of his fanciful ability to see in a shining stone (i) a silver shield over a knight's tomb, and (ii) a 'magic cave' or 'palace built by faeries of the rock' (viii. 406–26): and next contrasts his own strong control of all such fantasies with that of Coleridge. There is, elsewhere, critical reference to Coleridge's 'Platonic forms of wild, ideal pageantry' (vi. 298). A 'snow-white church' may be compared to a 'thronèd lady' (iv. 21); but more representative are the Druid temple and 'antique' abbey of ii. 101–7; or the mountain-chapel contrasted with a temple 'rich with pomp and gold' called, significantly, a shelter from 'sun and shower' (xiii. 229–31). There are vast metaphoric 'temples' at vi. 741 and viii. 339, and 'mountain solitudes' are a 'solemn temple' at xiv. 139. The architecture of Cambridge, including Newton's statue, is noticed at the start of Book III. London's monuments have more elaborate attention in Book VII. Though the poet's preliminary expectations of London are compared to 'airy palaces', 'gardens built by genii', 'golden cities' deep in Eastern wilds (vii. 77–87) and 'gorgeous ladies under splendid domes' (vii. 124), the full description is a most remarkable appreciation of England's various architectural and monumental records in closest relation to jostling crowds, street-scenes of all sorts, the sordid and the garish: probably more valuable a contemporary document of the sort than any other extant. Later (viii. 560–89) this very realistic impressionism is strangely built into a direct symbolism, London being compared to a haunted cave whose roof is a mass of

baffling complexities resolved slowly into significant
shapes: a dome-formation thus recurring. But for the
most part *The Prelude* promotes a gospel far enough from
conscious, and therefore geometrical, formulations of the
eternal. The most powerful geometrical-religious passage
(XIII. 312–49) concerns a backward intuition into 'darkness', whence rises a scene of Druidical ritual and an
ancient sacrifice with spears and arms of 'mighty bone',
'dismal flames', groans, and a mystic 'pomp' for 'both
worlds', those of 'the living and the dead'. A kinship with
other glooms and, indeed, Wordsworth's later Christianity, if it can so be called, is evident. More gentle are
the 'long-bearded teachers' with 'white wands' pointing
heavenward swaying to a ritual music. All is suggested
by a monumental, circular, and astrological designing.
Rocky Druidical remains at once natural, vast, human and
yet superhuman in their impact necessarily fascinate
Wordsworth.

Wordsworth distrusts all easy symbolisms, all 'nature's
secondary grace' and the 'charm more superficial' of
natural works used as 'moral illustrations' (XIV. 315–19).
Certainly he does not avoid altogether Coleridgean symbolisms: his own life-story is a stream whose 'natal
murmur' comes from a 'blind cavern' (XIV. 194–6). But
in Book VIII (70–97) he carefully repudiates natural and
architectural paradises of the *Kubla Khan* sort, preferring
his bleak native scenery to 'that famed paradise of ten
thousand trees' or 'Gehol's matchless gardens' made
beyond 'China's stupendous mound' for 'delight of the
Tartarian dynasty'. Coleridge's oriental 'Khan' is clearly
hinted. The description—the italics are mine—is expanded:

> There, in a clime from widest empire chosen,
> Fulfilling (could *enchantment* have done more?)
> A sumptuous dream of flowery lawns, with *domes*
> *Of pleasure* sprinkled over, shady dells
> For eastern monasteries, *sunny* mounts
> With *temples* crested, bridges, gondolas,

Rocks, dens, and *groves* of foliage taught to melt
Into each other their obsequious hues,
Vanished and vanishing in subtle chase,
Too fine to be pursued; or standing forth
In no discordant opposition, strong
And gorgeous as the *colours* side by side
Bedded among rich plumes of tropic birds;
And *mountains over all*, embracing all;
And all the landscape *endlessly enriched*
With waters *running, falling*, or *asleep*.

This might be taken as symbolic of creation as a whole in
its colourful, iridescent patterning. But 'lovelier far', we
are told, is the 'paradise' where the poet was reared; where
man works with free dignity and 'choice' of labour to be
contrasted with the 'patient toil of myriads' working for
an oriental despot. Wordsworth admits the intoxicating
effect of a 'half-hour's roam' in the more garish paradise,
leaving behind a 'dance of images' to disturb his sleep for
weeks: acting not so very differently from the mysterious
and disembodied, though gigantic, 'forms' already observed. The rejection is further developed. He describes
(VIII. 111–293) pointedly, in order to refuse, many traditional impressions of delight, including Arcadian and
Hellenic myths, Shakespearian pastoralisms such as those
of *As You Like It* and *The Winter's Tale*, Spenserian
fictions of faery-land. He is not at home with traditional
nature-pietism, such as outgrown customs of may-pole
dances, wreaths laid on porch or doorway, youth and maid
off before dawn to drink and deck with garlands a 'sainted
well'. The times, either 'too sage' or 'too proud', have gone
beyond this, while his own experience has been more
stern. So he rejects Pan and his 'tutelary music'. These
may serve for Mediterranean coasts where shepherds pipe
'liquid notes of love', but deeper sounds are to be his, of
moor and mountain, the vast Atlantic's voice, ungovern-
able forces of nature, winds howling dismally over 'awful
solitudes'. 'Craggy ways', 'frozen snow' are his brothers
in a land where vast nature dictates sternest 'tasks'. In a

c

terrific passage he images the forms cradling his boyhood's experience. This is how he saw a shepherd:

> When up the lonely brooks on rainy days
> Angling I went, or trod the trackless hills
> By mists bewildered, suddenly mine eyes
> Have glanced upon him distant a few steps,
> In size a giant, stalking through thick fog,
> His sheep like Greenland bears. . . .   (VIII. 262)

Or the same figure may be suddenly 'glorified' by the
setting sun, or lifted 'above all height', solitary and sil-
houetted, as some Chartreuse cross upraised on mountain
pinnacle for worship. What has the 'gay Corin of the
groves' living 'for his own fancies', dancing with Phyllis,
to say to this glimpse of 'man suffering among awful
Powers and Forms' (VIII. 165)? Admittedly, they cut poor
figures. Notice that Wordsworth presents an unromantic,
it seems an unsexual, world. The Nordic imagination
often travels south for inspiration. Wordsworth here refuses. He is happier at home standing beneath some rock
before the storm

> listening to notes that are
> The ghostly language of the ancient earth.
>   (II. 306–22)

He is a Norse poet, happiest in bleak solitudes, for whom
we must go to Old English poetry, *The Wanderer* and
The Seafarer, for a parallel.

The style of *The Prelude* is peculiarly bare, with long
stretches that avoid any heightening through traditional
associations of royalty, martial glory, gold, sun, or sexual
romance. Stock poetic figures are, normally, absent; nor
are new ones created in their stead. We 'inherit' an
'empire' as 'natural beings' (III. 192): but such extravagance is rare. The bare and simple is, as a rule, considered
sufficient, though sometimes an attempt at elevation
through periphrasis or unnecessarily cumbersome phraseology emerges unsuspected. Many opportunities of
metaphoric excitement through comparison of the in-

animate with animal or human vitality are passed by as
unworthy adjuncts in a poem whose declared subject is a
record of that precise fusion. Wordsworth feels himself
to be making a valuable advance, but he fails to recognize
the wide psychological sovereignty exercised by many
of the symbols he distrusts. He refuses to fall in love
poetically with human traditions and there is a corresponding failure in verbal colour and, often, in word or
paragraph music. This, for example, has a traditional
appeal and living richness rare in *The Prelude*:

> . . . the sullen water far beneath,
> On which a dull red image of the moon
> Lay bedded, changing oftentimes its form
> Like an uneasy snake.   (VI. 704)

There is little appeal to senses of smell, taste, or touch.
*The poem celebrates a union with all that is sensuously
stern and cold; and, finally, with the non-sensible world.
Great poetry often tends, at the limit, to such a consummation, but it normally grapples on first to the sensuous
and erotic. Here Wordsworth makes the end of great
poetry his whole subject; indeed, his starting-point.

The Prelude is peculiarly non-sexual. The silence in so
general a statement is remarkable. When at Cambridge
Wordsworth complains of superficiality, and contrasts the
'chattering popinjays' and their gaudy life with those
austerities of a past age he would have preferred (III.
443–78), the implications are puritanical. We have a
reference to 'slight shocks of young love-liking' (IV. 317);
and once, as we have seen, he revisits a place of dark
associations with a loved companion. There is, too, a
passage which holds a Coleridgean admission of some
importance:

> Oh! next to one dear state of bliss, vouchsafed
> Alas! to few in this untoward world,
> The bliss of walking daily in life's prime
> Through field or forest with the maid we love. . . .
>   (XIII. 120)

But in Book XIV he explicitly repudiates such blissful love of 'the one who is thy choice of all the world' as in itself and in its necessary limitations a 'pitiable' delight in comparison with the fuller mystic awareness (170–80). This awareness it is which forces his emphasis on 'solitude', 'calm', 'tranquillity', and 'quietude'. He worships the 'tranquillising power' of contemplation, a 'sorrow that is not sorrow but delight' (xiii. 246), blending with wintry scenes and 'calm and dead still water' (ii. 170). He focuses, more clearly than most, the deepest and darkest destinies of human personality, but in the process misses the fiery core of human existence. Even though his doctrine of contemplation were wholly right, it could not, in itself, make poetry for long: Francis Thompson's *Hound of Heaven* being only a great poem because the hero remains unconverted until the last stanza. Instead of mastering volcanic energies by an artistic serenity, he falls back, very often, on description of serenity itself, describing the poetic process or result and missing poetic achievement. It is as though he were consciously preferring something else to poetry. Indeed, he more than once expresses admiration for simple, homely, untutored, yet rock-like characters who scorn poetic laurels:

> Theirs is the language of the heavens, the power,
> The thought, the image, and the silent joy:
> Words are but under-agents in their souls;
> When they are grasping with their greatest strength
> They do not breathe among them.   (xiii. 271)

He slights those idolatrous paganisms necessary to poetic success. His kinship with the Church is clear and his movement towards it inevitable. He loves ruined monasteries and feels a nostalgia for the freezing ascetic austerities of past generations of Cambridge students. Such clearly blend into his feeling for some vast transcendent otherness. He rests back on the peace of those tragic serenities as on a mother's breast; or stands beneath dwarfing mountain masses as a child before its father.

In those he senses a pressing eternal, a God; and like Milton feels himself to be labouring 'ever in his great taskmaster's eye'.

Yet criticism may well appear somewhat witless in face of his grandest imaginative flights or most sublime intellectual discussions. In the last book (XIV) we have both together. As the poet climbs on Snowdon at midnight the moon suddenly appears, revealing a 'silent sea of hoary mist', hills humped up over what seems a mysterious ocean of solid vapours stretching endlessly 'into the main Atlantic'; the moon above 'naked' in a cloudless sky; and innumerable roarings of cataracts (11–62). All is the 'type', that is, manifestation, 'of a majestic intellect' (67). The poet elaborates (63–129) his doctrine of the creative mind holding 'converse' with such worlds. Such minds only are 'Powers', their 'affections' raised from 'earth to heaven'. Yet the totally unnecessary suggestion that they show 'cheerfulness for acts of daily life' hints, I feel, an insincerity, since such a continuity scarcely exists. However, such transcendent manifestations as this passage explores are said to be works of love, without which all is dust (168–70); which love works likewise through all more obviously happy natural appearances, which must, however, be complemented by deeper thoughts (170–87). Sexual love is, in itself, impotent. 'Spiritual love' exists only through 'imagination', which is at once 'absolute power and clearest insight' and exalted 'reason' (188–92); and points to 'eternity' (205). Such higher integration is each man's lonely business:

> Here must thou be, O Man!
> Power to thyself; no Helper hast thou here. . . . (209)

Yet it is, if accomplished, all embracing, and not all austere either, leading on to a 'feeling intellect' and a softness, maternal as a 'nursing mother's', with something of 'female softness' (225–9): with which we may compare the feminine emphasis in Nietzsche's not dissimilar gospel of power. Wordsworth definitely says his sister's companionship has assisted this development and saves him from a too Miltonic esteem of the 'love' and 'beauty' that holds 'terror', the admission being very important (231–65). Moreover Coleridge, to whom the whole *Prelude* is addressed, has helped to relax the 'overweening grasp' of fear, render the 'self-haunting spirit' more rational, and make the mysteries of life and death, time and eternity, more serene (275–300). So both friends become 'Prophets of Nature' (444). The poet's 'power' is akin to Nature's (xiii. 312). Probably the finest essence of Wordsworth's explicit wisdom is compacted in this last book of *The Prelude*.

We turn now to *The Borderers*. The action grows from a bleak atmosphere. In a thick wood the music of birds drops 'deadened' (ii. 675); it is 'nipping cold' (ii. 727)—the impression recurs—and there is an 'odd moaning' (ii. 751). Oswald watches by 'a dim lantern's light' (iii. 1202), in 'a dismal night' the wind 'howls' (iv. 1765), the storm 'beats' (iv. 1882). We have the typical 'single', and 'black', tree and 'solitary crow' (v. 2098, 2102); and another tree 'ragged' and 'bent' (iii. 1294) on a lonely moor. Terrible scenes are devised: the 'half-ruined castle' and dungeon-entrance (ii. 724) where the first attempt at murder is staged, a castle where Clifford has 'held infernal orgies' seasoning wickedness with 'the very superstition of the place' (ii. 660–1). The dungeon-entrance is similar in effect to Coleridge's cave in *Remorse*. Then there is the bleak moor where Marmaduke deserts the blind old man. It is so cold he shivers in the sunshine (iii. 1265), and the desolate setting is ironically called a 'pretty prospect' and 'masterpiece of Nature' (iii. 1275): wickedness here toning with an aesthetic judgement similar to those of *The Prelude*. The cruel action works up towards

> A desolate prospect—a ridge of rocks—a Chapel on the summit of one—Moon behind the rocks—night stormy—irregular sound of a bell.   (iv)

The bleak world certainly throws up this divine, though nature-embedded, structure, but for the most part our atmosphere corresponds exactly to those darkly troubling intuitions of *The Prelude:* here they are definitely entwined with a deliberate evil, and given corresponding human action. We have, indeed, a powerful concentration of many Wordsworthian essences. The distracted and ever-mourning woman of *The Thorn* appears in Oswald's awful descriptions of one of Clifford's victims pacing each night in all weathers round an 'infant's grave', 'still round and round', her lips 'for ever moving' (I. 378–95; II. 570–9).

As in *Remorse* the villain, Oswald, is pivotal to both plot and thought-scheme. He is a cold, philosophical villain, cynical concerning 'fools of feeling' (II. 558). He urges Marmaduke to execute a criminal sort of justice, despising those whose 'reverence' for 'life' spares human vermin (II. 583–8); while their brigand society makes such justice happily possible (II. 595–8). His words carry a darkly dangerous logic:

> it is
> In darkness and in tempest that we seek
> The majesty of Him who rules the world.
> Benevolence, that has not heart to use
> The wholesome ministry of pain and evil,
> Becomes at last weak and contemptible.
>
> (II. 615)

Which points variously to *The Prelude* and those strange sonnets on the death-penalty written years later. Oswald scorns the 'nightmare Conscience' (II. 866) and Marmaduke's 'weak scruples' (II. 883). Like Ordonio in *Remorse* he questions all accepted values. Why should we destroy 'a worn-out horse' or a 'withered tree' so easily, yet balk at an old man? (II. 927–9). His purpose is to reduce, or elevate, Marmaduke to his own state: he works subtly, sometimes pretending agreement with scruples. He reiterates the necessity of justice continually and speaks bravely before the bandit-gathering on the imperviousness

of true justice to pity, saying how women and old age
have made 'weakness a protection', distorting at once
reason and true morality (ii. 1073–91). The softer
Christian emotions are negated: the old man's prayers are
counted hypocritical (ii. 1096). Later (iii. 1142–74) he
soliloquizes on the dual principles of passion and proof,
instinct and reason, himself praising passion, that is, self-
assertion, and refusing to wrong its 'majesty' by those
trivialities of time, person, and place that constitute the
'spiritless shape of Fact', a phrase clearly showing a
tangential similarity in Oswald's to Wordsworth's own
recurring philosophy. Oswald's evil actions grow,
indeed, from that very darkness intolerant of all normal
manifestations so powerfully celebrated in *The Prelude*.
He is in the world of 'naked spirit' I have elsewhere
observed in *Macbeth*. He attacks (as did Nietzsche) an
enervate religious acceptance:

> A whipping to the Moralists who preach
> That misery is a sacred thing. . . .   (iii. 1160)

Nothing, he says, more quickly or surely degrades a man.
He supports direct self-expression and meditates, like
Wordsworth so often, on the human mind:

> These are strange sights—the mind of man, upturned,
> Is in all natures a strange spectacle;
> In some a hideous one—hem! shall I stop?
> No.—Thoughts and feelings will sink deep, but then
> They have no substance.   (iii. 1168)

Memory, he says, records actions only. The soliloquy is
of primary importance to our understanding of Wordsworth. Oswald is (iii. 1427–34) said to 'spin motives'
out of 'his own bowels' (like Iago); sadistic reference is
shadowed by the phrase 'incontinence in crime'; and we
are told 'power' is 'life', 'breath', and 'being' to him, so
that what he cannot 'govern' he will 'destroy'. Though a
'reasoner' he has his own 'uncouth superstition', believing
in 'spirits' and 'the Sun' (iii. 1439–47). Pride and her

daughter, Cruelty, are near 'madness', and such 'restless minds', unloved and unloving, seek for sympathy 'in dim relation to imagined Beings'. His destruction of Marmaduke is called a sacrifice 'to those infernal fiends' (III. 1448–58). *The Prelude* is again most vividly suggested.

Oswald congratulates Marmaduke on his accomplishment of the crime (III. 1484–1567). The just man obeys only 'his own bosom'; Marmaduke has cast off a tyranny, broken free of the 'torpid acquiescence' characterizing 'emasculated souls', realizing that the 'only law' is that 'flashed' by 'the light of circumstances' on 'an independent Intellect'. He may now move yet further through *both* 'good and evil'. Though men may stigmatize him as a 'murderer' and condemn him to 'solitude', that very eagle-like solitude is the mark of greatness. Man, however, must have some 'fellowship': but, if good angels fail, there are others less well-reputed that can serve instead. 'Extremes' meet 'in this mysterious world', 'opposites' 'melt into each other'. The doctrine is somewhat Germanic, resembling one step in Nietzsche's, while the value of Nietzsche's final result may assist our sympathies for Wordsworth's bold attempt. For Oswald is, partly at least, heroic. 'Great actions', he says, always involve great suffering, and though all action be finally trivial, suffering 'shares the nature of infinity'. He is a man who wills and enjoys his own tragic criminal being, and from that eminence scorns the 'light dancing of the thoughtless heart', and all toys unfit for the grimness of human existence. To live in 'forgetfulness of pain' would be idiocy, while remorse, as such, cannot stand against profound thought. In a universe where all depends on the irrational play of chance, where a cat's sneeze might prevent a crime, the strict logic of remorse is, he says, quite misplaced. Fact by itself signifies nothing.

His purpose accomplished, he tells Marmaduke his own life-story. Once on a voyage he was deeply wronged, according to the crew, by the captain. The ship is becalmed and short of water:

> for many days
> On a dead sea under a burning sky,
> I brooded o'er my injuries, deserted
> By man and nature.   (iv. 1697)

The impressions correspond to those in *The Ancient Mariner*. Later, he seizes the opportunity of marooning the captain on a desert island, only to discover eventually that he has been wickedly misinformed. He retreats to a convent, in bitter, almost lifeless grief:

> Three sleepless nights I passed in sounding on,
> Through words and things, a dim and perilous way.
>   (iv. 1774)

The lines recall Newton 'voyaging through strange seas of thought, alone' (*The Prelude*, iii. 63). He feels enslaved, yet embraces action, with 'energy' unconquered, restless, his sleep horribly bound to daylight reason with more 'continuity and substance' than any waking life (iv. 1776–94). Campaigning in Palestine, he would retreat alone 'through woods of gloomy cedar' among *Kubla Khan* settings of 'deep chasms' and 'roaring streams', or, standing on a hill by moonlight, perceive

> What mighty objects do impress their forms
> To elevate our intellectual being,   (iv. 1809)

wondering at the curse forcing 'a thing so great' as man to prey on itself. Returning from these 'forms' to worldly affairs, he feels himself a 'Being' who had passed 'alone'

> Into a region of futurity,
> Whose natural element was freedom. (iv. 1818)

That is, he feels himself a superman, beyond all human valuations. Fame merely registers a correspondence with a petty normality, while 'obloquy' is synonymous with 'merit'. 'Hate' or 'fear' disguised as 'scorn' is the reward of true, substantial service (iv. 1820–31). He is now untouched by 'shame' or 'fame', and approaches life as a 'monarch'. Like Nietzsche he repudiates the subtle webs of priestcraft, and is even grateful to those who first in-

volved him in crime (IV. 1833–44). Next Marmaduke
half-realizes the part Oswald has played towards himself.
Oswald admits it, suggesting they be now 'fellow-
labourers' to 'enlarge man's intellectual empire'; saying
he was driven by desire for sympathy to make Marmaduke a copy of himself; and seeming to urge that a vitalized consciousness depends on evil action (IV. 1854–71).
Wordsworth's satanic gospel outdistances all literary
rivals. Oswald means it:

> Young Man, the seed must lie
> Hid in the earth, or there can be no harvest;
> 'Tis Nature's law.   (IV. 1875)

The accent is one of experience and wisdom; and the
thought has strange, if perverted, correspondences with
Christian doctrine. Consciousness of evil is vitally necessary to both: but Oswald is—or feels—redeemed by his
own strength and unshirking acceptance.

He is Websterian, especially in the vivisectional
curiosity behind his enjoyment of 'experiment' (III. 1623),
and also in his proud rhetorical fling when about to die: if
his voice's 'echo' brings down 'a heap of rubbish' on his
head, that is no 'dishonour' (V. 2314). He is a deliberate
embodiment in self-conscious action of certain dramatic
tendencies that forecast Emily Brontë, Herman Melville,
and Dostoievsky.

Opposed are the blind old man and his daughter
Idonea, whose function is mainly passive, to be hideously
and irredeemably wronged. Parenthood is always highly
charged with sanctity in Wordsworth: we cannot give a
'holier name' to 'God himself' than that of 'father' (I. 543).
The old man is 'pious' and 'saintly' (III. 1246). He is,
too, helpless:

> Murder—perhaps asleep, blind, old, alone,
> Betrayed, in darkness!   (II. 901)

Blindness—we have met it before—increases his awful,
other-worldly, dignity and passive power. The beggar-
woman, Oswald's tool, repents and fears 'the curse of that

blind man' (ii. 951). At a crack of 'hell-rousing' thunder
he remarks, like Lear, how guilt may 'shudder' while the
helpless and innocent are guarded by Providence (ii.
788–92). With kindly nature he is in true sympathy.
Alone on the cold moor he murmurs:

> Hush!—'tis the feeble and earth-loving wind
> That creeps along the bells of the crisp heather.
>
> (iii. 1263)

Later he speaks of the lark whirring from the fern (iii.
1285). To Marmaduke's demonic fantasies he opposes a
stern reproof:

> Lost Man! if thou have any close-pent guilt
> Pressing upon thy heart, and this the hour
> Of visitation—   (iii. 1305)

and

> Learn, young Man,
> To fear the virtuous, and reverence misery,
> Whether too much for patience, or, like mine,
> Softened till it becomes a gift of mercy.
>
> (iii. 1337)

He speaks of himself, like Lear, alone 'under the arch of
heaven', helpless, doomed it would seem 'by the good
God, our common Father' (iii. 1343–5). He is left alone
by Marmaduke on the bleak moor; and we see him next
struggling towards the chapel above the cliffs and crying
to those who pray before its altar (iv. 1651–5). If Oswald
appears a blood-brother of Iago, the old Herbert reminds
us of *King Lear*, a play, like so much of Wordsworth's
persons and natural objects, bleak, aged, and reverend.
Herbert is terrible in his helplessness, and symbolizes
that in creation which stimulates, or should stimulate, the
awful compulsions of pity.

The hero, Marmaduke, like Wordsworth himself, is
set between these dark satanic promptings and this
reverence for helpless age, while his agony pivots, precisely as does Hamlet's, on the reiterated concept of
'justice', and the problem of personal action. He is a

young man of 'generous qualities' (ii. 621) to whom
compassion 'is natural as life' (ii. 626). Oswald's emphasis on the proposed sacrifice of Idonea to Clifford
urges him towards murder. He feels something like a
'transition' in his 'soul' (ii. 636). Yet, when opportunity
comes, he fails:

> . . . in plumbing the abyss for judgement,
> Something I strike upon which turns my mind
> Back on herself, I think, again—my breast
> Concentres all the terrors of the Universe:
> I look at him and tremble like a child.
>
> (ii. 782)

He is hopelessly divided, poised above an 'abyss' and un-
settled in direction: 'Which way so e'er I turn, I am per-
plexed' (ii. 878). He is forced into something very like
the mental world of *The Prelude*:

> Last night, when moved to lift the avenging steel,
> I did believe all things were shadows—yea,
> Living or dead, all things were bodiless,
> All but the mutual mockeries of body. . . .
>
> (iii. 1213)

A star recalls him, but he now thinks himself a fool

> To let a creed, built in the heart of things,
> Dissolve before a twinkling atom!   (iii. 1219)

That is, he embraces what might be called a visionary
nihilism sinking deeper than all surface appearances.
'Young' as he is—Wordsworth was himself only twenty-
seven when he wrote the play—he already claims wisdom
wider than Oswald's, and could, he says, reason of 'love
in all its shapes'—a significant phrase—and the 'diverse
aspects' of morality. He is penetrating below all accepted
valuations. Of two kings, one by war strews the ground
with human carcasses and is generally acclaimed; the
other 'sits i' the sun' and 'floats kingcups in the brook'
and is despised for wasting his time. To Marmaduke
either both are fools or both wise. In such a world, where
all established values are hypocritical, a man may as well

be prepared to murder his own child, if necessary (III.
1223–44). Meeting Herbert, the old man, on the moor
(III. 1269), he first soliloquizes in terms of a bitter, universalized, mockery; then says how the ghost of a murdered man might on this bleak moor have 'fine room' to
'squeak and gibber in' (III. 1304). Wordsworth's favourite
impressions harmonize with the action. Marmaduke's
softer nature rises, with memories of an earlier love, only
to be crushed:

> I am cut off from man;
> No more shall I be man—no more shall I
> Have human feelings!   (III. 1327)

Finally, he aims, as does Wordsworth himself in the
sonnets on *The Punishment of Death*, to cast the responsibility for 'justice' on God, leaving the old man's death
to Providence. Next, alone in a wood, he murmurs:

> Deep, deep, and vast, vast beyond human thought,
> Yet calm.—I could believe that there was here
> The only quiet heart on earth. In terror,
> Remembered terror, there is peace and rest.
>   (III. 1466)

You can fall back on dreadful imaginings, even crime,
as a source, somehow, of peace: a strange, but Wordsworthian, doctrine. Crime is, as it were, an action splitting
open the daylight world and revealing the outer darkness,
the eternal otherness. Marmaduke's story moves on to
knowledge of his betrayal and an agonized meeting with
his loved Idonea who curses, not knowing his identity,
her father's murderer (v. 2176); with thoughts of 'phantoms' who take the 'shape of man' and 'instigate' to evil
for cruel sport at man's distress (v. 2083–6). At the
end, we have

> darkness deepening darkness
> And weakness crowned with the impotence of death!
>   (v. 2285)

He bitterly mocks Oswald's advanced 'morality', but is
now 'raised above, or sunk below, all further sense of pro-

vocation' (v. 2289–96). The alternative is important. His destiny now is only to 'endure' (v. 2301). He becomes one of Wordsworth's beyond-pain solitaries. He passes over thoughts of a hermitage and suicide. Instead

> a wanderer must I go
> The Spectre of that innocent Man, my guide.
> No human ear shall ever hear me speak;
> No human dwelling ever give me food,
> Or sleep, or rest: but over waste and wild,
> In search of nothing that this earth can give,
> But expiation, will I wander on . . . (v. 2344)

Though compelled by 'pain and thought' to live, he loathes life and awaits Heaven's merciful release.

The play is weighted with what Wordsworth calls 'things substantial' (v. 2087), used in the Shakespearian sense (as in *Measure for Measure*) of spiritual, invisible, energies or essences. Solitude is emphatic: all beasts but man, we are told, all 'die in solitude' (v. 2153). Man adopts violent action as self-flattery because it 'asks not thought', whereas

> The deeper malady is better hid;
> The world is poisoned at the heart. (II. 1035)

We are all 'of one blood', our veins filled 'at the same poisonous fountain' (IV. 1739). Various aspects of the one grim reality, or energy, are presented. Both the good and evil, the old man and his child and Oswald, grow from the same world of rugged nature, awe, satanic destiny and endurance. The experience presented as a unity in *The Prelude* is here split into different persons, scenes, and actions, variously sympathetic or otherwise. In both, something is missing. There is slight feeling of any happy energies. True, the borderer-clan does something to establish nobility of action, like that of the Moors in *Remorse*, and the use of horns twice functions as in *Zapolya*. But the emphasis is weak. Marmaduke is set between (i) the unmoral, because absolutely *free*, and independent judgement, with consequent dangerous action,

and (ii) an aged passivity; between the power-instincts of
Oswald and the reverential and pitiful emotions raised by
the old man. Romantic and sexual desires certainly help
to force the conflict, and certain phrases, quoted above,
hint a perversion of sexual energy; but the erotic is never
here both vivid and positive and does nothing, even distantly, to *heal* the wound. In *Macbeth* you feel somehow
a rich and well worth-while splendour within the hero
that touches erotic glamour. In the Eros alone power and
gentle love, here antithetic, aspire to a proud unity, may
become identical; and perhaps nowhere else, unless
through a Christian symbolism. One would not wish
The Borderers other than it is: yet its naked disclosure of
extremes out of any contact with an erotic and unifying
principle is symptomatic and intensely interesting. For
the circle mystically completes itself as Oswald pointed
out and Marmaduke too observes:

> Conflict must cease, and, in thy frozen heart,
> The extremes of suffering meet in absolute peace.
>
> (v. 2215)

That might be taken for a Wordsworthian motto: the
bodiless extremes, the alpha and omega, are there, but the
alphabet itself absent. The poet, having seen the evil in
all action, is therefore happiest with the darkness *behind*
creation and the supervening quietude of the eternal.

The deep problems involved may be clarified by a
translation into national terms. Oswald's ethic then at
once appears less insane, closely resembling that of
Machiavelli and his successors in modern Europe; and
is, indeed, the ethic of many respectable *groups*, especially
where justice is concerned. That is why the crucial
question of justice and the infliction of death is handled
very much as in Wordsworth's sonnets on the death-
penalty written fifty years later. Wordsworth had had
cause to ponder the rights and wrongs of social action,
and this play condenses, brings to a fine point, the issues
involved in dramatic and closely personal terms. We are

pointed by it towards passages in *The Prelude* on the
French Revolution. There is the same provisional faith
in an 'independent intellect' (xɪ. 244), and there Wordsworth endures a confusion similar to Marmaduke's, and
is even driven by desire for some 'dramatic' tale, at once
more lively and less 'guarded' than political theorizing
(282-9). *The Borderers* is precisely such a dramatic disclosure. Like Marmaduke and the Solitary in *The Excursion*, Wordsworth concludes by giving up all 'moral
questions' (305), tangled hopelessly in all problems of just
action.

To return, for a moment, to *The Prelude*. As with
Milton, its finest effects and most energic movement of
verse concern dark impressions relating to the depths of
personality: in such nakedly spectral existences—'naked'
is a reiterated impression in *The Prelude*—you cannot distinguish properly the satanic from the divine. With these
Wordsworth enjoys a poetic, technical, union, but, since
he treasures them as absolutes, is turned back on himself
like Marmaduke. But a poet should continually suffer the
annihilation of his mind, almost his personality, in face of
word, image, or person; be lost in passionate approval of
this, that, or the other thing or energy that his own lonely
personality might reject; and from this coition springs the
bright new life as Athena, armed, from Jove's head, when
at once a more *parental* feeling suffuses the new birth.
Agapé corresponds to the completed form, the tranquillity, of art, as *eros* to its contained conflicts. Now Wordsworth, having known that ultimate tranquillity on his own
terms, often refuses the basic conditions of poetic art; he
describes in passages of dark mystery instead of recreating
in terms of a more universal and daylight symbolism. His
subject-matter is itself of *agapé* quality, and leads on to
barren ethical asseverations and an almost morbid insis-
tence on pitiful age and graveyards; while *The Borderers*
hints a relation of such un-erotic, unhappy powers, to a
satanic evil. If expressed in action, as there, they neces-

D

sarily become satanic: hence Wordsworth fears action.
Yet he knows well that a rhythm, a balance, is intrinsic to
nature and tells (xiii. 1–10) how she originates emotion
and calmness: that is, *eros* and *agapé*. These are both
(i) her glory and (ii) her strength; and genius is of the
same kind, thriving 'by interchange of peace and excita-
tion', 'energy' being needed to seek truth and 'stillness of
mind' to receive it. All this he knows; and all his most
favourite doctrines are, as statements, ultimately true.
I observe a limitation not so much in doctrine as in poetic
creation. Nor is this charge altogether fair. For of the
two major works so far discussed, which are also his two
most powerful full-length creations, the one is specifically
written to describe the forces *behind* his later work, and
the other was, in his judgement, a youthful experiment
withheld from publication. Neither was published until
the last decade of Wordsworth's prolific literary career:
then only was he 'induced' to publish *The Borderers*. That
life is one long attempt to modify his sight of the nakedly
spectral powers into a more positive doctrine of nature and
human existence. This doctrine will lack vigour, appearing egotistical and heavily didactic, with a tendency to
distrust all fiery agonies and splendours, and concentrate
on the graver duties, of man.

Tintern Abbey and *Michael* may be said to define the
transition. The one beautifully describes the calmness of
the creative mood—again describing rather than using—
through which a 'living soul' is born from physical
quiescence; and continues with a noble sense of underlying spirit infusing, buoying up into existence, all
natural and cosmic manifestations; and concludes with
'the still sad music of humanity'. The other shows a
typical old shepherd of rock-like strength and grave
morality whose loved son has been ruined by the vicious
encroachments of city-life, eternally, and alone, climbing
a hill to build with grey stones the sheepfold planned in
happier days: and this terrible, and lonely determination
to *build* from a rock-like and impregnable simplicity and

bleakness symbolizes Wordsworth's life-work. A contrast of that sheepfold with Coleridge's flashing dome in *Kubla Khan* almost distinguishes the two poets; yet Wordsworth is too full of surprises for that. We can, however, see *The Prelude* and *The Borderers*, with, too, many shorter poems touching the grotesque or horrible, such as *The Idiot Boy* and *Peter Bell*, as in some sense corresponding to Coleridge's glamorous nature—for Wordsworth's bleak scenes are, to him, glamorous; and, still more, to the caves of death, those 'caverns measureless to man' which Wordsworth's own reference of 'caverns' to the depths of personality recalls. From these we move to (i) positive human vision (Coleridge's Abyssinian maid), and (ii) architectural sanctities (Coleridge's dome). We might remember how Goethe's Faust descends to the Mothers, dark origins of creation, before his Hellenic quest.

II

The *Ode on Intimations of Immortality* is probably Wordsworth's most finally satisfying human work. Here he houses many favourite intuitions in majestic light; marries his dearest inward feelings to a highly charged impressionism, pastoral and royalistic; and faces the intoxication of a sunlight creation. It is his only poem at once human, happy, and powerful. The ode stands the test of his description of great poetry in *The Prelude*; in it that 'host of *shadowy* things' ('shadow' is an important word in Coleridge too) finds its 'proper home'; all mysterious 'substances' are suffused with 'light divine', the 'turnings intricate of verse', a phrase peculiarly apt to this poem, aiding poetic mastery. Though the subject still be childhood, the poem is more technically erotic than most, a symbolic union with the child-symbol performing a central and most important resolution of dynamic immediacy: poetic excitement locked imperishably to live as a tranquil yet pulsing memorial of creative joy. Technical and formal elaboration, whether in symbolism

or rhyme-scheme, forces the poet into an especially condensed precision. Art is born from a jerking of consciousness outside and above itself, throwing responsibility on
to a higher centre, and technical strictures are the medium
through which this other domination is conjured into
existence. That sense of young joy so often mentioned
in *The Prelude* now very subtly possesses the reader too:
we are inside Wordsworth's own ecstasy. In *The Prelude*
a very personal feeling tends, except in the great numinous
passages, to suffuse bare narration of objective fact.
Though the central experience of *The Prelude* is directly
included, its method is here diametrically reversed: a subjective experience is, through a clear technique, perfectly
objectified.

The poem is far from easy. The term 'immortality'
means 'death negated': it is a dramatic word and may be
equated with life itself provided some recognition of death
is incorporated. Such recognition our ode gives, celebrating life victorious over death. In poetic study we
must never limit too closely a vast unknowable which the
poem itself is created to define. So, though Wordsworth's
ode, like Shakespeare's *Pericles* or Shelley's *Prometheus*,
is a vision of immortality or life victorious, it need have
nothing to say about life-after-death. It is rather a vision
of essential, all-conquering, life. The symbols which
carry this over to us are flowers, springtime joy, bird
music, all young life, and, pre-eminently, the child.

The 'spring' references need not be emphasized: they
are clear and obvious. But the 'child' is so important that
I note first its continual presence in the poem. 'Early
childhood' occurs in the title, and at the head of the poem
are the lines commencing, 'The Child is father of the
Man'. 'Child' and 'birth' images are frequent. The sunshine is 'a glorious birth', the 'young lambs' bound as to
the tabor. Happy youth is in the air:

> Thou Child of Joy,
> Shout round me, let me hear thy shouts, thou happy shepherd-
> boy!

Again,
> And the children are culling
>   On every side,
> In a thousand valleys far and wide,
> Fresh flowers . . .

and,
> The babe leaps up on his mother's arm.

We have a whole stanza devoted to the slow fading of that glory we bring from birth:
> Our birth is but a sleep and a forgetting. . . .

We trace the 'growing boy' through his pilgrimage from life to death. Next Nature is the 'mother' to this wanderer, he her 'foster-child'. Then we have another long stanza describing the child at play:
> Behold the child among his new-born blisses,
> A six years Darling of a pigmy size!

The description is vividly realized. The child is next invoked as 'mighty prophet' and 'seer blest'. The 'little child' is 'glorious' in his immortal heritage, something magic and mystic, far more wonderful than any platitudinous 'simple creed of childhood'. Then we are brought to a dream of paradise in terms of 'children' who 'sport upon the shore' of eternity. Finally, we return to our spring setting, the birds' song, 'young lambs', and the 'new-born' day. The poet envisages life victorious in terms of the child. This is our approach to immortality.

We have the poet's references to his own childhood's faded magic, to the time when all nature
> To me did seem
> Apparelled in celestial light,
> The glory and the freshness of a dream.

The radiance is gone:
> But yet I know, where'ere I go,
> That there hath passed away a glory from the earth.

Next, he expresses sorrow that he alone should have shown grief amid universal joyousness. A second wave

of poetic rapture floods on in this and the next stanza;
then, again, the bitter remembrance alternating. A tree,
a field, both speak of 'something that is gone':

> Whither is fled the visionary gleam?
> Where is it now, the glory and the dream?

Then he expands this personal recollection into the general
pilgrimage of mortality from birth, the fount of life, to
life, the beginning of death.

The dawn-star of birth sets on the horizons of paradise.
'In infancy' there is, at it were, a heavenly blaze around
and within us, the original beam casting its radiance on
all things. But, as the years pile on their leaden weight,
the prison-house closes on the immortal birth, mortality
lays heavy irons on the limbs and wings of life. The
'growing boy' has a certain faculty of sight left him, and
'beholds the light'; and, though swiftly drawn from 'the
east', the dawn of life, he is yet 'Nature's priest' for a
while. This 'nature' is, then, the transfigured nature of
radiant vision, the 'vision splendid'. Finally, in manhood,
the cold light of 'common day' casts its sickling eclipse
on the dawn-fire glimmering from birth, birth being not
only life's origin but its *heart*. The child, though slowly
drawn down the dim corridors of mortality, yet sparkles
with the consecrated dews of the paradise he has left, and
is to be regarded as central: in so far as man is separated
from birth, which is life, he dies.

Yet the poet confuses us with two uses of 'nature'.
One is the nature transfigured, indistinguishable from
the antenatal glory, indeed itself the essential life of which
that glory is an intellectual aspect. But we also have quite
another 'nature'. Earth is a kindly foster-mother to the
divine life born to her arms: 'yearnings she hath in her
own natural kind.' So

> The homely nurse doth all she can
> To make her Foster-child, her Inmate Man,
>   Forget the glories he hath known
> And that imperial palace whence he came.

In these passages 'natural' and 'earth' are to be contrasted with the divine. This, then, is rather the 'nature' of clouded vision: the nature of Wordsworth's manhood. Now, after the great central invocation, which I inspect later, the poem again returns to this secondary nature, joying

> That nature yet remembers
> What was so fugitive!

His manhood is leavened and purified by fitful recollections, and such memories bring him 'perpetual benediction'. They take the form of

> obstinate questionings
> Of sense and outward things,
> Fallings from us, vanishings,
> Blank misgivings of a Creature
> Moving about in worlds not realized,
> High instincts before which our mortal Nature
> Did tremble like a guilty thing surprised. . . .

Observe how here 'sense and outward things' are 'questioned'. This is an intellectual falsification. In the moment of child vision, nature was itself the divine glory, and the youth therefore 'nature's priest'. Remembering the quality of that vision, without being able to re-experience it in direct contact with the actual, the mind is forced into an idealism which regards the other, lesser nature, as 'questionable'. The poet thus moves in formless worlds, traversing the wide spaceless vacancies of abstract and inhuman recollection, without the creative power to fuse such vision-longing with immediate experience: the process at times evident in *The Prelude*, which is, we may remember, merely a recollection of child-moments in maturity, and not necessarily an authentic autobiographical record. This 'mortal nature', once the vision is gone, is truly a thing of meanness; and indeed a whole universe separates the one nature from the other. So these recollected life-glimmerings, vague and fitful

though they be, have yet tremendous authority, and are,
indeed, in this poem given a fine and concrete expression:

> But for those first affections,
> Those shadowy recollections,
> Which, be they what they may,
> Are yet a fountain-light of all our day,
> Are yet a master-light of all our seeing;
>   Uphold us, cherish, and have power to make
> Our noisy years seem moments in the being
> Of the eternal silence: truths that wake
>   To perish never. . . .

The lights of that death-in-life which we live. They
'perish never'; not subject to mortality, because, though
'recollections', they are yet 'shadows' of some transcendent victory, existing with immortal power; and so time
itself, 'our noisy years', becomes but a passing moment in
the one vast immediacy of the eternal.

Our poem thus imagines the immortality in terms of
(i) the child, imaged objectively as a thing enjoying its
existence perfectly; and (ii) moments of vision, themselves to be related to the experiences of childhood. The
two alternate. Neither by itself is wholly satisfying to us
or to the poet suffering his loss of delight. He can see the
shepherd-boy in youthful happiness, but he himself is sad;
he can remember his own one-time visions, yet they
return but fitfully, and then in terms of themselves and
vague, 'shadowy' abstractions, rather than nature, thus
lacking a certain reality. The immortality will be perfectly incarnated when these two approaches are married;
when the poet's own desire is fused with an object, that
object or image alight with the poet's immediate vision.
Now our two aspects of immortality have been aspects of
childhood: and the heart of our poem is a passionate
invocation of the child. Here the poet falls into visionary
love with his own symbol, and *majestically recreates before
our eyes the thing he has lost.* The fusion is not 'recollected':
it is in the poetic act. Two styles are, moreover, blended:
that of *The Prelude* with that of the more technically

objective sonnets. The fusion Wordsworth elsewhere describes is here immediately at work. The poet marries his own birth-visions to the child-symbol. The elements are things of life, and the technical process a creative act, so that we have a miraculous birth, a vivid poetic life shooting its life-ray into the heart of life. The climax of the ode rings out a prophetic and human splendour unique in Wordsworth. Nor has it been properly understood.

This, the vital centre, is preceded by the stanza carefully describing the child at play. The poet first studiously actualizes the symbol with which his passion is to be fused; and indeed closes his grand invocation by again imaging the child in its expressly human actuality. In the invocation we have our vision of the child as immortality. The immortal fire blazes out from this moment of created vision, and the lost immediacy, now incarnated in poetry, is recaptured in its full richness and splendour. The rest of the ode, with all its vivid imagery, is really the structure for this the central towering height, or heart. I quote it in full:

> Thou, whose exterior semblance doth belie
>   Thy Soul's immensity;
> Thou best Philosopher, who yet dost keep
> Thy heritage, thou Eye among the blind,
> That, deaf and silent, read'st the eternal deep,
> Haunted for ever by the eternal mind,—
>   Mighty Prophet! Seer blest!
>   On whom those truths do rest,
> Which we are toiling all our lives to find,
> In darkness lost, the darkness of the grave;
> Thou, over whom thy Immortality
> Broods like the Day, a Master o'er a Slave,
> A Presence which is not to be put by;
>   [To whom the grave
> Is but a lonely bed without the sense or sight
>   Of day or the warm light,
> A place of thought where we in waiting lie;]
> Thou little Child, yet glorious in the might
> Of heaven-born freedom on thy being's height,

Why with such earnest pains dost thou provoke
The years to bring the inevitable yoke,
Thus blindly with thy blessedness at strife?
Full soon thy Soul shall have her earthly freight,
And custom lie upon thee with a weight,
Heavy as frost, and deep almost as life!

Of this there is much to say. I can only suggest a few ideas.

Coleridge did not like it. He did not understand it. This is what he said:

> Now here, not to stop at the daring spirit of metaphor which connects the epithets 'deaf and silent', with the apostrophized *eye*: of (if we are to refer it to the preceding word, philosopher) the faulty and equivocal syntax of the passage; and without examining the propriety of making a 'master *brood* o'er a slave', or the *day* brood *at all*; we will merely ask, what does all this mean? In what sense is a child of that age a *philosopher*? In what sense does he *read* 'the eternal deep'? In what sense is he declared to be '*for ever haunted*' by the Supreme Being? or so inspired as to deserve the splendid titles of a *mighty prophet*, a *blessed seer*? By reflection? by knowledge? by conscious intuition? or by *any* form or modification of consciousness?

Again, referring to the four lines which, following the Oxford Wordsworth, I have left bracketed:

> Surely, it cannot be that this wonder-rousing apostrophe is but a comment on the little poem, 'We are seven'? that the whole meaning of the passage is reducible to the assertion, that a *child*, who by the bye at six years old would have been better instructed in most Christian families, has no other notion of death than that of lying in a dark, cold place? And still, I hope, not as in a *place of thought!* not the frightful notion of lying *awake* in his grave!

I have quoted from the *Biographia Literaria*, chapter xxii. Now that is the kind of approach to poetry in which criticism too rashly precedes interpretation; or, put otherwise, judgement is independent of understanding. I cannot here defend Wordsworth in detail, though it would be very easy to do so. It is surely unnecessary, and,

if necessary, likely to be futile. Once we rise to the plane
on which the poet addresses us, each phrase that Coleridge
criticizes becomes of apocalyptic power. Coleridge, for
example, is quoting this stanza as an example of Wordsworth's use of 'thoughts and images too great for the
subject'. Too great! Might he not have remembered
Isaiah's 'And a little child shall lead them'? Or, 'Except
ye become as a little child ye shall in no wise enter into
the kingdom of heaven'? The thought of child-desecra-
tion called from Jesus His only words of utterly cold, un-
relenting, and pitiless judgement. And in Shakespeare's
most terrific play, the only force able to withstand the
world-quaking rampant death is a little child, victorious:

> What is this
> That rises like the issue of a king;
> And wears upon his baby-brow the round
> And top of sovereignty?

Why should the mighty force of creation be too slight a
symbol of immortality? The Kingdom of Heaven itself is
compared to a tiny mustard seed, and what universes of
paradise, of earth, of hell, may be compacted in a child!
So, not any literature, nor teaching, nor even the 'word'
of God Himself, is the true centre of our religion; rather
the Incarnation, the Birth of the Holy Child. We may
resolve our paradoxes by seeing the child as an expression,
or symbol, of life. Either the paradox, or symbolism: they
are often alternative.

The child is the new-minted coin of life, its freshest
currency, stamped with the impressure of the latest
signature of paradise. It is thus an 'eye among the blind'
possessing sight; deaf, silent, passive, its very *being* is a
light and a vision. The child is a new eye of life. In later
years we most often sleep. But in poetry, religion, music,
love, in all ecstatic experience, we may wake to essential
life, which is immortality. In that his very existence is an
awakening to life, the child is indeed 'a mighty prophet'
or blest 'seer'. Nor is he on a lower plane: wherever there

is birth and newness, there is sublimity. That is why
height-born mountain-torrents regularly symbolize birth.
Full possession of this miracle is the aim of all poetry
and prophecy. The child is therefore one

> on whom those truths do rest
> Which we are toiling all our lives to find,
> In darkness lost, the darkness of the grave.

The child is life, the man, death. Because the child is a
symbol of so vast a conception, greater than itself, itself
emblematic of sovereign life, its 'immortality' is said to
'brood' over it like 'the day', a *domed* empyrean of light,
overarching, expansive, illimitable, and of this the child
is a 'slave' or symbol, a momentary expression. Momentary, in terms of time, or logic; yet when fused with con-
templating passion, as here, the passion-child is immortality itself, the child being a symbol only when isolated,
but actually blending with the poet's emotion and clustering imagery to create the mystery of which it is a reflection.
Or, in terms of one of Coleridge's objections, that the
child is in no valuable sense conscious of divinity any
more than a tree or a ship, we may say indeed that the child
alone has life, but not life fully conscious of life, but that
that very consciousness the poet himself provides, so that
his creation is both child in purity and man in experience.
In such marriage of the symbol with poetic passion is
created the greatest poetry, and by such welding of a
childlike faith with profound experience have been forged
the greatest lives on earth.

Consider the lines I have bracketed; the lines which
Coleridge criticized, though with some fine remarks
(following shortly afterwards) on 'splendid paradoxes'
irritatingly irreconcilable with his misunderstanding of
the poem which suggests them. Our intellectual consciousness is 'the darkness of the grave'. The second 'grave'
must be considered likewise mainly metaphoric. 'To
whom' balances the 'on whom' and 'over whom' preceding.
The paraphrase of the bracketed lines runs thus:

From whose higher standpoint the grave of the intellectual
consciousness is as a lonely bed of death, without any feeling
or seeing of light or warmth, a dayless existence, a place
of *thinking* where we lie in perpetual waiting.

The child is to be equated with the Eden of Genesis, and
the intellectual consciousness, in the realm of the knowledge of good and evil, is Death. Beyond that, there is the
Tree of Life, which makes gods of men: whither all
poetry, prophecy, and religion direct us. Now what more
pregnant images for the worst sufferings of our intellectualized existence could be found than these: darkness,
the grave, loneliness, a continual prisoned waiting, continual actionless thinking. 'Denmark's a prison': so
the Hamlets of this world, and the Wordsworth of *The
Borderers* is one of them, are condemned by their very
greatness to live a life of death, thinking in their graves.
'A frightful notion', said the critical intelligence of
Coleridge. Frightful, indeed. If we want further proof
that this is the proper sense, consider the conclusion of the
stanza, where, the momentary spark of recognition
beginning to fade, the poet returns to a sharp logic:

> Full soon thy Soul shall have her earthly freight,
> And custom lie upon thee with a weight,
> Heavy as frost, and deep almost as life!

'Earthly freight', 'lie upon thee', 'weight', 'heavy as frost',
'deep almost as life'. What do these suggest if not the
horrors of living burial, with the weight of the cold earth
frozenly pressing on the thing sunk almost as deep as its
existence: that is, all but irredeemably. Notice how
strangely Wordsworth's love of deathly cold is inverted
here to a more normal, a more healthy, sense-valuation.

I conclude that Coleridge's criticism is based on a
fundamental misunderstanding. Nor is this all. Wordsworth himself deleted the crucial lines. The Oxford note
runs: 'Found in edd. 1807 and 1815; omitted from
ed. 1820 and all subsequent issues in consequence of
Coleridge's adverse criticism.' I have observed that this

ode pursues a direction different from that of Wordsworth's normal poetic interests. Its surrounding effects (of spring, sunshine, joyous creatures, the lamb, &c.) are, indeed, precisely those seen accompanying the erotic fervour rejected as 'pitiable' in *The Prelude*, xiv. 170–80. Did he not himself understand what he had written? Did he, too, miss the whole point of his poem?

And so the ode dims to a noble conclusion, where the poet assuages his banishment from life eternal by vague intuition that in some sense the pilgrimage into mortality is necessary and just. With him, we must believe it so, or name the universe a medley and human existence a farce. But these thoughts are not our essentials here; or, rather, only important as circling routes to the summit, which is the centre. We must see the ode spatially, not merely temporally: that is, must view its pattern simultaneously outrolled, the beginning and end as framework, the outer rose-petals, the centre its fiery heart, wherein we have our vision of the child, transfigured by poetry. At the close this transfiguration becomes an eternity given not the abysmal darkness of *The Prelude*—which is, with the exception of certain fine ocean-images, as in the great Snowdon passage in Book XIV singled out by Mr. Charles Williams, a singularly *inland* world—but a more Shakespearian symbol:

> Hence in a season of calm weather
>   Though inland far we be,
> Our souls have sight of that immortal sea
>   Which brought us hither,
>   Can in a moment travel thither,
> And see the children sport upon the shore,
> And hear the mighty waters rolling evermore.

Which recalls many Shakespearian passages, Timon's sea-shore grave, *The Tempest* and Ariel's song 'Come unto these yellow sands . . .', &c. The water vivid in *The Excursion* and the Sonnets becomes here of direct metaphysical and romantic importance. Where the emphasis is expressly human, as in Shakespeare and Byron, we often find the sea more cogent as a symbol of infinitude than mountain heights or architectural magnificence.

If I may use again my *eros* and *agapé* mechanism, I suggest that here, though the child-content as such tends in the usual Wordsworthian direction, yet it is so tinglingly realized and given such full romantic associations that we can call it erotically conceived. The technique is, too, peculiarly vivid in its fusion of poet with symbol. There is thus a queer reversal of *eros* and *agapé* with respect to content and form. We can say that Pope's *Éloisa* is a fine example of the normal 'emotion recollected in tranquillity'; *The Prelude* often (not always) gives us tranquillity recollected, almost diluted, in more tranquillity; and, as though to get the balance right at all costs, the *Immortality Ode* offers a peaceful substance (the child) dynamically (as in its 'leaping up'), almost erotically, apprehended. Of course, in any artistic creation you get these elements in both dynamic reciprocity and peaceful accomplishment; coition and child. In all good poetry the form is finally quiescent. My stresses are relative. Poetry, alike in its technique and message, exists to raise us beyond this *eros* and *agapé* antinomy: which is really one with the wider antinomy of life and death.

Wordsworth's most ambitious poem is *The Excursion*, and none so strikingly exhibits both his noblest strength and most pathetic deficiencies. Here he attempts a panoramic view of man's individual and social being. There are grand scenic descriptions, but also lengthy passages in sermonic dialogue-form, heavily didactic. The doctrine is unoriginal, mainly retrospective and backward in tendency, static, and clouded by consciousness of death. Simple duties, parental care, and children receive approbation, but sexual energies as such are neglected, impregnated with distrust, or definitely evil. The whole is dominated by a carefully reiterated sun-imagery and continual placid water-impressions. These aim to give his statement cosmic sanction. The result is often unfortunate, since such fertility-impressions do not blend with the doctrinal severity.

The persons are (i) the poet himself, (ii) the Wanderer, (iii) the Solitary, and (iv) the Vicar. The discussion-group gathers in that order. The poet's function is mainly relative. The Wanderer, a philosophical pedlar, is an idealized exponent of wisdom gained through wide experience; the Solitary, who alone has human vitality, a man of troubled history, disillusion, bitterness, yet with springs of generosity and profundity; and the Vicar intended as a *deus ex machina* who gives all the right answers with the accents of infallibility. Wordsworth's favourite essences clearly reappear, though not at maximum strength: the Wanderer is a descendant of the leech-gatherer, the Solitary of Oswald, while such poems as *Michael* or *The Blind Beggar* are constantly suggested. The whole is an attempt to interrelate these with each other in close reference to north-country life, fertility-impressions, mountain-scenery, and a high moral doctrine.

The poem is in two halves. Books I–V concern lay-discussions only, and are to that extent to be considered limited; whereas Books VI–IX are dominated by the Vicar. The Wanderer is introduced as, pretty nearly, a perfected Wordsworthian instrument, thoroughly matured by suffering and deeply embedded in a placid death-awareness. After recounting a calamitous story he defends his interest by saying that 'in mournful thoughts' there often is, and always might be, found 'a power to virtue friendly' (i. 632–4). The story has serenity and a severe beauty. When, however, the poet is delighted by sight of maypole festivities and sounds of merry music and wishes to join the gay company, the Wanderer characteristically insists they journey instead towards the unhappy Solitary to derive 'good recompense' for the 'day's toil' from sight of one 'lonesome and lost' (ii. 158–60); and merrymaking is soon replaced by a funeral, with, in close association, the Solitary.

The Wanderer gives a preliminary description of the

Solitary's history of church ministry, happy marriage, bereavement, recovery under excitement during the French Revolution, resultant 'overweening trust' and 'contempt of holy writ', and, finally, with faith and self-respect gone but a wrong pride remaining, 'voluptuousness' of cynicism and 'self-indulging spleen' (II. 164–315). We meet him, however, comforting a child, and he is presented as a far from unsympathetic figure. His auto-biographical account is given a setting of rocks whose altar-like structure drops 'shadowy intimations' of some mightier than human agency (III. 87–91). His self-diagnosis is striking. When he deserts 'depths of natural passion' in an attempt to make 'society' a 'glittering bride' we have a compressed miniature of Wordsworth's life-work (III. 735–7). Disillusioned, he indulges in 'liberty of life':

> Here Nature was my guide,
> The Nature of the dissolute; but thee
> O fostering Nature! I rejected. . . .   (III. 807)

The distinction is valuable. His tangential relation to Oswald is witnessed by the 'dim and perilous way' journeyed by both (III. 701; *The Borderers*, IV. 1775). But he realizes, and *The Borderers* tells us why, the poten-tial horrors of action. His business is to roam and observe, not feel:

> And, therefore, not to act—convinced that all
> Which bears the name of action, howsoe'er
> Beginning, ends in servitude—still painful,
> And mostly profitless.   (III. 893)

A sharp, almost harsh, self-comment, if read as a Words-worthian confession. He sees the American savage beaten by Western organization yet enjoying the truer, more passive, dignity, watching reflected in the vast Mississippi his own 'innate capacities of soul' (III. 934). The Wordsworthian repudiation of action here and else-where is intensely significant.

The Wanderer, however, comes forward with 'despon-

E

dency corrected' in Book IV, rather heavily referring
nature's miracles to the divine spirit and urging the regenerating effect of activity in close contact with earth;
to which the Solitary interposes a far more convincing
insight into cosmic energies. The Wanderer urges the
superiority of superstition over cold science (IV. 611–30),
and next traces man's early religious instinct through
Hebraic, Persian, Babylonian, and Chaldean beliefs,
ending with an appreciation of Greek mythology. The
Solitary remains sceptical and asks where are the 'genuine
seats of power' (IV. 771–8). The Wanderer in answer
eulogizes the shepherd boy's existence and explains how
in ancient Greece the pastoral imagination created mythological beings to express nature's vitality; whereon the
Solitary suggests that Northern puritanism—we may
remember *The Prelude*—would give such idolatrous
beliefs short shrift; but the Wanderer asserts a basic
kinship in point of sincerity and spiritual contact (IV.
847–940). You can watch Wordsworth trying to clarify
his persistent *technical* difficulty. We have next an exploding of scientific rationalism, with a fine phrase on the
human body 'so fearfully devised' (IV. 941–94). The
Wanderer emphasizes the manifold ways of spiritual
advance, and truly observes that the Solitary's narrative
has witnessed, in its own despite, the eternal truths; and
concludes by reiterating the educative value of natural
'forms', and their relation to human ideals; with a forward glance at some newly vital science.

Henceforward the Vicar is to take control. His appearance is, however, preluded by a noble description of the
Church, discussion of church rites, and some powerful
churchyard meditations. Especially fine is the Solitary's
exquisite remark on the

> easy-hearted churl,
> Death's hireling, who scoops out his neighbour's grave,
> Or wraps an old acquaintance up in clay,
> All unconcerned as he would bind a sheaf,
> Or plant a tree.   (v. 234)

and his magnificent meditation on

> the unvoyageable sky
> In faint reflection of infinitude
> Stretched overhead, and at my pensive feet
> A subterranean magazine of bones. . . . (v. 342)

The Solitary wins, without question, high poetic honours. One cannot say as much for the Vicar: indeed, the three main persons prove convincing in inverse order to the poet's surface intention. The Vicar's graveyard reminiscences grow extremely wearisome. The author's synopses speak for themselves. Two accounts, however, I may touch briefly. There is (vi. 674–777) the 'instance of an unamiable character' (Argument), a woman of powerful personality who among humble flowers 'towered like the imperial thistle'; in whom, however, power is inverted to 'avaricious thrift' and 'a strange thraldom of maternal love'. She is by nature indisposed 'to aught so placid, so inactive, as content', and the result is a 'dread life of conflict'. Seized by illness, though thinking herself submissive, she is 'fretted', 'vexed', and jealous, and dies with a flaming gesture towards the eternal. She is less 'unamiable' than many of Wordsworth's favourites. There is, too, a vividly characterized clergyman of 'resolute virtue' (Argument), who, vital in body and mind, leaves a brilliant society for a lonely country vicarage, to which he devotes an inexhaustible energy. In old age he still

> Retained a flashing eye, a burning palm,
> A stirring foot, a head which beat at nights
> Upon its pillow with a thousand schemes. . . .
> (vii. 210)

After years of happiness his family dies, one after the other. Yet he remains

> A man of hope and forward-looking mind
> Even to the last!   (vii. 276)

He is Browningesque.

Most of the stories are tedious and sound a reiterated note of colourless tranquillity. The goodness held up for admiration is mostly passive, and it is hard to enthuse over the blind, the deaf, the widows and babes, and catalogue of deaths, for long. The verse is often cumbersome as when a fine young man makes 'the inglorious football' mount to 'the pitch of the lark's flight', and causes even the 'indefatigable fox' to dread his 'perseverance in the chase' (vii. 741–6). He is, it is true, another example of energy, for a while: but in due course we find him seized by 'convulsions dire' (vii. 870); he is carried to his grave on a fine, sunny day; and all is well. The attempt to induce spiritual tranquillity by didactic verse is not happy. Wordsworth urges, through the Pastor, that the 'heaven-born poet' should not relegate the powers of his 'sacred shell' to encouragement of any passionate unrest, of which enough exists already, while attempting instead to describe good lives for our example and encouragement (vii. 361–86): passing by the ability of poetry to *transmute* the evils of energy, to reveal, rather than dogmatize on, the purposes of eternity. Book VIII has, however, some powerful comments on England's increasing mechanization and industrialization, with both sharp criticism and an awareness of potential marvels within scientific advance if virtuously controlled.

Wordsworth fails only by attempting what is outside his powers and, indeed, his deepest purpose. The Pastor's son and a friend are introduced and enthused over, as magnificent specimens of boyhood, and one has only to compare the incident with the creation of Arviragus and Guiderius in *Cymbeline* or Andreas in Coleridge's *Zapolya* to feel an unbridgeable gap. A full-blooded, at once sunny and physical, humanism is rather unhappily attempted, and the poem continually warmed, or intended to be, by sun-reference. There is an address to the sun with general brightness, music, and colour at ii. 111–37. The Solitary is 'all fire' (ii. 516), a child is 'sun-burnt' (ii. 530). The poem's second half is introduced by a glittering description of a 'crystal Mere', woods, stream, &c., with the 'grey church-tower' rising above (v. 77–91). But such emphasized brighter impressions, of which there are many, do not mix properly with the austere theme; and 'sons of the morning' (iv. 232) is here an over-ambitious phrase. You cannot quite play with the sun as though it were a private possession. Apollo can take a terrible revenge on a rival, as Marsyas found, and much of Wordsworth's *Excursion* is flayed into a barren, colourless, skeletonic bareness. The word 'naked' occurs over and over, applied to crag, headland, rocks, earth, plain, branch, and house. It is one of Wordsworth's favourite impressions, though quite divorced from erotic sensation and to be vitally distinguished from Shelley's more fiery-physical use.

There are, however, certain separate pieces that fall into line with Coleridge's *Kubla Khan* symbolisms. Human life is felt (as in *The Prelude*, xiv. 194–205, 251–6) as a stream *descending* from rocks:

> The mountain infant to the sun comes forth,
> Like human life from darkness. (iii. 34)

The softening of a 'stony region' in a woman's heart by the birth of her child is compared to God's smiting of the rock to bring forth a stream (vi. 916–23). The Solitary meditates on a savage superstition that humanity's 'first parents' leapt from 'a rocky cave' (iii. 238–43); and later compares 'the stream of human life' to the Hindus' conception of 'holy Ganges' rising from a 'skyey fount' and winding 'a stately course' towards a 'living ocean'; or like Niger (or Coleridge's river) sinking 'engulfed' in 'impenetrable sands' and 'utter darkness' (iii. 254–62). His own life has been like a *mazy* 'mountain brook', whose murmurs

> make known
> Through what perplexing labyrinths, abrupt
> Precipitations, and untoward straights,
> The earth-born wanderer hath passed; and quickly,

That respite o'er, like traverses and toils
Must he again encounter.

'Such a stream', he says, 'is human life' moving towards 'the *unfathomable gulf* where all is still' (III. 967–91). Such are 'the crooked paths of time and change' (IV. 183). But above time lifts the higher dimension, Coleridge's dome, 'Time's eternal Master' (VI. 520), a phrase resembling the immortality brooding as 'a master o'er a slave' in the *Immortality Ode*. The Wanderer praises 'infinite majesty', the 'shadow' of whose 'might' falls across our world (IV. 99–101). The vertical dimension is suggested when a loved one is conveyed by death

> to inaccessible worlds, to regions
> Where height, or depth, admits not the approach
> Of living man.   (III. 642)

Human aspiration is compared to 'a pillar of smoke' rising with 'majestic energy' (IV. 142); and, at a moment of social and revolutionary mysticism, there rises 'a golden palace', a dazzling wonder blending earth and heaven (III. 713–22). You feel these more Coleridgean and Shelleyan images pushing through the barer narrative which itself ends with a paradisal setting, the Vicar's home and garden, his lovely children and 'summer-house' on a 'rocky garden-mount', his daughter as a 'silver fawn' (VIII. 491–3). Wordsworth embraces the idyllic pastoralism rejected in *The Prelude*, and we have a boat-journey on the 'silvery' and 'blue' (IX. 421) lake, and a picnic. The corresponding architectural symbolism occurs, with an interesting dome:

> 'Observe', the Vicar said, 'yon rocky isle
> With birch-trees fringed; my hand shall guide the helm,
> While thitherward we shape our course; or while
> We seek that other, on the western shore;
> Where the bare columns of those lofty firs,
> Supporting gracefully a massy dome
> Of sombre foliage, seem to imitate
> A Grecian temple rising from the deep.'   (IX. 495)

The long poem works up to this climax wherein religious orthodoxy flirts with the sunny paganism Wordsworth mourns for in his sonnet 'The world is too much with us...'. His domes are, however, normally more naturalistic or solemn. The sky is a 'dome' at iv. 34. There is the story of the 'unamiable female' (whose 'dread life of conflict' is compared to the 'agitation' of a mountain-brook) who at death sees the planet Jupiter set 'above the centre of the vale' as a thing eternal, in an 'untroubled element', safe from sorrow (vi. 734–40, 757–66).

The poem often expresses its otherwise scarcely infectious sense of eternal purposes in direct symbolism. The Wanderer tells how the Solitary's eye has kindled during his narrative 'like an altar lit by fire from heaven' (iv. 1121). Though his tale has been a *Kubla Khan* river flowing 'like the fabled Lethe' in 'creeping sadness' and through 'oblivious shades of death and night', it has caught continually the 'colours of the sun' (iv. 1122–6)—Coleridge's flashing dome. We continue with a shell-symbolism recalling the Arab-dream:

> I have seen
> A curious child, who dwelt upon a tract
> Of inland ground, applying to his ear
> The convolutions of a smooth-lipped shell;
> To which, in silence hushed, his very soul
> Listened intently; and his countenance soon
> Brightened with joy; for from within were heard
> Murmurings, whereby the monitor expressed
> Mysterious union with its native sea.
> Even such a shell the universe itself
> Is to the ear of Faith; and there are times,
> I doubt not, when to you it doth impart
> Authentic tidings of invisible things;
> Of ebb and flow, and ever-during power;
> And central peace, subsisting at the heart
> Of endless agitation.   (iv. 1132)

The use of 'inland' and a sea-eternity may be compared with similar impressions in the *Immortality Ode*. The

passage valuably interprets shell-symbolism in both
Wordsworth and Shelley. See the equation of 'faith' with
the mind-nature union of the *Recluse* fragment; and notice
the final awareness of opposites, rhythm and repose, rest-
lessness and peace. When writing in these terms Wordsworth is emotionally inclusive. Here 'reasoning power'
makes the 'eye blind', closing the passages 'through
which the ear converses with the heart' (iv. 1152–5): he
is for the moment with Shelley and Keats in humanistic
trust. He goes on to image a 'shock of awful consciousness' when the dome of night descends on and completes
the roof of those 'lofty', encircling, Druidical rocks,
framing a temple 'of dimensions vast', fit for anthem-
ings that 'glorify the Eternal'; and continues with dark
Coleridgean rock-recesses, caverns and rivulets, a
'fabric huge', and the 'concave of the dark blue dome';
all as a 'far-stretching view into eternity' (iv. 1156–89).
The poem shows a balancing of such naturalistic and
cosmic structures against others purely ecclesiastical,
and we have the fine church description (v. 138–70) of a
'sacred Pile', in all its roughness yet rugged strength, its
rudely painted divine images, 'sculptured oak', 'marble
monuments', and 'sepulchral stones'. However, our
finest visionary impressionism comes from the Solitary.
He tells, at the end of Book II, how they carry a sick
man, recently lost in mountain fog and storm, over mist-
wrapped rocky passes. 'A single step' suddenly takes
them from out the skirts of vapour and:

> opened to my view
> Glory beyond all glory ever seen
> By waking sense or by the dreaming soul!
> The appearance, instantaneously disclosed,
> Was of a mighty city—boldly say
> A wilderness of building, sinking far
> And self-withdrawn into a boundless depth,
> Far sinking into splendour—without end!
> Fabric it seemed of diamond and of gold,
> With alabaster domes, and silver spires,

And blazing terrace upon terrace, high
Uplifted; here, serene pavilions bright,
In avenues disposed; there, towers begirt
With battlements that on their restless fronts
Bore stars—illuminations of all gems!
By earthly nature had the effect been wrought
Upon the dark materials of the storm
Now pacified; on them, and on the coves
And mountain-steeps and summits, whereunto
The vapours had receded, taking there
Their station under a cerulean sky.
Oh, 'twas an unimaginable sight!
Clouds, mists, streams, watery rocks and emerald turf,
Clouds of all tincture, rocks and sapphire sky,
Confused, commingled, mutually inflamed,
Molten together, and composing thus,
Each lost in each, that marvellous array
Of temple, palace, citadel, and huge
Fantastic pomp of structure without name,
In fleecy folds voluminous, enwrapped.   (II. 831)

In the midst he sees as it were a throne, with correspondences of gigantic stature, glorified; vast as 'forms
uncouth of mightiest power' and 'awe' such as those of
Hebrew prophecy. The vale of human existence lies
beneath: this is the 'abode of Spirits in beatitude'. So

                    my heart
Swelled in my breast—'I have been dead', I cried,
'And now I live! Oh! Wherefore *do* I live?'
And with that pang I prayed to be no more! (II. 874)

How sharply that tiny soliloquy condenses the problem of
human survival in terms of a new revelation of human
personality. But, for the rest, see the light handling of
massive substance; the subtle interchange of solidity and
ethereality, of natural magnificence with human art; the
building up a consciousness of the titanic in stature to
realize the titanic in quality. A superhuman energy and
action creates supernal placidity. What 'mutual inflaming'
of creation's marvels—there is love of all sorts within it—

and what transmuting of fiery agony to a 'molten' joy!
This experience is, later, called

> Confusion infinite of heaven and earth
> Dazzling the soul.   (III. 721)

In so condensed a descriptive set-piece Wordsworth can
accomplish the syntheses his wider narrative schemes
lack. Remember the dying man whom this very storm
and these mountains have killed, being carried to his rest.
Here lies exposed the meaning of those mysterious
feelings of grandeur in association with death and horror
so often found in *The Prelude*. A strange clarity now
vanquishes the poet's other reluctance to engage himself
too far in poetic idolatries, in jewels, domes, palaces, and
thrones. Having glimpsed the archetypal wonder he
throws off all critical precepts of his own fashioning and
lays the richest splendours of human fabrication at the
feet of glory.

The description, perhaps, lacks complexity: it is an
outpouring of unrestrained magnificence. Let us conclude
with a passage of subtler tone, more unobtrusively
marrying nature and human experience, and therefore
less obviously symbolic. 'Within the soul', says the
Wanderer, abides a faculty that turns all hindrances to
'contingencies of pomp', thereby increasing her own
exaltation:

> As the ample moon,
> In the deep stillness of a summer even
> Rising behind a thick and lofty grove,
> Burns, like an unconsuming fire of light,
> In the green trees; and, kindling on all sides
> Their leafy umbrage, turns the dusky veil
> Into a substance glorious as her own,
> Yea, with her own incorporated. . . .   (IV. 1062)

So a reserve of 'power' in man can transmute all evils of
mortality.

Though such subtle interweaving of thought with
naturalistic impression is rare in *The Excursion*, the poem
has its own noble and austere demand on our attention.

There is throughout an inherent falsity in attempt to sanction austerity with water-paradises and sun-splendours, but the doctrine, as doctrine, is gravely insistent. The human interests, as such, sag: we must not expect anything else. The energic sources of existence are, as in *Paradise Regained*, mostly denied. We watch a failure to embody transcendence in human terms, with a corresponding surrender to paradisal and architectural symbols. The rest of Wordsworth's work to be observed is largely concerned with various structures: castles, domes, churches. To these I now pass, requiring of the reader that he keep in detailed memory Coleridge's *Kubla Khan*, with its domed architecture dropping a shadow across a nature of chasm, fertility, 'mazy' river, cave, and 'sunless' sea.

III

Remembrance of Coleridge's *Kubla Khan* symbolism and Wordsworth's own move from *The Borderers* and *The Prelude* to *The Excursion* will clarify our approach to the various sonnet-groups and other sequences. These aim at direct and, on the whole, optimistic description of nature and human works, the nature often being symbolically felt and the works concerned mainly architectural. With these are interwoven Wordsworth's favourite and severe doctrines, personal, political, and religious.

Imagery sometimes recalls *Kubla Khan*:

Thus when thou with Time hast travelled
Toward the mighty gulf of things,
And the mazy stream unravelled
With thy best imaginings. . . .

(The Longest Day)

The reminiscence 'sunless' is interestingly present in some lines (*On the Death of James Hogg*) treating of Coleridge's own death:

The rapt One, of the godlike forehead,
The heaven-eyed creature sleeps in earth;
And Lamb, the frolic and the gentle,
Has vanished from his lonely hearth.

> Like clouds that rake the mountain-summits,
> Or waves that own no curbing hand,
> How fast has brother followed brother,
> From sunshine to the sunless land!

There are natural architectures. *Yew-Trees* has a 'pillared shade' and 'sable roof', with 'Death the Skeleton' and 'Time the Shadow'. *The Triad* introduces us to 'domes of pleasure' (cp. Coleridge's 'sunny pleasure-dome') in a stanza of fanciful delicacy. In *Hart-Leap Well* the knight records the stag's place of death with a sumptuous 'pleasure-house', carefully described, to be a place of love and merry-making; with, however, a typically Words-worthian repudiation of callous enjoyments built on slaughter, and a final victory for nature. *Memorials of a Tour in Scotland, 1814,* III, describes an elaborate 'pleasure-ground on the banks of the Bran, near Dunkeld', with an intense prose and poetry realization of the usual effects: 'magic', a 'splendid apartment' itself 'dizzy and alive with waterfalls', amazing reflections; a 'hollow dome', mirrors, dazzle, colour; next contrasted with an effigy 'sculptured out of living stone', various darker and more sacred impressions, an 'abbey's sanctity', 'mountain solitude', granite, and the wind's 'melancholy moans'; a condemnation of artificial delights beside 'the depths' of true art. But he is often forced back on some such object. When the strange poem *Gold and Silver Fishes in a Vase* sees the 'transparent cell' as 'type of a sunny human breast' *Kubla Khan* is not far off; in *Liberty*, the poem's sequel, it draws nearer, the fish being removed to a 'pool in the pleasure-ground of Rydal Mount'; and becomes finally almost explicit in phrases such as 'the golden Power' and 'the silver Tenant of the crystal dome'.

The River Duddon is a sonnet sequence of some interest. It starts (1) with a rejection of 'Alpine torrents' and 'ice-built arches radiant as Heaven's bow' (Coleridgean in tendency) and welcomes instead the 'birthplace' of a 'native' stream. The river is a 'cradled Nursling of the mountain' (4); the association of river-sources with birth is consistent. It next goes in 'curves', as a 'glistering snake' with 'sinuous lapse' (4). Nature-imagery is slightly ornate or geometrical as when birch-trees make a 'silver colonnade' (5) and river-bed stones show a 'studied symmetry' (9): with which a normal, idyllic, love-interest entwines at 7, 10, 22, and 25. Plastic images start up: Naiad dwellings as 'bright liquid mansions' stronger than 'palace and tower' (12), a niche in the chasm seeming as if carved for 'some statue' (15), leading on to Indian cliff-carvings in America (16), and Druid ritual (17). Such blend into Christian architectures, Seathwaite Chapel raising thoughts of 'sacred Religion' as 'mother of form and fear' (18), or other medieval structures, as in the 'embattled House' whose 'massy keep' drops a *shadow* from its cliff (27). The Kirk of Ulpha (31) is 'as a star' in a 'black cloud', a 'fruitful palm-tree' in Arabia, the 'boundless canopy' of an Indian tree. The river is a symbol of innocence (30), bound for eternity (33). From a paradisal nature is gradually formed the sacred and eternal, the river entwined with various buildings. The river-sequence concludes (34) with explicit reference to human life, its transience, eternal meaning, and ever-fleeting indestructibility. 'The Form remains, the Function never dies'; though bound for a 'silent tomb' we are 'greater than we know'. Wordsworth tends more and more to re-express that mysterious greatness in terms of native ecclesiastical, or other, architectures.

A short collection entitled *Inscriptions* is very significant. The poet's own 'pensive strains' (the idiom is often idyllic) are set beside Sir George Beaumont's wooing of 'the silent Art' (i.e. painting). Impressions occur of 'memorial stone', 'temples' and 'columns', 'hallowed urn', trees as 'pillars', and a 'darksome aisle'; and the 'awful Pile' where Reynolds lies buried. The first four poems concern Sir George Beaumont's estate at Coleorton. In the fourth ruins are contrasted with the intellect's ability to raise 'from airy words alone' (cp. 'air' in *Kubla Khan*) a 'pile, that ne'er decays'. The fifth, written on an outhouse on an island at Grasmere, compares it with buildings of 'proportions more harmonious', nearer to 'ideal grace', and honours its simplicity with meditations of a slightly decorative, artificial, kind leading to faery-impressions of dream and romance. The seventh celebrates the ruins of 'a little Dome' or 'Pleasure-house' designed by a certain Sir William but never completed. The 'outrage' must be forgiven. The reader is warned that,

> if, disturbed
> By beautiful conceptions, thou hast hewn
> Out of the quiet rock the elements
> Of thy trim Mansion destined soon to blaze
> In snow-white splendour,

he had best remember Sir William's pleasure-dome and desist. 'Snow-white' is Coleridgean. The eleventh poem (inscription on a rock) is so too. The poet saw the rock upholding a marvellous monument, a kind of Taj Mahal, white as 'marble', pure as 'ether', as if in honour of some buried hero; his fancy 'kindled', and in sunlight the structure 'glistened' and 'blazed' proudly; but the miracle is only of 'frost', and melts. The wondrous 'fabric', however, is given exquisite description. In the next poem 'thoughts' are as 'bubbles' under ice, a wind-swept meadow or troubled sea, with death a 'shadow' from the 'rock eternity'. The collection concludes with a rocky stream felt as emblematic of the human mind. Sir George Beaumont, with whom we started, is celebrated again in the *Elegiac Stanzas* on his picture of Peele Castle. Wordsworth first imagines the castle 'sleeping on a glassy sea'; associates it with the magic transmutations of poetry; considers it, like other domes, 'a treasure-house divine' and 'chronicle of heaven'. Such fancies he contrasts with tragic experience and that 'pageantry of fear' the picture offers, and rejects the castle-paradise precisely as Tennyson rejects his Palace of Art:

> Farewell, farewell the heart that lives alone,
> Housed in a dream, at distance from the Kind!

Instead, we ·must welcome fortitude and patience. The typical symbolisms often recur negatively, to be rejected: even so, they help to define the other acceptance.

Miscellaneous Sonnets illustrate Wordsworth's consistent reliance on this brief form. Action and human analysis are replaced by meditations on art itself: poetry, music, painting, and, continually, architecture. Nature feeling is, of course, constant, and usually bright and glittering. The moon and Venus are vividly addressed, birds are idyllic, water-drops glitter, and the sea is a symbol of peace. Pagan mythology assists frequently, and faery-impressions and even faery-personifications are allowed. Sleep is honoured, as in Shelley and Keats. There is a tendency to concentrate on poetry or other arts. Wordsworth writes sonnets on sincerity in poetry and critics (III. 27); on the sonnet-form itself (I. 1; II. 1); on 'a violent tribe of Bards' (I. 34). One sonnet (III. 83) is called 'a plea for authors'. Paintings bulk heavily: the painter Haydon is addressed twice (II. 3; III. 26), and sonnets are written on a portrait of Henry VIII (III. 4), the Duke of Wellington (III. 29), and a pictured figure in 'saint-like trance', one hand lifted (III. 31). The art is praised in terms of its static vitality (as in Keats's *Grecian Urn*) and 'soul-soothing' introduction to the eternal (I. 9); and again as a time-conquering power (III. 32). Philoctetes is imagined as 'a Form sculptured on a monument' (III. 12). *Kubla Khan* mechanisms assert themselves. 'New-born waters' (III. 21) and 'new-born rivers' (III. 22) carry on a usual water-birth association. Shawford Brook goes in a 'tempting maze' (I. 16). Death is a cave (I. 28); so is, psychologically, poetry (II. 17). Three sonnets powerfully describe Yorkshire caves, with associations of hell-tormented spirits, prehistoric giant art, and tidal waters (II. 33–5); while 'The Torrent at the Devil's Bridge, North Wales', with its 'dread chasm', woods, and 'everlasting snows', is such as exerts power over all poets 'young or old' (III. 10). As for symbolic structures, we have tranquillity as an 'azure disc' (II. 15),

poetic mountains (I. 5), an 'aerial rock', 'imperial castle'
and 'votive towers' catching the 'golden sunset', with,
too, a 'sinuous vale and roaring stream' (I. 11); spiritual
peace is a 'temple' in a sonnet starting with sea-description
(I. 30), stars are 'mansions' for blest spirits, and all of
nature's handiwork is 'dome or vault or nest' (II. 25). A
delicately Coleridgean sonnet mentioning Addison's
'Vision of Mirza' treats of soft music, 'visionary arches',
and a 'sacred' music-built mountain (I. 8). Sunset sky-
formations make an 'Indian citadel' or 'Temple of
Greece' (II. 11), but such a 'sky-built dome' is next considered symbolic of gaudy insubstantialities (II. 12).
Though direct symbolic force is sometimes absent, the
continual attention to structures is significant. They are
various: a simple cottage (I. 2, 4), a 'Pile of Turf' as a
'rude Mausoleum' (III. 23), a ruined castle (III. 8),
another castle (III. 21), Worcester Cathedral (III. 19), the
'wide-spanned arch' of Furness Abbey (III. 47–8), a
church spire (III. 40), an 'old grey stone' like some ancient
tomb (II. 10), Roman antiquities (III. 20). Moreover,
just as nature is here most often glittering, so human
civilization has its flashing surfaces and aspiring arts.
From Westminster Bridge London at dawn appears
beautiful as nature:

> . . . silent, bare
> Ships, towers, domes, theatres, and temples lie
> Open unto the fields and to the sky;
> All bright and glittering in the smokeless air.
>
> (II. 36)

The 'spires' and 'domes' of Oxford are likewise honoured
(III. 2). Such realistic descriptions tone into those more
symbolical, architectural metaphor (as in I. 34) being an
increasingly important Wordsworthian approach to all
inward and cosmic adventures. In his 'mind's eye' a
cloud-like 'Temple' rises from darkness, a 'bright work'
symbolic both of human art and divine meaning: Faith
has her 'arch', Love her 'towers' sinking deeper than death,

and Hope her 'spire', a building against which no hell-
phantoms can exert their power (III. 44). These sonnets
show smooth sea, gushing rivers, bright nature; mountains; pagan mythology; continual references to the arts
—to music as well as poetry, painting, and architecture,
the last with strong religious implications.

I am concentrating on image and symbol, but the many
religious, social, and historic sentiments enwoven would
need, necessarily, more extended notice. Such are naturally
still stronger in *Poems Dedicated to National Independence
and Liberty*. Nature is felt as ultimately identical with
man's nobler self and all those political ideals to which
he aspires: as in the reference of political martyrdom to
powers of air, earth, and skies in *To Toussaint L'Ouverture*
(I. 8) and the fine 'Two voices are there . . .' on the *Sub-
jugation of Switzerland* (I. 12). Star, sea, and 'naked
heavens' contribute to the austere and simple purity de-
manded by the sonnet on Milton (I. 14). A 'glittering
brook' is an image of superficiality (I. 13), but the 'flood'
of 'open sea' symbolizes 'British freedom' (I. 16). Though
criticism of Britain is harsh, her enemies are worse (I. 21):
Threat of invasion inspires patriotism (I. 25). The
poems of Part II range wide geographically. The sentiments are noble, with strong sense of true power coming
from *within* (II. 29) and a contrast of armed might with
a more reserved, yet infinitely powerful, national will
(II. 32). The sequence works up to the celebration of
British national success in three powerful odes. The first
(II. 39), dated 1814, imagines the descent of Saint George
as a 'glorious Form'. The poetry is highly pictorial with
victory-garlands twined by virgins and matrons, crimson
banners, ritual-ceremony with girls in 'dazzling white'
and 'rosy boys'. A sunny dome, with sleep, occurs:

> Anon before my sight a palace rose
> Built of all precious substances,—so pure
> And exquisite, that sleep alone bestows
> Ability like splendour to endure:
> Entered, with streaming thousands, through the gate,

I saw the banquet spread beneath a Dome of state,
A lofty Dome, that dared to emulate
The heaven of sable night
With starry lustre; yet had power to throw
Solemn effulgence, clear as solar light,
Upon a princely company below,
While the vault rang with choral harmony,
Like some nymph-haunted grot beneath the roaring sea.

The ode descends next to the 'silent art' of sculpture and
monument, 'consecrated places' and 'imperishable columns'
to eternalize heroism, and concludes with the muses as
'Pierian sisters', and thoughts of poetry asserting 'Britain's
acts' to be as 'lofty' as any in 'man's heroic prime'.
Wordsworth's later work teems with variously pagan
or Christian architectures, ceremonial and music. The
'choral harmony' here is repeated in another ode (II. 45),
dated 1815. 'Justice triumphs, Earth is freed.' On the
'shore of silver Thames', in the 'mighty town' to which
'persecuted men retreat', a 'new Temple' is imagined
as rising, a bright 'Fabric', a star of peace and grace.
Ecclesiastical ritual within Westminster Abbey uniting
the living and dead is called forth to celebrate heroism,
with 'visual pomp' and organ-music soft and thunderous,
and a white-robed choir. England's 'martial service' is
approved by the great God of pestilence and drought,
volcano and earthquake, swallowing towns and cities, a
god almighty, using nations for a righteous purpose; the
awe-inspiring thought pointing us back to *The Prelude*
and *The Borderers* and forward to the sonnets on the
death-penalty. This great and terrible God of Battles is
honoured in terms of church ceremonial. Another ode
(II. 46), dated 1816 and written for an official thanksgiving, has further elaborations. Paradisal nature-imagery
accompanies 'towers of righteousness'. England's office
is felt as strongly ethical in service to the 'citadels of
truth'. Her greatness is hymned:

To Thee the exterminating sword is given.
Dread mark of approbation, justly gained!

The long, somewhat repetitive, poem returns to nature-imagery and the sun and

O, enter now his Temple gate!

with organ cathedral music, and a 'Throne of grace'. Wordsworth's feeling for organ music, and, indeed, much else in his poetry, is strongly Miltonic.

There is some fine poetry in Wordsworth's odes. *Vernal Ode* has a compactness and symbolic force repaying attention. The bee is the centre of a passage at once interpretative and descriptive. Nature is cleverly contrasted, not all to its disadvantage, with higher dimensions ('shadow' recurs throughout with the proper *dimensional* significance), her own cyclic revival from 'unfathomable deeps' themselves witnessing eternal essence. The ode starts with a supernatural appearance, like our recent Saint George, poising in 'middle air' and floating to earth:

Upon the apex of that lofty cone
Alighted, there the Stranger stood alone;
Fair as a gorgeous Fabric of the east
Suddenly raised by some enchanter's power,
Where nothing was; and firm as some old Tower
Of Britain's realm, whose leafy crest
Waves high, embellished by a gleaming shower!

The two buildings are in juxtaposition. One might define much of Wordsworth as the attempt to integrate the one into the other; to inflate English history and England's buildings with the magic significance of *Kubla Khan*.

Wordsworth's later work reads as a search for various 'objective equivalents' to his sense of the eternal: hence the reiterated structures. These serve as substitutes for strong human action. *Memorials of a Tour on the Continent* (1820) is one succession of such poems. Here are some titles: *In Presence of the Painted Tower of Tell, at Altorf* (20), *The Town of Schwytz* (21), *The Church of San Salvador, seen from the Lake of Lugano* (24), *The Column*

intended by Buonaparte for a Triumphal Edifice in Milan (29).
Wordsworth sees Bruges 'attired with golden light' as
with 'a robe of power', and with avenues of 'stateliest
architecture' (2), and, again, enshrining the 'spirit of
antiquity' in 'sumptuous buildings', the whole city 'one
vast temple' (3). Between Namur and Liége he sees grey
rocks 'like old monastic turrets' (6); is disappointed at the
'puny Church' with 'feeble columns' at Aix-la-Chapelle,
the 'Seat of Charlemagne' (7); wishes for the 'help of
Angels' to complete the 'Temple' of Cologne Cathedral,
and strains of music to create an 'empyreal', heavenly,
ground for 'immortal Fabrics' of the *Kubla Khan* variety
(8); is entranced by the 'venerable pageantry of Time',
'beetling' ramparts and towers and cloistral arches, on the
banks of the Rhine (9); writes a hymn for boatmen
approaching the rapids under the Castle of Heidelberg
(10); is pleased by a 'votive stone' touched by the 'golden
finger' of sunset (14); writes of Engelberg, the Hill of
Angels, with impressions of hymns in 'middle-air', 'holy
structure', and 'resplendent apparition' (18). The ruins
of Fort Fuentes call forth a poem with a preface of
detailed architectural description, including notice of a
child statue in 'pure white marble' surviving intact after
disaster (23). A sabbath morning in the Vale of Cha-
mouny suggests *Processions* (32), a poem concerned with
'living monuments', 'solemnities' in 'long array', marches
round an altar; with various reminders of pagan ritual,
'Roman pomps', and Corybantic extravagance; and a
return to Christian ceremony, with the 'white-robed
shapes' resembling the 'living stream' of 'glacier pillars'
issuing from 'the impenetrable heart of that exalted
mount'. The collection is summed up in a concluding
poem (38) on the poet's 'contending themes' of cataract
and city, mountains as 'wrinkled sons of Time' and his own
Fancy as an 'airy bridge'; with sentiments political and
religious entwined with mountain-strength and cathedral
music, and his own consciousness again an 'arch of airy
workmanship' with earth below and heaven beside, and

Time as a river pressing remorselessly on. In such terms Wordsworth meditates over and over again the interactions of the temporal and the eternal.

Memorials of a Tour in Italy (1837) is similar with a heavier emphasis on ecclesiastical art. The first poem, *Musings near Aquapendente*, has the favourite Wordsworthian image of a seeming-still torrent (cp. *Address to Kilchurn Castle*, 38), a 'cone-shaped' hill, and later a 'glorious temple', 'Baptistery's dome', 'cathedral pile', 'tower's shadow', 'convent-crested cliff'; with thoughts of the 'pure poetic spirit', and compliments paid to 'words', 'word-preserving arts', and historic Powers 'by poesy irradiate'. He calls on 'Christian traditions' to reveal their splendours 'on the brow of ancient Rome': 'sanctuaries', 'catacombs', cross, orisons. Time is a *Kubla Khan* stream whose gifts sink 'out of sight' mysteriously. The relation of history to imagination is elaborated (4–6), with rights accorded to each. 'Eternal things' are contrasted with 'change' (3), time with eternity (18). St. Peter's 'everlasting Dome' concludes a sonnet (2). At Florence the poet stands under the 'shadow' of a 'stately Pile' and its 'dome' (19), or before a Raphael picture (20). He is deeply involved not so much with men as with vast nature, eternal memorials and transcendent structures; with the 'rich stores of Nature's imagery' and 'divine art' (26). He concludes with *The Pillar of Trajan*, meditating on 'mutilated arches' and 'temples' doomed to 'change'. Round the enduring and time-beautified ruin man's passionate and *fluid* history beats as a sea; on it embossed figures, as on Keats's urn, continually ascend, 'group winding after group with dream-like ease', like the woodbine's 'spiral grace'. It is 'murmuring but one smooth story for all years', again recalling Keats; standing as a 'memorial Pillar', record of a 'haughty' but forgotten Empire amid 'the wrecks of Time', 'glorious Art' defying all temporal power. Trajan 'mounts, in this fine illusion, toward the skies', till Rome starts forth from 'silent marble' and lives as 'a vision of the mind'. So sculptural

or other plastic art blending vitality with stillness continually serves to resolve the opposition of temporal fluidity
and eternal structure.

I cannot do justice to the thinking enwoven with these
structures: they are always, of course, more than pictorial. One watches a growing interest in the Christian
Church. Wordsworth satisfactorily fuses his various
interests in the *Ecclesiastical Sonnets*.

These trace the history of the Anglican Church.
Wordsworth seeks on the 'heights of Time' the source of
this 'Holy River' (I. 1), England's Church being a 'growing Rill' (I. 5), a stream (I. 37). Christian faith is a
'sacred well' (I. 2). Nature is thus incorporated into our
ecclesiastical series. The poet defends the right of poetic
'fancy' to serve religion (I. 18). We watch Christianity
replacing the 'baleful rite' (I. 3) of the Druids and next
its various fortunes under Roman, Saxon, Danish, and
Norman invaders. 'Fanes', 'holy rites', and 'ceremonials'
keep actual observances before our eyes (I. 7). There are
many examples. Though Christian structures are contrasted with *Kubla Khan* temptations of 'fair houses'

> And temples flashing, bright as polar ice,
> Their radiance through the woods,   (I. 8)

the 'silver Cross' has its own resplendence (I. 14). A recapitulation of the famous image defining man's life as a
bird intruding into a brilliant banquet-hall and vanishing in darkness may be allowed to make correspondence
with Coleridge's river (I. 16). The 'sacred structures'
of monasteries instil simple but valuable faith (I. 24),
and even work to preserve pagan culture (I. 25). The
Crusades are attributed to 'the mightiest lever known
to the moral world, Imagination' (I. 34), but the humbling
of England before papal authority is deplored (I. 37).
A blend of national and religious allegiances is the whole
purpose of these essentially British sonnets.

It is, however, admitted that the Church of Rome
thunders 'from her spiritual tower' (II. 2) against brutish

passions and, in spite of lapses, assists righteousness. A Cistercian monastery spreads gentleness round its 'holy spires' (ii. 3) and monks free serfs from 'legalised oppression' (ii. 4). Their leavening influence is praised (ii. 5, 6). Crusaders return to lie in 'cross-legged effigy' on 'chancel floors' (ii. 8). The unity of Christendom is attested by 'works of Art', and 'countless Temples' rise symbolical of the Faith (ii. 9): but horror of superstition makes the sonnet *Transubstantiation* (ii. 11) contrast burning 'tapers', 'odorous incense', 'greedy flame', and all the paraphernalia of ritualism with the great 'Invisible' and rough Nature's 'craggy' sincerities. Two more sonnets indulge in natural fervour (ii. 12, 13). Wicliffe is honoured in terms of a stream (ii. 17); monastic self-indulgence and pagan revelry wrong the 'arched roof' of their setting (ii. 20); nuns are sympathetically discussed (ii. 22–3), legendary saints given a glamorous sonnet (ii. 24), and the Virgin Mother naturalistic praise (ii. 25). Rome, so long the 'aerial keystone' to the 'arch of Christendom' (ii. 26), sees her power decline. A remarkable sonnet (ii. 27) hears the 'ghostly tenants of the wind', while Tiber, Ganges, and Nile, all sacred *rivers* of the ancient world, lament her fall, if only in sympathy for her more pagan affinities. Yet the impressions involved of demons, 'monstrous urn', forest and cave, make this sonnet powerful beyond most of its companions, and drive it on to consideration of Mohammedan schemings

> 'Mid spectral lakes bemocking thirsty men,
> And stalking pillars built of fiery sand.

We shall find such sand-pillars in Coleridge. Wordsworth next honours the Bible as our sole remaining security, deplores the 'revival of Popery' that makes altars 'smoke' again with 'frankincense' (ii. 33), and passes through various famous martyrdoms to the 'silver car' of Elizabeth (ii. 38), Hooker in association with 'spicy shores of Araby' (ii. 39), and the Reformed Church (ii. 40). The variously tranquil and volcanic influence of religion is

finely compared (II. 43–4) to a 'Virgin-Mountain' wearing
a 'brilliant crown of everlasting snow' (the image denotes
Elizabeth) changing to 'blasts of tempestuous smoke'
(i.e. civil wars). Part II ends with a noble comparison of
God's steadfast purpose with (i) the firmament and (ii)
the 'chambers of the deep'. Wordsworth's naturalistic
sympathy is never denied by his ethical and ecclesiastical
interests, and the sea often accompanies religious emotion.

In Part III a sonnet called *Latitudinarianism* sets
Church inspiration beside

> . . . a Platonic piety confined
> To the sole temple of the inward mind,

and moves to a eulogy on Milton (III. 4). *Clerical Integrity* sees Nonconformists driven from their 'altars' by
an 'inward sense' of rectitude (III. 6). When the second
Pilgrim Fathers sonnet (III. 14) sees concord and charity
moving in circles 'transcendent over time', the circular
eternity is interesting. A sonnet of fine naturalism praises
England's 'places of worship', her 'Christian fanes',
spires, steeples, chapels 'lurking among trees' (III. 17).
Various sonnets discuss the Church calendar and Church
ritual:

> As through a zodiac, moves the ritual year
> Of England's Church.   (III. 19)

Sonnet-titles include Baptism, Sponsors, Catechising,
Confirmation, Sacrament, Marriage Ceremony, Funeral
Service, and other such rites. *Regrets* (III. 33) prettily
blends the ecclesiastical and richly natural; *Old Abbeys*
speaks of 'monastic Domes' and venerable ruins, with a
moral drawn from temporal change (III. 35); *New Churches*
(III. 38) sees 'sacred truth' as a 'flood' and joys in the
arrival of new 'temples' and 'sabbath bells'. Churches
rise among oaks 'of Druid memory' and daisies where
once may-garlands were woven (III. 39): that is, they grow
organically, rooted in England's natural and spiritual
history. Though for us no such 'appalling' ritual is used
as when 'dread hosannas' sound while from 'clouds of

incense' the rood, or cross, glimmers as a pine-tree through 'Alpine vapours', yet each building has its cross outside, greeted by the sun, wooed by the incense of morning (III. 40). An intermesh of the naturalistic and the austere is more satisfying than in *The Excursion*: the themes are, of course, shorter, and human persons less involved. The sequence concludes with some magnificent architectural descriptions, highly charged with various eternal significances. *Cathedrals* (III. 42) sees these 'everlasting Piles' as 'types', or 'symbols', of the 'spiritual Church'; admires their 'sumptuous aisles' and 'intricate defiles'; watches the tower seem to *grow* (as the dark rock in *The Prelude*) while the watcher moves, making, as it were, a ladder to train the heart and will upwards. King's College Chapel, Cambridge, has three sonnets (III. 43–5). It is a work of 'fine intelligence', with 'lofty pillars', a 'branching roof', all 'self-poised', with 'ten thousand cells' of intermingling light and shade in which music lingers undying like thoughts born for 'immortality'. As evening falls the stained windows in this 'awful perspective' hide their portraitures, the 'stone-work' glimmers, while martyr, king, and saint glow with 'solemn sheen' and fade; but— and the contrast suggests that of death blossoming into immortality—music 'bursteth into second life', and every stone is kissed

> By sound, or ghost of sound, in mazy strife.

Such a building is not 'perishable'. Within Westminster Abbey all 'bubbles' of folly burst, its foam melts: as so often, the temporal is as water, though the great sea itself may symbolize the eternal. Saint Paul's is 'a younger pile'

> whose sky-like dome
> Hath typified by reach of daring art
> Infinity's embrace.

In which the relevance of our whole sequence to *Kubla Khan* and other such symbolisms is summed. We end with two naturalistic sonnets. The first sees the incarnate Christ as a human tabernacle, 'like ocean burning with purpureal flame', or an Alpine mount rosy at morn and evening; and strains for 'unimpeded commerce with the sun' (III. 46). In the last, futurity sleeps darkly as a coiled snake, but may yet be awakened by the Word of God: that is, our future is as assured as the very 'stream' we have been tracing. Something there is in this story out-living nations and death and 'mighty kings': the 'living Waters' grow slowly purer, and roll, brightening, to-wards the 'eternal City'.

Though certain tonings be bright enough, Words-worth's awe-inspiring structures are the most successful. These throw us back on memory of *The Prelude* and its haunting awe. His best early nature and mature archi-tectures are pre-eminently grave. Among the last things he wrote are those great but almost terrifying sonnets on the *Punishment of Death*. 'O, restrain compassion' sounds queerly, under any circumstances, as a phrase of consi-dered poetic judgement. The Roman Consul dooming his own sons is a prototype of duty. Death is, we are told, not the worst evil; and the laws deep-planted in man's conscience must not lack support from govern-ment. The argument is, I think, justly related to the stern workings of 'the one Paternal mind', the great unknown God of battles and earthquakes; the contention very significantly repeating that of Oswald, the villain of Wordsworth's early Satanic play *The Borderers*. But only a subtle dishonesty solicits indirectly the sanction of Christ, with whom neither Wordsworth nor Milton are, I feel, quite at home. However, fine things are said:

> What is a State? The wise behold in her
> A creature born of time, that keeps one eye
> Fixed on the statutes of Eternity.

Even though human life be the 'shrine' of an 'immortal spirit', over which it seems no tribunal should exert final authority, though 'Eternity and Time' have most subtly 'interwoven claims and rights' demanding 'heaven-born' mercy, yet there remains a danger of letting the 'finite sense' measure 'Infinite Power, perfect Intelligence'. Therefore, remembering that imprisonment and penal extradition may prove more cruel than death, the law, like Marmaduke at a criminal moment—and the strangeness of the comparison holds significance—leaves 'the final issue in *His* hands' who is eternal love. You could argue that Wordsworth dares a grim realism which other poets shirk, but when he sees the condemned man brought as a 'kneeling penitent' before the altar, the sacrament softening his heart and bringing tears to his eyes, one may question the emotional integrity. Wordsworth expects the judge to tremble at his own sentence, and listeners to 'shudder'; yet when the 'sacrifice' is called not unmeet 'for Christian Faith', the ritual-word shadows a certain communal enjoyment of a criminal's execution which sinks into atavistic possibilities which the rational intelligence would probably deny. However, social conditions improve, and the penalty will eventually fall into disuse: 'Oh, speed the blessed hour, Almighty God!' These sonnets are, I think, noble, sincere, and, finally, un-Christian: whereas I should call Nietzsche's opposite view (in *Zarathustra*) at once unsocial and deeply Christian. The balance is held by Shakespeare in *The Merchant of Venice*. But, whatever our opinions, the reference of these sonnets, in choice of subject and treatment, to both the satanic doctrine of *The Borderers* and the enjoyment of corpse-horrors in *The Prelude*, is necessary. The wheel comes full circle: Wordsworth ends where he began.

Wordsworth's attempts at a sunny nature, pagan mythology, or glittering architecture are variously short-lived, half-condemned by himself, or unsatisfactory. Harmonious structures are being used to blend mountain-worship with 'geometric truth.' Such more positive expressions are, of course, far harder to *realize* than are his ghostly presences. It seems that a weakness in mastery of the human problem forces him back variously on (i) a deathly otherness, dark mind-hauntings, and (ii) second-

hand description of the arts. Music unifies the two: a
mental, abstract, mysterious, and other-worldly art. I
have not emphasized Wordsworth's feeling for sound.
It is as important as in Milton; as when the sea makes
with its 'eternal motion' a 'sound like thunder, ever-
lastingly' (*Miscellaneous Sonnets*, 1. 30), or when mountains and cataracts are the two voices of Liberty:

> For, high-soul'd Maid, what sorrow would it be
> That mountain floods should thunder as before,
> And ocean bellow from his rocky shore,
> And neither awful voice be heard by thee!
> *(Independence and Liberty*, 1. 12)

The Miltonic music itself is compared to the sea: 'Thou
had'st a voice whose sound was like the sea' (*Independence and Liberty*, 1. 14). This ocean-voice, the voice of
eternal being, was finely honoured in the *Immortality
Ode*:

> And hear those mighty waters rolling evermore. . . .

Probably Wordsworth's genius attains its most characteristic expression in his ode *On the Power of Sound*.

His summary of the argument alone witnesses the
philosophical care expended. As so often, deepest layers
of the mind receive a cave-formulation:

> A Spirit aerial
> Informs the cell of Hearing, dark and blind;
> Intricate labyrinth, more dread for thought
> To enter than oracular cave.

The reverential awe corresponds to that sense of mystery
and power in the 'mind of man' urgent throughout
Wordsworth. This poem, like the *Immortality Ode*, fuses
the haunting depths with a precise daylight, though often
highly metaphysical, projection. All sorts of *sounds* are
noticed: sighs, shrieks, warblings, hosannas, requiems,
a nun's throbbing fear, a 'sailor's prayer', a cottage-
lullaby. There are no facile exclusions: the lion's roar is set
by the lamb's bleating. A single line does much to realise

a bird unknown to most of us:

Toll from thy loftiest perch, lone bell-bird, toll!

Impressions pile up of huntsman's music among rocks and caves and church bells, 'bridal symphony' and milk-maids' ditties. Song comforts blindness, peasants and slaves find that it empowers their labours, it draws pilgrims towards the distant shrine. Moreover, at a time of civic awakening, the soul of Freedom finds expression no words can supply in a tune; while in war-time a civilian populace may be thrilled to fervour by a martial music whose origin is strangely akin to that of happier peace-melodies, dancing graces, and romantic joy. Wordsworth penetrates the soul of harmony more ultimate than life or death. From more 'mazes' we pass to temple-psalms and black-thunder-music, God-awful harmonies; yet with a prayer that only noble actions be our theme, that music may preserve (as in Goethe's *Faust*) the suicide from death and steel the martyr or patriot for his end. A profound stanza compares the disturbing effect of music on an idiot to the inroads of conscience in mankind, music coming from divine and mysterious sources 'above the starry pole', seat of all wisdom and virtue. The first music origins, the Caliban-promptings, of the race, are observed, its 'voice and shell' awaking softer emotions than nature implants. Hell bows, the upper 'arch' rejoices. Myths of Amphion and Arion find their place: the one concerning building by music, as in *Kubla Khan*; the other, a contrast of some master-music to watery monstrosity, with a dolphin docile for riding as any horse, pointing to the alligator-boys in Shelley's *Witch of Atlas*, and Yeats's *Byzantium*. We have Pan-pipings, a leopard's eyes sparkling to the 'cymbal's clang', dancing fauns and satyrs; but against these life-ecstasies—the old Wordsworthian contrast—we move suddenly to cold earth echoing on a coffin and the prison-bell sounding for the convict's execution. There is something awful in Wordsworth's unremitting remembrances. He strives for a comprehensive understanding:

For terror, joy, or pity,
Vast is the compass and the swell of notes:
From the babe's first cry to voice of regal city,
Rolling a solemn sea-like bass, that floats
Far as the woodlands. . . .

Wordsworth's sea has Shakespearian undertones. The poet pathetically cries—and his life-work is in the cry—for some *moral music*, some reasonable scheme for man, tuning with the inward deeps of harmony; asks that the 'unsubstantial' might submit to those 'chains' of 'sight' which weight all ages of poetry, for poetry must blend intellectual space-sight, earthly experience, with that uncapturable music. The geometric mind is therefore also involved: which leads to a Pythagorean interpretation of the universe in terms of 'tones and numbers'. The still heavens are alive with spheral music. The mist-crowned headlands planting foundations in rough sea—the usual contrast—know 'that Ocean is a mighty harmonist', and the pinions of Air 'delegates of harmony'. But suddenly, as before, comes the harsh contrast of the final line: 'Stern Winter loves a dirge-like sound.' Yet may 'wind' and 'chords', nature and art, blend in thanksgiving; and, 'to magnify the Ever-living', unite in blended mystery sound with '*words*', that is, finally, with poetry and therefore with the purposes of man's earthly existence. May the 'lone eagle' of the mountains attune its 'hungry barkings' to the hymn of 'flaming Seraphim'. 'Deep' calls to 'deep' under a more Christianized, or at least Hebraic, symbolism, in which all our former realistic and mythological impressions are subsumed.

Sound is ultimate. Wordsworth writes, as so often, of that behind creation, its womb, nurse, and grave. The alpha and omega of existence is thus no object but a 'voice':

A Voice to Light gave Being;
To Time, and Man his earth-born chronicler;
A Voice shall finish doubt and dim foreseeing
And sweep away life's visionary stir.

Compare that with the sight-metaphysic of the *Immortality Ode*: this is perhaps the more deeply and truly Wordsworthian of the two. The last trumpet shall open graves and quench stars, with man's noisy years, as in the earlier ode, but moments in the eternal silence. Is harmony itself 'bond-slave'—again an echo from the sister-poem—to that eternity? No. For at the last shall exist not time's ephemeralities, not nature or cosmic geometries, not even music in abstraction, but the 'Word': whereby the supremacy at once of both poetry and Christianity is asserted over other allegiances, artistic or spiritual. All Wordsworth is here compacted. Thought and feeling range over his expansive life-work. Here time and eternity, nature and those mysterious forms of *The Prelude* are at work; man individual and social; man demented— in the idiot stanza; the geometric mind, pagan myth, and harsh contemporary realism; together with the ortho-dox religion of his land—all are placed. As so often, it is a poem about an art, but the art deepest in Wordsworth— the invisible, the haunting and mysterious, art, of music; or, rather, just of sound, the sob and surge of eternal seas, the ultimate language of the depths of being; sound which is all but silence.

Wordsworth's life-work reads as a continuous effort to re-express the nakedly spectral appearances of *The Prelude* and the sheer Machiavellian evil of *The Borderers* into (i) a bright and glittering nature, and (ii) shapes of ecclesiastical and national organization. Often enough he succeeds. His sonnets have sharp definition and detonation and an especially compressed power. But, after *The Borderers*, no full-length poem of satisfying *action* results. The flights are short and descriptive, and depend on other arts. Moreover, though Wordsworth's utterances on all final problems and unblenching re-membrances of sternest destinies are of noble worth, they lose by reiteration and isolation. Energies are neglected rather than eternally transmuted, while his eternities tend towards the abstract, or at least are diffused into several independent structure-symbolisms. There is a failure in face of erotic powers. That is why, except in short poems, sun-feeling and dewy glitterings, though frequent, remain somewhat ineffectual. Ethically, Wordsworth never breaks new ground. The established values remain intact, whereas poetry's more normal business is to *reclaim* territory from evil possession, to redeem rather than reject, seizing on essential good: of which the great prophet is Nietzsche. Though as a whole lacking such creative leverage Wordsworth's work abounds in profound *comments* on the creative powers and numerous exquisite poems on art itself. Wordsworth's kinship with Milton is fairly obvious and driven home by the central and inclusive nature of his ode on *Sound*, while in mysticism he draws near the inward and meditative doctrines of Indian philosophy. Yet he is also essentially Nordic and very fond of Druidical, or other all but prehistoric, remains. He is rather like Shakespeare's Prospero. As for the fusion of mind with nature to create the living paradise outlined in the *Recluse* fragment, to that Shelley and Keats bear stronger *immediate* witness than Wordsworth: a limitation balanced, perhaps forced, by his far greater range of social and national realism.

He compares his life-work to a cathedral. *The Prelude* and *The Excursion* 'have the same kind of relation to each other' as the ante-chapel has to the body of a Gothic church. As for his minor poems, they are 'cells', 'oratories', and 'sepulchral recesses' (Advertisement to *The Prelude*). Or we may call it a grim version of *Kubla Khan*: from deathly caverns of the mind, mountains, and nature variously solemn and sweet, through human poems, mostly dimmed with suffering, yet occasionally brighter, towards a multiplicity of structures either glittering or shadowed with eternal awe; the whole overcast with memories of death as a darkly brooding otherness, at once a threat, a compulsion, and an awaited peace.

II

COLERIDGE'S DIVINE COMEDY

I

I SHALL concentrate first on *Christabel*, *The Ancient Mariner*, and *Kubla Khan*. Within a narrow range these show an intensity comparable with that of Dante and Shakespeare. As with those, strong human feeling mixes with stern awareness of evil, without artistic confusions. Coleridge's main negation tends to a subjective sin-fear: his use of *fear* is, indeed, the secret of his uncanny power, this being the most forceful medium for riveting poetic attention.

Christabel is one nightmare; so, pretty nearly, is *The Ancient Mariner*; and *Kubla Khan* at one point strikes terror. Coleridge is expert in nightmarish, yet fascinating, experience. The human imagination can curl to rest, as in a warm bed, among horrors that would strike pallor in actual life, perhaps recognizing some unknown release, or kinship: as in Wordsworth, who, however, never shows the nervous *tension* of Coleridge. These three poems, moreover, may be grouped as a little *Divina Commedia* exploring in turn Hell, Purgatory, and Paradise.

Christabel is akin to *Macbeth*. There is darkness (though moon-lit), the owl, the restless mastiff. There is sleep and silence broken by fearsome sounds. The mastiff's howl is touched with deathly horror: 'some say she sees my lady's shroud'. Opposed to the nightmarish are images of religious grace. This first part is strangely feminine: the mastiff is a 'bitch', the heroine set between Geraldine and the spirit of her own mother as forces of evil and grace respectively. 'Mary Mother' and 'Jesu Maria' find a natural home in the phraseology. Some sort of sexual desecration, some expressly physical horror, is revealed by Geraldine's undressing. She insinuates herself into Christabel's religious, mother-watched, world;

G

she is mortally afraid of the mother-spirit and addresses her invisible presence with extreme dramatic intensity. As so often a seemingly sexual evil is contrasted with a parental good, yet Geraldine gets her opportunity through Christabel's charity, and when she lies with her is imaged as a mother with a child. Some hideous replacing of a supreme good is being shadowed, with an expression of utter surprise, especially in the conclusion to Part I, that so pure a girl can have contact with so obscene an horror. It is something Christabel cannot confess: she is power-less to tell her father. She is under a spell. The evil is nerve-freezing yet fascinating. There is vivid use of light in the tongue of flame shooting from the dying brands, and before that Geraldine's first appearance in the moonlight is glitteringly pictured. Stealth, silence, and sleep are broken by sudden, fearful, sound. In Part II we get perhaps the most intense and nightmarish use of the recurring serpent-image in our literature: both in Bracy's dream of Christabel as a 'sweet bird' (the usual opposite) with a 'bright green snake' coiled round it and Christabel's tranced hissing later, mesmerized by 'shrunken' serpent eyes. The poem expresses fear of some nameless obscenity. Christabel, we gather, has a lover, but he is of slight importance in the poem as we have it, though there is reason to suppose the conflict between him and Geraldine was to have been made dramatically explicit.

Christabel helps our understanding of *The Ancient Mariner*, which describes the irruption into the natural human festivity of a wedding party of the Mariner's story of sin, loneliness, and purgatorial redemption. These somewhat Wordsworthian elements are set against the 'merry din', the 'loud bassoon'. The wedding guest is agonizedly torn from human, and especially sexual, normality and conviviality.

The story starts with a voyage into 'the land of ice and of fearful sounds'. There is snow and fog. From this the Albatross saves them: it is as 'a Christian soul'. Its snowy whiteness would naturally grip Coleridge: he is fascinated

by whiteness. The bird seems to suggest some redeeming
Christ-like force in creation that guides humanity from
primitive and fearful origins. Anyway, the central crime
is the slaying of it and by their wavering thoughts the
crew 'make themselves accomplices'; and the dead bird
is finally hung round the Mariner's neck 'instead of the
cross' as a sign of guilt. Indeed, the slaying of the Albatross in the Mariner's story may correspond to the death
of Christ in racial history. It is, moreover, an act of unmotivated and wanton, semi-sadistic, destruction, explicitly called 'hellish'. As a result the ship is calmed in
a tropic sea. Parching heat replaces icy cold. The 'land
of ice and snow' may be allowed to suggest primeval
racial sufferings or primitive layers in the psychology of
man; and yet also, perhaps, something more distant still,
realms of ultimate and mysterious being beyond nature
as we know it, and of a supreme, if inhuman, purity and
beauty. The central crime corresponds to the fall, a
thwarting of some guiding purpose by murderous self-
will, or to loss of innocence in the maturing personality,
and the consequent suffering under heat to man's present
mental state. In poetic language you may say that whereas
water parallels 'instinct' (with here a further reach in 'ice
and snow' suggesting original mysteries of the distant and
primeval), flames, fire, and light hold a more intellectual
suggestion: they are instinct becoming self-conscious,
leading to many agonies and high aspirations. The bird
was a nature-force, eating human food, we are told, for
the first time: it is that in nature which helps man beyond
nature, an aspect of the divine purpose. Having slain it,
man is plunged in burning agony. The thirst-impressions
recall Eliot's *Waste Land*, which describes a very similar
experience. The new mode is knowledge of evil, symbolized in the 'rotting' ocean, the 'slimy things' that crawl
on it, the 'death-fires' and 'witches oils' burning by night.
It is a lurid, colourful, yet ghastly death-impregnated
scene, drawn to express aversion from physical life in dissolution or any reptilian manifestation; and, by suggestion,

the sexual as seen from the mentalized consciousness as an alien, salty, and reptilian force. It is a deathly paralysis corresponding, it may be, to a sense of sexually starved existence in the modern world: certainly 'water, water everywhere, nor any drop to drink' fits such a reading.

Next comes the death-ship. 'Nightmare Life-in-Death' wins the Mariner's soul. This conception relates to deathly tonings in literature generally, the *Hamlet* experience, and the metaphorical 'death' of Words-worth's *Immortality Ode*. It is, significantly, a feminine harlot-like figure, and is neatly put beside Death itself. She 'begins her work' on the Mariner. The other sailors all die: observe how he is to endure *knowledge* of death, with guilt. He is 'alone on a wide wide sea' in the dark night of the soul; so lonely—compare Wordsworth's solitaries—that God Himself seemed absent. The universe is one of 'beautiful' men dead and 'slimy things' alive, as in Shelley's *Alastor*. The 'rotting sea' is now directly associated with the 'rotting dead', while he remains eternally cursed by the dead men's 'eyes'. At the extremity of despair and therefore self-less feeling, his eyes are suddenly aware of the beauty of the 'water-snakes' as he watches their rich colours and fiery tracks: 'O happy living things'. The exquisite prose accompaniment runs: 'By the light of the moon he beholdeth God's creatures of the great calm.' A fertilizing 'spring of love' gushes from his 'heart' and he blesses them *'unaware'*— the crucial word is repeated—with unpremeditated recognition and instinctive charity. Immediately the Albatross slips from him and sinks like lead into the sea. An utterly organic and unforced forgiveness of God conditions God's forgiveness of man.

The exact psychological or other conceptual equivalents of poetic symbolism cannot be settled. If they could, there would be no occasion for such symbols, and my use of the term 'sexual' might seem rash to anyone unaware of the general relation of snakes and water to

sexual instincts in poetry, as in *Antony and Cleopatra*
and Eliot's use of water and sea-life. Christabel's en-
forced and unhappy silence whilst under Geraldine's
serpent spell may be directly related to the water-snakes of
The Ancient Mariner. She, like the becalmed ship, is helpless; perhaps, in her story too, until a certain frontier, involving spontaneous, but not willed, recognition, is reached.
Just as she cannot speak, that is, confess, so the Mariner,
when, as it were, saved, spends the rest of his life confessing.

The immediate results of conversion are (i) gentle
sleep after feverish and delirious horror, and (ii) refreshing
rain after parching heat. These are imaginative equivalents and may be said to touch the concept of *agapé* as
opposed to *eros*, and are here logically related to Christian
symbols. A sense of purity and freedom replaces horror
and sin. Energy is at once released: the wind blows and
the dead rise and work, their bodies being used by a
'troop of spirits blest', who next make music, clustering into a circle, with suggestion of Dante's paradisal
lives. Now the ship starts to move like Eliot's similar
ships in *The Waste Land* and *Ash Wednesday*; yet no
wind, but rather the 'lonesome spirit from the South-pole',
is causing the motion, and demanding vengeance still.
Why? and who is he? Coleridge's prose definition
scarcely helps. He works 'nine fathom' deep—in man or
creation, at once instinct and accuser, and not quite stilled
by conversion. At last he is placated by the Mariner's
penance. Next '*angelic* power' drives on the ship. There
is more trouble from the dead men's eyes and another
release. As the ship draws near home, each body has a
burning seraph upright above it. These seraphic forms
that twice seem conditioned by dead bodies, yet not, as
individuals, precisely the 'souls' of the men concerned,
must, I think, be vaguely identified with the concept of
human immortality, the extra dimension of their upright
stature over the bodies being pictorially cogent.

At home there is the 'kirk', the woodland 'hermit', and
safety. After such fiery experience the normality of the

hermit's life, its homely and earthy quality, is emphasized.
We meet his 'cushion' of 'moss' and 'oak-stump' and his
daily prayers. He is a figure of unstriving peace such
as Wordsworth sought, associated with earth and solid
fact after nightmare and transcendent vision. Extreme
sensual and spiritual adventure has brought only agony.
Therefore:

> O sweeter than the marriage-feast,
> 'Tis sweeter far to me,
> To walk together to the kirk
> With a goodly company.

It is an embracing of *agapé* with a definitely lower place,
if not a rejection, accorded to *eros*; a welcoming of earth
and refreshing rain ('the gentle rain from heaven' is an
agapé-phrase in Shakespeare) with a rejection of the sun
in its drawing, tormenting, heat. I doubt if there is any
relieving synthesis implicit in the 'youths and maidens'
that go to church at the end of the poem with the Wordsworthian 'old men and babes': the balance is scarcely in
favour of youthful assertion. The final lesson is a total
acceptance of God and his universe through humility,
with general love to man and beast. But the specifically
sexual is left unplaced: the wedding-guest is sadder and
wiser henceforth, and presumably avoids all festive
gatherings from now on; though forgiveness of *reptilian*
manifestation remains basic.

This is Coleridge's *Purgatorio*, as *Christabel* is a fragmentary attempt at a little *Inferno*. Whether we can
call the central criminal act 'sexual' is arguable: it certainly resembles that in Wordsworth's *Hart-leap Well*, but
the Mariner's compulsion to tell his tale suggests rather
Eliot's Sweeney and his grim account. One might notice
that the imaginative tonings in *Lucrece* and *Macbeth* are
identical, and that 'sadism' may be only a conscious
recognition of a deeper relation than has yet been plumbed:
motiveless cruelty is, moreover, a general and most valuable
poetic theme, as in Heathcliff's ill-treatment of a dog.

Such thoughts help to integrate into the whole the mystery of an unmotivated action which, with the South-pole spirit itself, is left rationally undefined, as Shakespeare leaves the motives of Macbeth and Iago and the pain of Hamlet rationally undefined. The new life comes from acceptance of the watery and the reptilian, at which the sea no longer appears to be 'rotting', that is, dead, though all these drop out of the picture afterwards. The crime, together with rejection of the unrefreshing 'rotting sea' and its creatures, brings parched agony, but acceptance of those brings the other, heavenly and refreshing, water of rain. Also acceptance precedes repentance, not vice versa. A spontaneous, unsought, upspring of love alone conditions the down-flow of grace.

The poem is lively and colourful, as A. C. Bradley has well emphasized. The movement and appearance of sun and moon are described in stanza after stanza; and stars too. The sun peeps in and out as though uncertain whether or not to give its blessing on the strange scene. The poem glitters: the Mariner holds the Wedding Guest with a 'glittering eye', which, if remembered with his 'skinny hand', preserves a neat balance. The light is somewhat ghastly: as in the strange sheen of it on ice or tropic calm, and the witches' oils burning 'green and blue and white'. Green light is a favourite in Coleridge (cp. in *Dejection* 'that green light that lingers in the west'). The snakes move in 'tracks of shining white', making 'elfish' illumination. Their colours are 'blue, glossy-green and velvet black' and by night their every motion pencils 'a flash of golden fire'. The ghost-ship comes barred across the blood-red sun. The 'charmed water' is said to burn 'a still and awful red'. There is a very subtle interplay of light and colour. The Life-in-Death figure is a garish whore with red lips, yellow hair, white leprosy skin; the evil creatures are colourful; the supernatural seraphs brilliant. The whole is dominated by a fearful intensity summed in the image, rather dark for this poem, of a night-walker aware of a demon following his steps.

But the play of light and colour helps to give the somewhat stringy stanza succession and thinly narrative, un-
dramatic sequence of events a certain intangible poetic
mass. I doubt if the rhyme-links, the metrical rhythms,
even the phrase-life, so to speak, would be considered fine
poetry without this and, what is equally important, the
substance of idea and meaning we have been analysing.

The strangeness and ghastly yet fascinating lights of
the experience must guide our judgement of the solution.
The experience is of fearful fascination; a feverish horror
that is half a positive delight, mental pre-eminently; and
the return is a return to earth, the hermit's cell and mossy
stone, a return to reality and sanity. Whatever our views
of the implied doctrine there is no artistic confusion or
lack of honesty. The balancing of symbols, as in the
contrast of bird-life and the reptilian, is subtle as Dante's
(the *Purgatorio* has a very similarly reiterated observation
of the sun in varied position and mood) and Shakespeare's,
though without the massive scheme of the one or the
sympathetic range of the other. It is a little poem greatly
conceived. The supernatural figures dicing for the
Mariner's soul suggest, inexactly, the balancing of the
Eumenides against Apollo in respect of Orestes in
Aeschylus; while the 'lonesome spirit' from the South
Pole in its office of accuser performs exactly the function
of those Eumenides, furies of guilt and accusation. It is
replaced eventually by swift angelic power, as in Eliot's
Family Reunion the furies of *Sweeney Agonistes* turn into
angels.

Poetry of any worth is a rounded solidity which drops
shadows only on the flat surfaces of philosophical statement. Concretely it bodies forth symbols of which our
ghostly concepts of 'life', 'death', 'time', 'eternity',
'immortality' are only very pallid analogies. They are
none the less necessary, if we are to enchain our normal
thinking to the creations of great literature, and I next
translate the domed symbolism of *Kubla Khan* into such
shadow-terms corresponding to the original in somewhat

the same way as the science of Christian theology corresponds, or should correspond, to the New Testament.

The pleasure-dome dominates. But its setting is carefully described and very important. There is a 'sacred' river that runs into 'caverns measureless to man' and a 'sunless sea'. That is, the river runs into an infinity of death. The marked-out area through which it flows is, however, one of teeming nature: gardens, rills, 'incense-bearing' trees, ancient forests. This is not unlike Dante's earthly paradise. The river is 'sacred'. Clearly a sacred river which runs through nature towards death will in some sense correspond to life. I take the river to be, as so often in Wordsworth (whose *Immortality Ode* is also throughout suggested), a symbol of life.

Born on a *height*, it descends from a 'deep romantic chasm', a place 'savage', 'holy', and 'enchanted', associated with both a 'waning moon' and a 'woman wailing for her demon lover'. The river's origin blends romantic, sacred, and satanic suggestions. Whatever our views on sex it would be idle to suppose them anything but a tangle of inconsistencies. Moreover, the idea of original sin, the 'old serpent', and its relation to sex is not only Biblical but occurs in myth and poetry ancient and modern. We have not yet compassed the straightforward sanity on this vital issue which D. H. Lawrence said would, if attained, make both nasty sex stories and romantic idealisms alike unnecessary: a certain obscene and savage sex-desecration seems to have fixed itself as a disease in the human mind. That is why we find the virgin-symbol, in both paganism and Christianity, sublimated; especially the virgin mother. Sex is overlaid with both high romantic and low satanic conceptions, complexities, fears, taboos, and worship of all sorts, but the necessity and goodness of pure creativeness no one questions. Our lines here hint a mystery, not altogether unlike Wordsworth's dark grandeurs, blending satanism with sanctity and romance with savagery. They express that mystic glamour of sex that conditions human creation and something of its pagan evil magic; and touch the enigma of the creator-god beyond good and evil, responsible for eagle and boa-constrictor alike.

Whatever our minds make of them, sex-forces have their way. Nature goes on cheerily blasting families and uniting true lovers in matrimonial bonds of 'perdurable toughness', with an equal efficiency working through rake and curate alike, and not caring for details so long as her work be done. Goethe's poetry well presents this seething, torrential, over-mastering creative energy. Look now at our next lines: at the 'ceaseless turmoil', the earth-mother breathing in 'fast thick pants', the fountain 'forced' out with 'half intermitted burst', the fragments rebounding like hail, the 'chaffy grain beneath the flail', the 'dancing rocks'. What riotous impression of agony, tumult, and power: the dynamic enginery of birth and creation.

Then off the river goes 'meandering in a mazy motion': observe the rhythm of this line. The maze is, of course, a well-known figure suggesting uncertain and blind progress and is sometimes expressly used for the spiritual complexities of human life; and the general symbolism of mazes and caves throughout my present study might be compared with my brother's inspection of such symbolisms in the ancient world (*Cumaean Gates*, by W. F. Jackson Knight). After five miles of mazy progress the river reaches the 'caverns measureless to man', that is, infinity, nothingness; and sinks, with first more tumult (i.e. death-agony), to a 'lifeless ocean', that is to eternal nothingness, death, the sea into which Timon's story closes. This tumult is aptly associated with war: the principle of those conflicting and destructive forces that drive man to his end. The 'ancestral voices' suggest that dark compulsion that binds the race to its habitual conflicts and is related by some psychologists to unconscious ancestor-worship, to parental and pre-parental authority. We find an interesting analogy in Byron's *Sardanapalus*.

So in picture-language we have a symbolical pattern

not unlike Addison's *Vision of Mirza*, though less stiffly allegorical. As for Kubla Khan himself, if we bring him within our scheme, he becomes God: or at least one of those 'huge and mighty forms', or other similar intuitions of gigantic mountainous power, in Wordsworth. Or we can, provisionally—not finally, as I shall show—leave him out, saying that the poet's genius, starting to describe an oriental monarch's architectural exploits, finds itself automatically creating a symbolic and universal panorama of existence. This is a usual process, since the poet continually starts with an ordinary tale but universalizes as he proceeds: compare the two levels of meaning in *The Tempest*, where Prospero performs a somewhat similarly superhuman role to Kubla Khan here; or Yeats's emperor in *Byzantium*.

In *The Christian Renaissance* I wrote at length on the concept of immortality as it emerges from interpretation of poetry. I concluded that, though we must normally think in temporal terms and imagine immortality as a state after death, yet poetry, in moments of high optimistic vision, reveals something more closely entwined than that with the natural order. It expresses rather a new and more concrete perception of life here and now, unveiling a new *dimension* of existence. Thus immortality becomes not a prolongation of the time-sequence, but rather that whole sequence from birth to death lifted up vertically to generate a super-temporal area, or solidity. I used such a scheme to explain parts of the New Testament, Shakespeare, Goethe, and other poets: especially here I would point to my interpretation of Wordsworth's *Immortality Ode*. But I did not use *Kubla Khan*, my scheme being evolved from inspection of other poets.

I come now to the latter movement of our poem, whose form is not unlike an expansion of the Petrarchan Sonnet. This is the sestet. Observe that the metre changes: a lilting happy motion, a shimmering dance motion, replaces heavy resonance and reverberation. Our minds are tuned to a new apprehension, something at once assured, happy, and musical. A higher state of consciousness is suggested: and see what it shows us.

The dome's *shadow* falls half-way along the river, which is, we remember, the birth-death time-stream. This shadow—a Wordsworthian impression—is cast by a higher, more dimensional reality such as I have deduced from other poets to be the pictured quality of immortality. It is directly associated with the 'mingled measure' of the sounds coming from the two extremes. In Wordsworth, and elsewhere, immortality may be associated closely with birth, though that is by way of a provisional and preliminary approach to the greater truth; while in our own thinking it is found most often to function in terms of a life after death. But both are finally unsatisfying; birth and death are both mysteries that time-thinking distorts, and personal life beyond their limits a somewhat tenuous concept. The true immortality is extra-dimensional to all this: it is the *pleasure-dome itself*, arching solid and firm above creation's mazy progress and the 'mingled' sounds of its conflicts, just as in Wordsworth the child's immortality is said to 'brood' over it 'like the day': that is, arching, expansive, immovable.

The 'mingled-measure' suggests the blend and marriage of fundamental oppositions: life and death, or creation and destruction. These 'mingle' under the shadow of the greater harmony, the crowning dome-circle. Observe that it is a paradoxical thing, a 'miracle of rare device'; 'sunny', but with 'caves of ice', which points the resolution of antinomies in the new dimension, especially those of light and heat, for Eros-fires of the mind; and ice, for the coldness of inorganic nature, ultimate being, and death, the ice-caves being perhaps related to our earlier caverns, only more optimistically toned; light instead of gloomy, just as 'sunny' suggests no torturing heat. The 'caves of ice' may also hint cool cavernous depths in the unconscious mind (a usual Wordsworthian cave-association) blending with a *lighted* intelligence: whereby at last coldness becomes kind. These, ice and sun-fire, are the two elemental antitheses of *The Ancient Mariner*, and their mingling may lead us farther. We are at what might be called a marriage-point in life's progress half-way between birth and death: and even birth and death are themselves here mingled or married. We may imagine a sexual union between life, the masculine, and death, the feminine. Then our 'romantic chasm' and 'cedarn cover', the savage and enchanted yet holy place with its 'half intermitted burst' may be, in spite of our former reading, vaguely related to the functioning of a man's creative organs and their physical setting and, too, to all principles of manly and adventurous action; while the caverns that engulf the sacred river will be correspondingly feminine with a dark passivity and infinite peace. The pleasure dome we may fancy as the pleasure of a sexual union in which birth and death are the great contesting partners, with human existence as the life-stream, the blood-stream, of a mighty coition. The poet glimpses that for which no direct words exist: the sparkling dome of some vast intelligence enjoying that union of opposites which to man appears conflict unceasing and mazed wandering pain between mystery and mystery.

I would leave a space after 'caves of ice'. I am not now so sure about the sonnet form: those six lines are central. So next we have our third and final movement, starting with the Abyssinian damsel seen in a vision playing music. The aptness of a girl-image here is obvious. In Shakespeare and Milton music suggests that consciousness which blends rational antinomies, and so our poet equates the once-experienced mystic and girl-born music with his dome. Could he revive in himself that music he would build the spiritual dome 'in air'; that is, I think, in words, in poetry. Or, maybe, he would become himself the domed consciousness of a cold, happy, brilliance, an ice-flashing, sun-smitten, wisdom. The analogy between music and some form of architecture is not solitary: it receives a fine expression in Browning's *Abt Vogler*, a valuable commentary on *Kubla Khan*. The analogy is natural enough for either music or poetry: we talk of architectonics in criticizing poetry or a novel, for the very reason that literary or musical art bears to rational thought the relation of a solid, or at least an area, to a line. Tennyson's *Palace of Art* is a direct analogy, and Wordsworth compares his life's work to a 'Gothic Church'.

The poem's movement now grows ecstatic and swift. There is a hint of a new speed in the drawn-out rhythm of 'To such a deep delight 'twould win me . . .'. Now the three rhymed lines gather up the poet's message together with his consciousness of its supreme meaning with a breathless expectancy toward crescendo. Next follows a fall to a ritualistic solemnity, a Nunc Dimittis, phrased in long vowels and stately measured motion, imaged in the 'circle' and the eyes dropped in 'holy dread' before the prophet who has seen and re-created 'Paradise': not the earthly, but the heavenly paradise; the 'stately' permanence above motion, the pleasure-dome enclosing and transcending human agony and frustration. To tune our understanding we might go to such a passage as Wordsworth's:

> incumbencies more awful, visitings
> Of the Upholder of the tranquil soul,
> That tolerates the indignities of Time,
> And, from the centre of Eternity
> All finite motions overruling, lives
> In glory immutable.   (*The Prelude*, III. 116)

Which transmits a similar recognition.

Kubla Khan is a comprehensive creation, including and transcending not only the dualisms of *The Ancient Mariner* ('sun', 'ice', and sexual suggestions recurring with changed significance) but also the more naturalistic, Wordsworthian, grandeurs. Though outwardly concentrating on an architectural synthesis, it has too another, mountainous, elevation suggested in Mount Abora; and indeed the dome itself is a kind of mountain with 'caves', the transcendent and the natural being blended, as so often in Wordsworth. It must be related to other similar

statements of an ultimate intuition where the circular or
architectural supervenes on the natural: in particular to
the mystic dome of Yeats's *Byzantium*. The blend here
of a circular symbolism with a human figure (the Abyssinian maid) and images of human conflict may be compared both to Dante's final vision and an important
passage in Shélley's *Prometheus*. *Kubla Khan* is classed
usually with *Christabel* and *The Ancient Mariner*, both
profound poems with universal implications. The one
presents a nightmare vision related to some obscene but
nameless sex-horror; the other symbolizes a clear pilgrim's
progress (we may remember Coleridge's admiration of
Bunyan's work) through sin to redemption. It would be
strange if *Kubla Khan*, incorporating together the dark
satanism and the water-purgatory of those, did not, like
its sister poems, hold a comparable, or greater, profundity, its images clearly belonging to the same order of
poetic reasoning. Its very names are so lettered as to
suggest first and last things: Xanadu, Kubla Khan, Alph,
Abyssinian, Abora. 'A' is emphatic; Xanadu, which
starts the poem, is enclosed in letters that might well be
called eschatological; while Kubla Khan himself sits
alphabetically central with his alliterating 'k's. Wordsworth's line 'of first, and last, and midst, and without end',
occurring in a mountain-passage (*The Prelude*, vi. 640) of
somewhat similar scope, may be compared. The poem's
supposed method of composition is well known. How it
comes to form so compact and satisfying a unit raises
questions outside the scheme of my study. The poem,
anyway, needs no defence. It has a barbaric and oriental
magnificence that asserts itself with a happy power and
authenticity too often absent from visionary poems set
within the Christian tradition.

II

I pass to a cursory inspection of other poems grouping
them for convenience into something of a *Kubla Khan*
structure. We shall inspect Coleridge's ever-present itch

for transcendence in three main divisions: (i) naturai,
(ii) human, and (iii) divine. But the groups intershade and
each poem is at once naturalistic, psychological, and religious. I shall not consider Coleridge's often uncertain
dates of composition. We must keep *Kubla Khan* continually in mind and watch for certain typical tendencies:
a tortured craving for purity and associated imagery of
ice; a visionary, half-demented, insight; a nostalgia for
simple happiness; a pathetically agonized reaction to
human warfare and other social evils; with insistent use,
or experience, of fear.

His nature-approach shows often a delicate, nervous,
apprehension of shimmering, intangible, excellence (the
earthly paradise of *Kubla Khan*), as when in *This Lime-Tree
Bower my Prison* he stands 'silent with swimming sense'
and gazes on the 'landscape' till all seems

> Less gross than bodily, and of such hues
> As veil the Almighty Spirit, when yet he makes
> Spirits perceive his presence.

A mysterious personality is felt within and beyond nature.
Yet he is less whole-heartedly 'nature's priest' than
Wordsworth, and may distrust pantheism as he elsewhere
distrusts human love, and, indeed, poetry itself. *The
Eolian Harp* exquisitely senses a 'Fairy-Land' of 'twilight
Elfins', a 'witchery of sound', and 'melodies round honey-
dropping flowers' like 'birds of Paradise', until all is
confused so that 'one Life' is felt informing 'all motion'
with a 'light in sound, a sound-like power in light',
and 'rhythm in all thought and joyance everywhere'.
The deliberate sensory-confusion forecasts Shelley.
'Sunbeams' are 'diamonds' and the poet enjoys idle
'phantasies' of a Keatsian luxury. Coleridge variously
approaches territories to be later developed by others.

> And what if all of animated nature
> Be but organic Harps diversely fram'd,
> That tremble into thought, as o'er them sweeps

> Plastic and vast, one intellectual breeze,
> At once the Soul of each, and God of all?

See the tentative, philosophical approach, the delicate, nervous apprehension as of a snail's wavering antennae. The heresy is rebuffed by his companion, a 'meek daughter in the family of Christ', who bids him 'walk humbly with my God'. He at once retracts

> These shapings of the unregenerate mind;
> Bubbles that glitter as they rise and break
> On vain Philosophy's aye-babbling spring.

No talk of the 'Incomprehensible' is 'guiltless' except when, with 'awe' and 'a Faith that *inly* feels', one praises Him

> Who with His saving mercies healed me,
> A sinful and most miserable man. . . .

Poetic imaginations are condemned as glittering 'bubbles' —a truly signifying image recalling the dome of *Kubla Khan*—in comparison with religious inwardness, and here the conclusion is correspondingly, shall we say reverently, prosaic. This critical insecurity and lack of poetic confidence is important: Coleridge's orthodox belief, though elsewhere making magnificent poetry, here clogs his imaginative faith.

He often, however, preserves a happy balance of natural symbol and inward, or transcendental, meaning. Impressions of mountains, caves, cataracts, winding rivers, and woodland form a common poetic stock-in-trade, but the common meanings held by such symbols is not yet appreciated. Caves have been for centuries impregnated with semi-mystic significance. In poetry tragic or prophetic heroes, such as Timon, Prospero, Nietzsche's Zarathustra, and the Hermit in Coleridge's *Mad Monk*, retreat to them for psychic reasons: a retreat into oneself is hinted. In Coleridge's *A Tombless Epitaph* genius is said to pursue 'hidden' paths towards the 'Parnassian forest' and trace the river of inspiration '*upward* to its

H

source'; and we end in a specifically philosophic cave—
'haunt obscure of old Philosophy'—whose 'starry walls'
sparkle by torchlight as once to the 'odorous lamps' of
'Saint and Sage'. This cave is almost a mystic dome and the
impressionistic whole a valuable pointer for the reading
of Shelley. The cave-symbol may suggest sub-conscious
depths as when in *Ad Vilmum Axiologum* pure hearts in
response to deep poetry are compared to 'caves in the
ancient mountains'. An obvious extension may render
suggestion of either prenatal unconsciousness and therefore birth, as in Shelley's *Witch of Atlas* and Coleridge's
On a Cataract (to be noticed shortly); or of death, as in
Kubla Khan and *The Destiny of Nations*, where Night,
personified, flees to a 'cave of darkness palpable, Desert of
Death' sunk deep below Gehenna, and returns through
an 'uncouth maze' and 'drear labyrinth' to trouble mankind: a passage to which I shall return. Mazes and
labyrinths are usual enough. They may suggest snaky
evil as in a Fury's 'mazy surge' of hair (*Religious Musings*),
or the obstructions conditioning a high delight as when
a lover approaches his mystically conceived idol through
a 'leafy labyrinth' in *Lewti*. They may symbolize, as in
Kubla Khan, all temporal troubles, as in 'Love illumines
manhood's maze' (*Ode to the Departing Year*); or the
trials, probably psychic, of youth, the poet praying that
the Spirit descend on his child ere it tread 'youth's perilous
maze' (*On Receiving a Letter informing me of the Birth of a
Son*). When a violent rock-divided torrent goes 'in mazy
uproar bewilder'd' (*Mahomet*) the adjective and humanizing participle are intersignificant. In contrast to such
childhood is associated with a placid stream in the *Sonnet to
the River Otter*; so is the fairy innocence of young love in
An Effusion at Evening. In *Recollection* life's storms and
'wild'ring way' are contrasted with the 'dear native brook'
associated with former 'peace' and 'young poesy', in a
lovely passage holding that lucid interdependence of
nature and symbolic meaning generally favoured by
Coleridge:

Where blameless Pleasures dimpled Quiet's cheek,
As water-lilies ripple thy slow stream.

Here a willowy maze is happily associated with a crystal clarity disclosing the coloured stones of the river-bed, and all possesses, to the memory, a rainbow peace: moving nature is blended within laid, gem-like, patterns, and a maze dissolves in a rainbow's circular harmony. 'Gems' often, as in *Comus* and Byron's *respective* comparison of Aurora and Haidée to a 'gem' and 'flower' in *Don Juan*, suggest the eternal. The balance of the natural and transcendent so important in *Kubla Khan* is therefore plainly, though delicately, implied.

Such passages witness Coleridge's sensitivity to and precise use of water. His rivers symbolize life, variously toned for child-innocence, young love, mature unrest, or spiritual peace. The *Inscription for a Seat* speaks of the 'tide of life' and *The Improvisatore* of 'life's gay summer tide'. In *To Asra* love is felt 'welling' at the heart whose 'living fount' heaves and falls like 'vernal waters springing up through snow'; and this love becomes a great 'power' which, if transmuted to one whole of 'happy life' and given to its object, would realize 'eternity'. Love-power is the life-force and aspires to the eternal. This process of expansion Coleridge often feels himself to have missed: hence his insecurity, his frequent nostalgia for past experience, his often fragmentary work. *The Picture* tells his story: a lovely river-poem to be shortly analysed, where the river-symbol is subtly used, as in *Comus*, to project a cool purity apart from those romantic desires which nevertheless are also reflected in the watery glass, and apparently find new, if sublimated, expression at the close.

Whatever life's varied problems there remains the ultimate mystery and grandeur of 'nature struggling in portentous birth' (*Ode to the Departing Year*), a line whose natural and supernatural impact reflects precisely the tumultuous creation in *Kubla Khan*; where there was something very Germanic in the birth-and-torrent imagery, which indeed led me, during my analysis, to compare it with Goethe. Now the meanings I attributed to that cataract are explicitly expanded in a poem translated by Coleridge from an original by Count F. L. Stolberg, called *On a Cataract*, falling 'from a cavern near the summit of a mountain precipice':

> Unperishing youth!
> Thou leapest from forth
> The cell of thy hidden nativity;
> Never mortal saw
> The cradle of the strong one;
> Never mortal heard
> The gathering of his voices;
> The deep-murmured charm of the son of the rock,
> That is lisp'd evermore at his slumberless fountain.

The central mystery of creative energy and ever-present miracle is here a 'ceaseless renewing'. The 'moonshine' sinks as in 'slumber'

> That the son of the rock, that the nursling of heaven
> May be born in a holy twilight!

Which recalls the 'savage place' 'holy and enchanted' associated with a 'waning moon' in the similar torrent-birth description in *Kubla Khan*. The 'holy twilight' suggests variously the womb, prenatal unconsciousness, and sexual mystery. The balancing of 'nursling of heaven' against 'son of the rock' may be compared with Shelley's 'daughter of earth and water and nursling of the sky' in *The Cloud*: both hold human connotations. Here the birth-origin is, as usual, *elevated* and the 'wild goat in awe' looks up amazed at the 'inaccessible' height:

> Thou at once full-born
> Madd'nest in thy joyance,
> Whirlest, shatter'st, splitt'st,
> Life invulnerable.

Notice the phrase 'full-born', expressing birth's miraculous quality; and 'invulnerable'. The poem forms a valuable commentary on *Kubla Khan*, as do also *Tell's Birthplace* and *Hymn to the Earth* (both from Stolberg).

Coleridge often feels, like Wordsworth, a direct relation of nature to human wisdom and ethics. *France*, one of his finest odes, works out a doctrine of freedom in terms of spiritual experience rather than revolutionary materialism; which is precisely an experience of oneness with that nature of 'clouds' and 'waves' which 'yield homage only to eternal laws'. The midnight mountain-slope where storm-tossed branches make 'solemn music', 'glooms' where 'never woodman trod'—we meet them again in *Dejection*—the wildness and wayward harmonies of forest, ocean, and sun, are symbols of 'liberty' and that loneliness 'beloved of God' which their company inspires. The ode very clearly opposes this to the other, more political, liberty, and no poem so clearly exposes the word's profound content in the literature of this period. After forgiving the revolution its 'blasphemy', Coleridge has nevertheless watched it develop into aggressive action, and concludes that

> The Sensual and the Dark rebel in vain,
> Slaves by their own compulsion!

Below a certain psychic level material revolution is utterly useless and only wins new 'manacles', with 'blasphemy' replacing 'priestcraft'. Yet liberty exists, speeding still on 'subtle pinions', among winds and waves and trees:

> Yes, while I stood and gazed, my temples bare,
> And shot my being through earth, sea, and air,
> Possessing all things with intensest love,
> O Liberty! my spirit felt thee there.

The gospel is neat and truly profound. But, until the sensual is transcended, a hopeless man-nature dichotomy exists, and the question how to transmute human nature remains.

Coleridge uses mountains somewhat as he uses the dome and Mount Abora in *Kubla Khan*. Often they are definitely mystical, as when, in *Time, Real and Imaginary*,

the two figures are seen on a mountain described as 'some
fairy place'. Or the hill itself may be allegorized. *To the
Author of Poems* works out an allegory of poetic achievement. A 'poetic mount' is circled by 'coal-black' waters
from an 'oblivious fount', and all 'vapour-poisoned birds'
(i.e. minds clouded by the 'sensual') fall into it. Next,
beneath the 'lofty-frowning brow' and before any 'perilous ascent' is attempted, lies an attractive paradise, like
the *earthly* paradise of *Kubla Khan*:

> Not there the cloud-climb'd rock, sublime and vast,
> That like some *giant king*, o'erglooms the hill;
> Nor there the pine-grove to the mid-night blast
> Makes solemn music!

The mountain is symbolical of spiritual effort and ascendancy. The psychic implications of the pine-grove's wild
desolation is also important; whereas the lower paradise
enjoys instead bird-song, an 'unceasing rill', and 'jas-
mine bowers'. Such a paradise Coleridge often feels
himself to have left for ever. It corresponds to the fertile
nature of *Kubla Khan*, as the 'poetic mount' corresponds
to the dome or Mount Abora; but the 'frowning' height is
also given giant, regal attributes, relating to the monarch
Kubla himself and similar Wordsworthian presences. In
a poem to Charles Lamb (*To a Friend*) Coleridge writes
of a 'bleak rock, midway the Aonian mount'—the hill of
poetry—where

> There stands a lone and melancholy tree,
> Whose aged branches to the midnight blast
> Make solemn music.

He urges his friend, who, though from birth plunged into
poetry's 'wizard fount', has sworn off poetic composition,
to pluck from that tree a mysterious bough—symbolizing
a troubled, elegiac, poetry.

However, peace must always be the final aim, and in
To a Young Friend a companionship is imagined in terms
of a mountain-ascent, including the usual torrent, crag,
spring, and pine with 'old romantic limbs'. The world's

'vain turmoil' is left below: the ascent is partly psychic, and the hill next allegorized as the 'Hill of Knowledge' with 'secret springs', 'nooks untrod',

> And many a fancy-blest and holy sod
> Where Inspiration, his diviner strains
> Low-murmuring, lay. . . .

Its evergreens remain untouched by either age's frost or bigotry's fire. It is called 'sublime', and 'uplifted high' above the 'stirring world'. The explicit semi-allegoric interweaving of naturalistic impression with psychic qualities resembles that in Keats's *Psyche*, whose very rhythms are faintly present in the tone of

> Whose noises, faintly wafted on the wind,
> To quiet musings shall attune the mind. . . .

A transition from natural outline to spiritual pattern is usual in Coleridge. This 'Hill of Knowledge' may assist our understanding of the dome in *Kubla Khan* in terms of direct mental illumination. *Reflections on having left a Place of Retirement* describes the climbing of a 'stony mount' and a landscape with the inevitable winding river and a supervening sense of 'Omnipresence' as though 'God' had 'built him there a Temple': such a 'mount sublime' being itself all but a sacred edifice. Or again, a mountain may become a semi-human, *monarchic*, presence that speaks, as with Skiddaw in *A Stranger Minstrel*.

I pass to two greater poems. In *Dejection* one is caught up into a shivering yet delighted ecstasy to tune with midnight wind and eerie powers. Nature, as so often, is superstitiously tinged, with a 'green' brilliance at sunset and next a moon 'overspread with phantom light'. The poet, somewhat like Shelley in his *West Wind*, sees natural tumult as positive energy, and cries to driving rain to lash his spiritual apathy. Remember the becalmed ship of *The Ancient Mariner*. Yet he knows the 'fountains' of 'passion' and 'life' are within and objective phenomena alone can never restore the lost contact. What we give, that only we receive, and man's mind is at once nature's

'wedding-garment' and 'shroud'. This 'wedding', as in
France, gives 'the spirit and the power' and realizes 'a new
Earth and new Heaven' of which the 'sensual' and the
'proud' (intellectual pride, as in Pope, being intended)
can know nothing. However, 'fancy' and 'hope', once
enjoyed, are both now lost, and 'abstruse research' has
replaced the 'shaping spirit of imagination'. Yet our poem
itself restores the lost contact; what neither nature alone
nor desire alone can do, the creative faculty, as in Wordsworth's *Immortality Ode*, superbly realizes. So he banishes
'viper' thoughts and lets energy breathe through in a
wild stanza of satanic music to match the agony-scream of
a satanic wind:

> Thou wind, that rav'st without,
> Bare crag, or mountain tarn, or blasted tree,
> Or pine-grove whither woodman never clomb,
> Or lonely house, long held the witches' home,
> Methinks were fitter instruments for thee,
> Mad Lutanist!

Elsewhere superstition and fear are felt as necessary pre-
liminaries to wisdom; and now, like Wordsworth, the poet
objectifies his own torment by housing it in recognition of
satanic forces in nature. With them he is at home, in their
terms quickly touches those super-rational and mysterious
powers central to his craving. Therefore he loves the
festive 'Devil's Yule'. It is himself. Next the wind is a
'mighty' actor of 'tragic sounds', singing of battle-agony.
This, Coleridge's most paralysing aversion, is finely
assimilated and purified, as in the short but pivotal war-
reference of *Kubla Khan*. The storm's sudden change to
gentleness is vividly realistic, while also making a transition from Coleridge's experience of evil to Coleridge as he
sees himself. It sings

> of a little child
> Upon a lonesome wild,
> Not far from home, but she hath lost her way.

It cries for its 'mother'. 'Not far from home, but she hath

lost her way.' What an admirable, if limited, autobiographical comment! He ends by wishing the tempest (i.e. of existence) to be to the 'lady' he addresses (here supposedly Sara Hutchinson, but there is often enough a 'lady' in such poems of Coleridge) only as a 'mountainbirth' (like the cataract in *Kubla Khan*), while the stars (i.e. of eternity, the sky's dome) 'hang bright above her dwelling', silently watching the sleeping earth like Keats's star-eremite. Coleridge packs himself and his riotous but thwarted longing into this sweeping anthem. It swings and whirls, tugs at its centre like a flag in storm; then flutters and falls. Shelley's *West Wind* is more assured, more positive and purposive in its deep cadences and heavy modulations. This screams with Titanic energies, demon powers are astride the wind as it whistles and wails across lonely heights of subjective evil. Here an almost moral evil takes the place of Wordsworth's eternal glooms and ghostly presences, and raging activity that of the awful quietude Wordsworth usually favours.

Literature teaches us that such satanic power is set halfway towards the sublimest good. The *Hymn before Sunrise* bears to *Dejection* something of the relation of *Kubla Khan* to *Christabel* and *The Ancient Mariner*. It is bright, dazzling, and tremendous, isolating and expanding the 'height' and 'ice' impacts of *Kubla Khan* to magnificent purpose. No poem in English so perfectly fits the recurring mountain-cult into orthodox religious phraseology without a corresponding loss of the sublimely natural. The mountain is vaguely personified, recalling Kubla Khan *himself*, in such phrases as 'thy bald awful head', 'sovran Blanc', 'most awful Form'; and merges into a vast temple-dome symbolizing the eternal in 'crystal shrine' and 'habitation from eternity'. But also the poet gazes on the 'dread and silent Mount' until it all but vanishes into prayer and worship of the 'Invisible': just as the dome in *Kubla Khan* is built to music 'in air', so here vast mass expands into such immensity and upheaving significance that space is, as it were, out-spaced. Therefore it is also

music, a 'sweet beguiling melody', mingling, almost
erotically, with the poet's own 'Life' and 'Life's own
secret joy',

> Till the dilating Soul, enrapt, transfused,
> Into the mighty vision passing—there
> As in her natural form, swelled vast to Heaven!

'Crystal shrine' earlier blends now into 'icy cliffs': the
vision is one of architectural wonder, cold brilliance, and
natural majesty. But, though by night the mountain
communes with the stars, at daybreak it becomes itself one
vast 'rosy star' and 'coherald' of dawn: it not only faces,
but *is* the eternal dome-structure of heaven. It is both
awful and sublimely, radiantly, colourful:

> Who sunk thy sunless pillars deep in earth?
> Who filled thy countenance with rosy light?
> Who made thee parent of perpetual streams?

Notice the architectural analogy in 'pillars'; the recurrent yet unobtrusive humanizing in 'countenance'; and
the reminiscences of *Kubla Khan* in 'sunless', as also in the
association of parenthood with 'streams'. But here the
birth-terminations of the life-streams are felt as cavernous,
abysmal, deathly, the 'fiercely glad' torrents being called
forth by mysterious power from 'night and utter death',
'dark and icy caverns', to become things, as in our *Cataract*
lyric, of *'invulnerable* life', of 'unceasing thunder' and
'eternal foam'. Thus we have the eternal aspect of life's
ever-present force and activity: yet there is always the
other, more dome-like eternity of architectural design and
plastic form. In this poem the upward space-structure,
though shading into a temple, or shrine, is first natural,
while the lower, more temporal and moving, nature is,
in part, paradoxically still, a motionless wonder; for the
'ice-falls' obey a mighty voice and become under the
wizardry of cold 'motionless torrents' and 'silent cataracts' blending impossibilities like the other cataracts
'frozen by distance' in Wordsworth (*Memorials of a Tour*

in Scotland, x) and the synthesis of opposing elements in *Kubla Khan*. The interpenetration of rivers and domes— or all that these signify—is often, as in Keats especially, a major poetic exercise. That is why the cataracts at once become, in frozen stillness, miracles of wonder 'glorious as the gates of Heaven'. The poem's lifting mass up-piles to the chorus of torrents, ice-plains, and avalanches until all, as with the 'shout of nations', attribute their being to 'God':

> Rise, O ever rise,
> Rise like a cloud of incense from the Earth!
> Thou kingly Spirit throned among the hills,
> Thou dread ambassador from Earth to Heaven,
> Great Hierarch! tell thou the silent sky,
> And tell the stars, and tell yon rising sun
> Earth, with her thousand voices, praises God.

Observe the royalistic and sacred tonings: it is at once a sacred edifice and a mountain, a thing of earthly majesty and invincible transcendence. The mighty universe itself here lifts in song. The music existent in pure mass was never more splendidly developed.

This poem drives to an extreme Coleridge's habitual fascination for ice, frost, and snow. He has a poem *Frost at Midnight* balancing summer against 'tufts of snow' and 'silent icicles', the miracles of creation wrought by the 'secret ministry of frost'. Such impressions were vital to *The Ancient Mariner* and *Kubla Khan*. My earlier interpretation of 'sunny dome' and 'caves of ice' as together expressive of the sublimated intelligence receives support in two valuable fragments. In one a lady's spirit after death awaits the resurrection of that 'pure Tabernacle' which is her own 'virgin body'

> Far liker to a Flower now than when alive,
> Cold to the touch and blooming to the eye.
>   (*Fragment 7*)

The body is equated with a bright temple, light replaces warmth. *Fragment 9* describes the particular whitish brilliance symbolized by Mont Blanc, with a religious significance:

> Bright clouds of reverence, sufferably bright,
> That intercept the dazzle, not the Light;
> That veil the finite form, the boundless power reveal,
> Itself an earthly sun of pure intensest white.

Fragment 2 has a sea-mew 'white-gleaming' with 'arching wings' (like an albatross). The tendency expresses Coleridge's often half-unwilling and generally unhappy thirst for a pure transcendency at the risk of loneliness and coldness, as when he describes a life without sexual partnership in terms of cold splendour:

> Beneath the blaze of a tropical sun the mountain peaks are
> the Thrones of Frost, through the absence of objects to reflect
> the rays.   (*Blossoming of a Solitary Date-Tree*)

Where colours occur in his poetry they are sudden, vivid, almost feverish (as in *The Ancient Mariner*), and as much light as colour: as in the 'thin blue flame' of *Frost at Midnight*; the 'swimming phantom light' and 'silver thread' of the moon and the sky's 'peculiar tint of yellow and green' in *Dejection*; and Mont Blanc as one vast 'rosy star' at dawn.

We are now to examine certain poems approaching the supreme reality through human sympathies, love, and art. Human contacts seem of wider and more intimate poetic service to Coleridge than to Wordsworth. This service is both peculiar and fascinating. The semi-mystical poems here to be inspected are, however, based on a firm, indeed semi-religious, respect for normal family ties. Mother, child, and wife are all sacred:

> You were a Mother! That most holy name,
> Which Heaven and Nature bless. . . .
>   (*Ode to Georgiana, Duchess of Devonshire*)

A mother is 'the holiest thing alive' (*The Three Graves*). The human and divine blend. Numerous poems reveal a direct worship of child-simplicity (*On the Christening of a Friend's Child*, *A Child's Evening Prayer*, *Epitaph on an Infant*, &c.; sonnets on his own child; and numerous scattered examples). Moreover, a wife's name also holds

> A promise and a mystery,
> A pledge of more than passing life.
>
> (*The Happy Husband*)

The thoughts are simple enough: but I point to a continual, almost pathetic, reverence for simple human values to be contrasted with the demonic straining and compulsion elsewhere evident.

Coleridge's more important human poems are less simple. There is a strange lack of normal love-poetry: no direct and passionate heart-song such as Byron's 'There be none of Beauty's daughters', nor the buoyancy of Shelley's 'I arise from dreams of thee'. Though *Alcaeus to Sappho* is delicately physical, with blushes like a mountain-snow made rosy at dawn, the entwining thoughts of personality and soul are definitely elusive. Two ballads, *The Mad Monk* and *Love*, have a love-interest, but their symbolic and psychological meanings— *The Mad Monk* involving remorse for murder and love entwined which we may compare with the moral of *The Ancient Mariner*—are complex. Coleridge is an ardent devotee where Wordsworth appears cold:

> This yearning heart (Love! witness what I say)
> Enshrines thy form as purely as it may,
> Round which, as to some spirit uttering bliss,
> My thoughts all stand ministrant night and day
> Like saintly Priests, that dare not think amiss.
>
> (*Love's Sanctuary*)

Such semi-religious worship is usual. But his love-poetry is seldom either immediately engaged or forward in hopefulness, but rather reverently nostalgic, mourning the loss of youthful love-magic somewhat as Wordsworth's mourns the passing of child-vision. *Love's Apparition and Evanishment* tells of the loss of Hope, 'Love's elder sister',

and sees Love herself appear, now cold and unable to
infuse life. There is no hope of 'resurrection' in the heart's
'gradual self-decay'. This peculiarly wistful and painful,
yet often palely beautiful, intuition of loss recurs often,
even in his early poetry. *Lines on an Autumnal Evening*,
written in college days, addresses, in a somewhat traditional phraseology, the maiden-spirit of youthful love:

> When the bent flower beneath the night-dew weeps
> And on the lake the silver lustre sleeps,
> Amid the paly radiance soft and sad,
> She meets my lonely path in moon-beams clad.

A silvery, ethereal, and watery haze suffuses such reminiscence, coming 'like far-off music, voyaging on the
breeze'. The poem has a delicacy and soft, almost Keatsian, apprehension of flowery delight and concludes with
pained yearnings for 'infant Love' associated, indeed
almost identical, with a 'dear native brook' and its 'water-
lilies'. Placid, or softly flowing, water entwines with
'love', 'peace', and 'poesy'.

A certain coldness, at once painful and poetically
fertile, overspreads these attractive meditations. In *To
Two Sisters* the poet thanks the ladies concerned for
aiding one wasted 'with the poison of sad thought', like
a winter sun 'on unthaw'd ice', the recurring sun-ice
impression being used with a delicate precision. Their
kindness is in him *coldly* but *brightly* reflected, and a
soul-state indicated almost correspondent to that implied
by the 'sunny dome' and 'caves of ice' in *Kubla Khan*.
Their friendship is 'music', 'at once a vision and reality'.
Nevertheless, such highly spiritualized adventures are not
necessarily all-sufficing. Coleridge emphasizes the pains
and thwarted longings of too frigid, too loveless, an
existence in *The Blossoming of a Solitary Date-Tree*. I
apologize for repeating, and extending, my earlier quotation:

> Beneath the blaze of a tropical sun the mountain peaks are the
> Thrones of Frost, through the absence of objects to reflect the

rays. 'What no one with us shares, seems scarce our own.' The
presence of a one

> The best belov'd, who loveth me the best,

is for the heart, what the supporting air from within is for the
hollow globe with its suspended car. Deprive it of this and all
without, that would have buoyed it aloft even to the seat of
the gods, becomes a burthen and crushes it into flatness.

He is, himself, the icy mountain-peak: and Nietzsche, in
Zarathustra, presents once an exactly similar self-defini-
tion. Nor is it over-rash to see in this quaint balloon-
image a replica of that gorgeous and palatial bubble, the
specifically air-built dome in *Kubla Khan*. What sort of
spiritual iciness or sunshine love best favours such dome-
accomplishments and balloon ascents is, of course, a complicated question; but the state recorded, and its pain,
remains clear.

Coleridge's love-poetry has its own thin, silvery-voiced,
music divorced normally from all burning passions. Indeed, unless lost youth-visions be the theme, the poem's
subject is generally some lady of almost casual acquaintance
who serves as a handy stimulus. The poet addresses a
semi-poetic ideal; while the lady is usually an authoress or
artist and, as in *To Two Sisters*, at once 'music', 'vision',
and 'reality'—of the same category as the Abyssinian
Maid in *Kubla Khan*, who is practically a symbol of
poetic creation. The associations are pointed in a poem
To Matilda Betham written in praise of the lady's poetic
genius ('a sweet tune played on a sweet instrument'):

> The Almighty, having first composed a Man,
> Set him to music, framing Woman for him,
> And fitted each to each, and made them one!
> And 'tis my faith, that there's a natural bond
> Between the female mind and measured sounds. . . .

The recurring lady-poetry-music association is firmly and
self-consciously established. These various ladies might
almost be called means of addressing the poetic faculty:
which is, however, itself closely entwined, like Dante's
Beatrice, with recollections of youthful love-magic.

In *The Reproof and Reply*, addressed to a lady, the poet excuses himself for plucking flowers in a garden. We have a recurrence of *Kubla Khan* elements: a white-sparkling and sacred edifice high above nature's 'maze', a hill-side, a winding stream 'of music', and impressions of poetic art ('Helicon'), all blending into the personality of a lady explicitly associated with the muses of Greek mythology. *A Stranger Minstrel* takes us to Skiddaw and its heights and chasms. In his thought arises a 'form' suddenly causing the poet to wish for a certain 'lady of sweet song'. Skiddaw asserts that her gentleness would scorn so rugged a scene. The issue is interesting: has divine love-magic any real authority among the stern *powers* of mature travailing? Skiddaw has, indeed, often heard 'her magic song' and 'divinest melody'; being 'free'—freedom is a spiritualized concept—the lady, or the spirit of love, is omnipresent and 'unfetter'd by mortality', able to fly to a 'haunted beach' and its tossing seas or to where the 'maniac wildly raves, crying "Pale moon, thou spectre of the sky"'. The resemblance to the 'holy and enchanted' spot in *Kubla Khan* with its 'waning moon' and 'demon-lover', indeed to all Coleridge's demonic impressionisms, is interesting. But lyric love, the poem implicitly says, need have no fear of such. For it is, ultimately, one with, or, being human, greater than, the mountain, that is, the ultimate craggy and universal vastness. Therefore the 'mighty mount' desires that she honour him, as the Abyssinian Maid honours Mount Abora, with her 'witching melody'

> Which most resembles me,
> Soft, various, and sublime,
> Exempt from wrongs of Time!

Skiddaw here speaks 'like a *monarch* wooing': musical ladies, mountains, monarchs (corresponding to Kubla himself) are variously interwoven. This poem is written in honour of the poetical Mrs. Robinson: so is *The Snow-Drop*, celebrating her poem on that flower. She is said to have transported it by 'the potent sorceries of song', somewhat as art transports the figures and trees in Keats's *Grecian Urn*, to 'immortal' greenery and eternal life beyond winter. Love (personified) mistakes it for one from his own bower—art is here being compared with immediate love-experience—and next flies to a wondrous 'arboret' where Laura, the lady-poetess, lies each night reclined. It is a bower of love and sleep; or rather those graced by 'love' or 'fancy' are, instead of the sleep most are subdued by, wafted to realms of *imagination* 'up the insuperable steep' to the 'vast summit broad and smooth' —Coleridge's method, as elsewhere, of making a dome out of a mountain—where the immortal Phoenix conceals her nest, heavenly Lethe soothes cares, and all who come are, among soft breezes and gentle mists, healed and fitted to 're-endure' their 'earthly martyrdom'. We end with a gold harp (the dulcimer of *Kubla Khan*), with 'music' that 'hovers'—a favourite word—half-perceived, moulding the slumberer's dreams with remembrances of love and youth. A remarkable poem: hardly anything is left out. It is especially beautiful in certain variations on frost and whiteness, while its approach to visionary bliss by sleep and dream forecasts Shelley and Keats. Laura directly resembles Shelley's Witch of Atlas. Last of our immediate list is the *Ode to the Duchess of Devonshire*. The lady is praised both for 'genius' and for breathing in a 'more celestial life' than her aristocratic peers, since she versifies in the cause of liberty:

> O Lady, nursed in pomp and pleasure!
> Whence learn'd you that heroic measure?

She is not only a truer mother than many, but also twice a mother by reason of her poetry, created by reading— the analysis is valuable—her children's 'twilight thoughts' and 'nascent feelings'. The 'Angel of the Earth', whose duty it is, like the Earth-Spirit in Shelley's *Prometheus*, to guide the 'chariot-planet', and who 'trembling gazes on the eye of God', turns his face momentarily from that Sun to raise in the lady 'new-influences', and

I

Blest intuitions and communions fleet
With living nature, in her joys and woes.

Extreme, if never more than exquisitely lyric, reverence is accorded these poetical ladies. Indeed, they perform among Coleridge's collected poems precisely the kind of office held by the Abyssinian Maid within the structure of *Kubla Khan*.

In a very beautiful poem, *The Picture*, sub-titled *The Lover's Resolution*, the poet claims a new-found psychic freedom beyond the sexual, yet, and the comparison is important, 'lovely as light':

The master-passion quelled,
I feel that I am free.

The stern connotations of 'quelled' may suggest a certain danger, a too ruthless mental control, of instinct. Nevertheless, the new soul-state resorts to wild and rugged nature, felt as a fit Wordsworthian home for 'wisdom' and 'remorse'. The sick soul, indeed, like Goethe's Faust retreating from Margaret to craggy mountains, loves and worships here the spirit of 'unconscious life', with no groves 'where Love dare loiter'. Nature-imagery is next directly enlisted *against* the sexual: as in Wordsworth and Milton's *Comus*, where a river's purity is grouped with chastity against intemperance. Though now in 'triumph' and 'free', the poet deliberately recalls the loveliness he claims to transcend, thus subtly rendering it part of the higher state indicated. Delicately, tremulously, the wavering, watery and ethereal, imagery floats in air.

The brittleness of love's delight is noted in terms of stream-water and a lady lost in the 'woodland maze' of her lover's baffled longing. But the poet boasts of the river by which he now stands, covered by trees and 'doleful as a cavern well', where he feels 'emancipate from Passion's dreams', a 'freeman', enjoying the fierce cataract. The impressionism, most subtly used to objectify psychic states, is at once peaceful and wild, symbolizing release and strength. Next he finds a picture carved on bark wherein a sleeping child is shown pillowed on a sleeping dog: a symbol of final integration comparable with that of boys embracing alligators in Shelley's *Witch of Atlas*. The poet at once grows wildly excited about the artist, Isabel, calling her 'divinest maid' and 'daughter of genius', and starts anxiously in search of her. There is thus a progress from passion-mastery and rejection of love's allurements towards an art felt as an ultimate synthesis, and so on up to a new love-quest which includes suggestion of genius and the divine. The poem holds the key to all other poetical or musical ladies in Coleridge, including the Abyssinian Maid. River-impressionism flows through the whole and applies variously to the opposing emotional states, or strata, the poem aims to elucidate.

We are faced in all these poems by the tension of sexual instinct against artistic sublimation. One poem explicitly creates paradise in terms of literary art: it is called *The Garden of Boccaccio*.

Coleridge here applies to literature itself that very tremulous, sometimes fluid, sometimes, as it were, hovering, approach he elsewhere uses for an idealized watery and woodland nature. Here he feels literary art as, pre-eminently, a fusion of the fluid and statuesque, of sequence and pattern, content and form: which, indeed, it is, all poetry aiming to blend, as it were, the river and dome of *Kubla Khan*. So Boccaccio's work is an 'exquisite design', a 'faery', Keatsian, wonder, 'framed in the silent poesy of form', yet with a spiritual quality compared to a mist, a stream, music. It steals on his 'inward sight', touching as with an 'infant's finger', and is referred directly to 'selfless boyhood', the super-consciousness of art being all but equated in point of simplicity and magic with the consciousness of youth, which 'loved ere it loved, and sought a form for love'. We pass in review 'sea-worn caves' and 'prophetic maids' and many legendary and historic pageants loved in youth. Next, we concentrate on philosophy, now, certainly, a 'matron' and 'sober' enough—this is a late poem—yet 'radiant still and with no earthly sheen', but

once, in childhood, welcomed as herself a 'faery child',
and called in those days 'Poesy', descending from
'Heaven', unselfconsciously gleeful and innocent. Child-
purity, philosophy, and art are all but identified.

Imagery next becomes at once natural and artificial.
The garden is an Eden, yet civilized, with 'green arches',
a 'fountain clear', and 'restless pool'. The music-lady
recurs, functioning very like the Abyssinian Maid:

> 'Tis I, that sweep that lute's love-echoing strings,
> And gaze upon the maid who gazing sings:
> Or pause and listen to the tinkling bells
> From the high tower and think that there she dwells.

We have a lifting architecture in 'tower'. The poet is
'possest' of 'old Boccaccio's soul', and breathes 'an air like
life': that is, the super-life of art. Dreams of old Italy,
rich in courtesy, natural fertility, and architecture, lead to

> Palladian palace with its storied halls;
> Fountains, where Love lies listening to their falls;
> Gardens, where flings the bridge its airy span,
> And Nature makes her happy home with man. . . .

The bridge's 'airy span' helps the general feeling of a
Kubla Khan affinity. A flower 'wreathes the marble urn'
and 'weeps liquid gems'; a marriage of nature and human
art, of the river and dome in *Kubla Khan*, of the instinctive sap in creation and what Wordsworth calls the
'geometrical mind', being subtly patterned. The fluid
and the solid intermix, as in Keats. So 'every muse is
thine',

> And more than all, the embrace and intertwine
> Of all with all in gay and twinkling dance.

The synthesis of all literary art is pictured: 'O all enjoying
and all-blending sage.' Boccaccio's page is directly called
'mazy' since all the complexities of human life are involved, and the poem ends with a happy mixture of
'fauns' and 'wingèd saints', of 'Dian's vest' and a maid

half-devoted to 'vestal fires' with yet a 'sly satyr peeping through the leaves'. The purity is one of inclusion, existing not so much in any rejection as in a bird's-eye view: which is, after all, the most satisfactory approach to any maze.

We have disentangled a progress from normal sexuality —if indeed, such was ever Coleridge's, or any true poet's, possession—towards the specifically artistic consciousness, which is, however, generally entwined with some literary or musical feminine figure; while the whole progress is, as it were, *lighted* by a nostalgic memory of youthful love, felt as a still existing, but somehow mislaid, experience. Such pain within the artistic temperament is, of course, perfectly normal. The poet is jerked, often unwillingly, into the higher experiencing dimension; is forced to create and live from eternity. The Duchess of Devonshire was felt as 'twice a mother', bringing forth poems as well as children; creative in eternity as well as time. Coleridge elsewhere, after saying how Wordsworth's poetry echoes in the soul's deep 'caves', writes:

> This is the word of the Lord! It is spoken, and Beings Eternal
> Live and are borne as an Infant; the Eternal begets the Immortal:
> Love is the Spirit of Life, and music the Life of the Spirit!
> (*Ad Vilmum Axiologum*)

In Shelley such eternity-creation tends to produce intuitions of child, hermaphrodite, or seraph: these are symbolic of some higher, more fully integrated, state such as Nietzsche envisioned in his 'superman'. Coleridge is directly responsive to child-innocence, but the child, 'man's breathing miniature', may also, as in *To an Infant*, symbolize his own mortal helplessness: 'such a thing am I.' Man's ultimate dependency is emphasized:

> O thou that rearest with celestial aim
> The future Seraph in my mortal frame,
> Thrice holy Faith!

Man is a child in relation to eternity, to which he must
cling as the child clings to its mother. 'Seraph' may recall
both Shelley and the seraphs of *The Ancient Mariner*.
A strangely gripping poem, *Constancy to an Ideal Object*,
considers human 'thought' as a remarkable power alone
'constant' amid 'change'; a consciousness able to conceive,
and think itself into, eternity. It is an earnest of some
future state, some greater race, creating prophetically 'the
faery people of the future day', yet failing to warm itself.
The conception is of deep importance. As for love—'She
is not thou, and only thou art she'. The unknown Eros,
to borrow Patmore's phrase, speaks through 'some dear
embodied good', 'some living Love'; but without this central ideal man is a 'becalmed bark' on an 'ocean waste and
wide' whose 'helmsman' sits 'mute and pale his mouldering
helm beside'. The suggestion, as in *The Ancient Mariner*, is
one of slow rotting death. Though such thoughts are
next felt as self-created, their relation here to some 'faery'
race such as Wordsworth (in *The Recluse*) and Nietzsche
both envisioned is of direct importance. You get it
elsewhere:

> And while within myself I trace
> The greatness of some future race,
> Aloof with hermit-eye I scan
> The present works of present man. . . .
> (Ode to Tranquillity)

The vague evolutionary shadowing must not preclude
sense of the eternal: often in such passages one must consider the two conceptions as complementary.

One may suggest that a new psychological type is being
painfully created, though such scientific phraseology must
never limit our more mystical intuitions. *The Pang more
Sharp than All* deplores the loss of some indefinable Eros,
'Hope's last and dearest child without a name'. The
'hope' so reiterated by Coleridge involves regularly an
erotic, dream-romantic, essence. This Eros is, however,
something 'innocent', and *at once reserved and forward*, like

a child 'that tempts and shuns the menaced kiss': a very
neat description of that delicate love-potentiality inspiring
at once desire and inhibition, and forcing us towards the
paradox of Milton's *Comus*. The departed Eros has,
however, left aspects of himself 'of either sex', a sister and
a brother called respectively Esteem and Kindness. These
are shadows of that 'bright Boy', who is therefore, like
Shelley's Hermaphrodite in *The Witch of Atlas*, somewhat
bi-sexually imagined. He is, moreover, here described in
spheral terms—remember that spheres and domes are
close akin—resembling those containing the child in
Shelley's *Prometheus*:

> Ah! he is gone, and yet will not depart!—
> Is with me still, yet I from him exiled!
> For still there lives within my secret heart
> The magic image of the magic Child,
> Which there he made up-grow by his strong art,
> As in that crystal orb—wise Merlin's feat—
> The wondrous 'World of Glass' wherein inisled
> All long'd-for things their beings did repeat;—
> And there he left it, like a Sylph beguiled,
> To live and yearn and languish incomplete!

'Repeat' suggests the doctrines of recurrence to be found
in Shelley and Nietzsche. The soul, as often, is feminine,
a 'sylph': we may compare the slight but relevant poem
entitled *Psyche*, while our 'magic Child' or 'bright Boy'
is Eros—a lover of 'strong art', a child yet powerful,
without whom the soul is 'incomplete'.

Such poetry, with the *integration*-poem *Phantom or
Fact*, suggests a gradual way to spiritual fulfilment.
Though scarcely poems of power, they indicate a direction
assisting our understanding of Coleridge and the poetic
temperament in general. But, where Shelley has all fire
and ardour and Nietzsche a steady-burning confidence,
Coleridge is here insecurely poised: his progress is at
once tortured and subject to varied allegiances.

His poetic faith is often weak. In *Constancy to an Ideal
Object* the higher intuitions were felt as mainly subjective,

like the vision seen by a 'woodman' over the 'sheep-track's maze' through snow-mist. He

> Sees full before him, gliding without tread,
> An image with a glory round its head.
> The enamoured rustic worships its fair hues,
> Nor knows he makes the shadow he pursues. . . .

Kubla Khan is clearly suggested: beyond a 'maze' and 'mist' rises some stupendous, and colourful, glory which, like the pleasure-dome, drops its 'shadow' across the horizontal dimension. 'Gliding without tread' points on to the supernal car in Shelley's *Triumph of Life*. The *Improvisatore*, a queer play-poem discussing love, considers the often-deplored loss of vision:

> Those sparkling colours, once his boast
> Fading, one by one away,
> Thin and hueless as a ghost,
> Poor Fancy on her sick bed lay. . . .

'Sparkling colours' may be referred to Coleridge's fondness for combined light and colour and suggests further his sparkling, often colourous, heights, whether domes or otherwise. Now he fears such dreams are each merely a 'shadow' cast by some 'unsteady wish' that enjoys substantiality only in proportion as it shuts out 'Reason's light': that is, he distrusts poetry itself. We have a precisely similar use of the 'shadow' thought in *Constancy to an Ideal Object*. He passes to love, earlier called 'the fair fulfilment of his poesy'. Adam and Eve took one flower from Paradise. This, the rose, with all its summer magic, is next grouped with 'autumn's Amaranth', symbolizing matured experience of an even greater fragrance than 'passion's flowers'. All this—both rose and amaranth—the poet has lost. But was the magic ever really his? Had it 'outward being' or was it only 'his own true love's projected shade'? 'Real' or 'magic'? He is caught in the trammels of an uncomfortable intellectualism. We may notice especially the relation of poetic to amatory experience; the use of 'shadow' and 'shade', to which I shall

refer again; and the suspected deceit of such poetic
visions as *Kubla Khan*. Coleridge sees himself as one

> Who, soul and body, through one guiltless fault
> Waste daily with the poison of sad thought.
>
> (*To Two Sisters*)

Moreover, the pale and ethereal quality of his amatory
poems may suggest on occasion a too-little inclusive
spirituality hinted also by a few lines which an apostle of
Pope might regard as heretical:

> What is there in thee, Man, that can be known?—
> Dark fluxion, all unfixable by thought,
> A phantom dim of past and future wrought,
> Vain sister of the worm,—life, death, soul, clod—
> Ignore thyself, and strive to know thy God!
>
> (*Self-Knowledge*)

The soul is, as before, feminine. Coleridge is excessively
under the compulsion of transcendental intuitions. His
mind is eminently metaphysical, as in his passage on time
in *Limbo* or the note to *Time, Real and Imaginary*; while
his more directly intellectual and metaphysical propensities are always likely to lead back to such things as the
cogent, and powerfully reasoned, defence of immortality
in *Human Life*.

Often there is a clear sense of guilt with a consequent,
and powerful, emphasis on those demonic energies vivid
in *Christabel* and *Dejection*. In *Fire, Famine and Slaughter*
he identifies himself with war-evils elsewhere most hated
to create a satanic music not unlike that of the Weird
Sisters in *Macbeth*. *The Visionary Hope* poignantly con-
fesses agony from certain 'obscure pangs' tormenting
sleep with nightmares, though nameless Hope makes the
'love-stricken visionary' still prefer life to not-being: with
a half-formed, fleetingly embodied love, as so often, hinted.
Love is able to pierce 'disease' with heavenly light: but the
cry is despairing. *The Pains of Sleep* is a record of 'shapes',
'thoughts', and 'lurid light' tormenting with a sense of
wrong in the outer world, yet also striking an irrational

guilt and leading to 'life-stifling fear, soul-stifling shame':
phrases which burn deep into Coleridge's suffering. The
'unfathomable hell within' necessarily tortures sinners;
but why, he asks, choose one who only desires simple
love? The experience of sin is akin to that dramatically
housed in Ordonio in *Remorse*. We may feel his poetry
reveals more than Coleridge himself knows. Certainly
fear, vague guilt, and nightmare fertilize many of his more
powerful poems: through them, or natural phenomena
felt as demonic, he objectifies some inward, semi-sexual,
agony. Or again, he falls back, as in *Dejection* and *To an
Infant*, on a plaintiff, child-like, misery:

> Doubts toss'd him to and fro;
> Hope keeping Love, Love Hope alive,
> Like babes bewilder'd in a snow,
> That cling and huddle from the cold
> In hollow tree or ruin'd fold.
>
> *(The Improvisatore)*

'Doubts.' A too-metaphysical cast of mind is, it may be,
stifling some necessary faith in his own highest, and lowest,
instinctive powers.

The way—or, at all events, a way—to self-realization
is shadowed by certain lines on Wordsworth. These
expand the various adulations accorded to the poetical
ladies, with a supreme confidence in the poetic faculty.
After listening to Wordsworth reading *The Prelude* he
writes:

> Theme hard as high!
> Of smiles spontaneous, and mysterious fears
> (The first-born they of Reason and twin-birth),
> Of tides obedient to external force,
> And currents self-determined, as might seem,
> Or by some inner Power; of moments awful,
> Now in thy inner life, and now abroad,
> When power streamed from thee, and thy soul received
> The light reflected, as a light bestowed. . . .
>
> *(To William Wordsworth)*

Both instinctive joy and mysterious fear accompany

spiritual initiation; the mysterious reality indicated seems alternately subjective and objective in origin; while 'Power streamed from thee' resembles Nietzsche's vision of a super-state. To Wordsworth Coleridge attributes the integrity he desires:

> . . . thenceforth calm and sure
> From the dread watch-tower of man's absolute self,
> With light unwaning on her eyes, to look
> Far on—herself a glory to behold,
> The Angel of the vision!

See how, as, too, in Nietzsche's *Zarathustra*, the integrated self *is* the vertical structure overlooking temporal horizons. Poetically perhaps Coleridge, possibly twice in *Kubla Khan* and *Zapolya*, enjoyed a synthesis richer than his friend. His reverence is, however, uncompromising:

> The truly great
> Have all one age, and from one visible space
> Shed influence! They, both in power and act,
> Are permanent, and Time is not with them,
> Save as it worketh for them, they in it.
> Nor less a sacred Roll, than those of old,
> And to be placed, as they, with gradual fame
> Among the archives of mankind, thy work
> Makes audible a linked lay of Truth,
> Of Truth profound a sweet continuous lay,
> Not learnt, but native, her own natural notes!

The poet utters eternity and is therefore identical in office with Biblical prophets. 'Not learnt': Coleridge respects what Pope pithily called his 'priestless muse'. Yet he as often distrusts his own secular inspiration, and his most powerful utterances, outside the plays and *Kubla Khan*, are usually couched in directly orthodox terms. To those I now pass. This noble address, itself Wordsworthian in accent, serves as a transition from the human and artistic to the divine and transcendental; that is, from the Abyssinian Maid to Kubla's overarching dome.

Continually in Coleridge nature is felt as tremulous and

essences as 'hovering', half-seen, half-felt. Often, too, as in *Kubla Khan*, some higher intuition is phrased in terms of a mysterious 'shadow' thrown across human existence. These we have met already in *Constancy to an Ideal Object* and *The Improvisatore*, in close relation to transcendent, sparkling and colourful, visions; though with vague suspicion that such shadows are cast by the watcher's own reflection shutting out 'reason's light'. Yet the noble phrase applied to his friend overlooking temporal existence 'from the dread watch-tower of man's absolute self' admits a subjective origin with no corresponding lack of spiritual authenticity. Of such a possibility Coleridge is, of course, often aware:

> The body,
> Eternal Shadow of the finite Soul,
> The Soul's self-symbol, its image of itself;
> Its own yet not itself.   *(Fragment 22)*

Moreover, all mistaken superstition such as that of our woodman in *Constancy to an Ideal Object* is, in its way, a profitable pointer. Superstition is felt as entwined with religion:

> O! Superstition is the giant shadow
> Which the solicitude of weak mortality,
> Its back toward Religion's rising sun,
> Casts on the thin mist of th' uncertain future.
>   *(Fragment 42)*

Coleridge's use of 'mist' is always precise. This respect towards superstition may be related to his own, and Wordsworth's, occasional reliance on satanic impressions as in some inexplicable way a poetic road to divine possessions. We can see all these as, in reality, shadows of the transcendent, and the shadow-image may be used with divine significance:

> For though 'tis Heaven Thyself to see,
> Where but thy *shadow* falls, Grief cannot be!
>   *(A Hymn)*

We should group and inspect the frequent mechanisms of

(i) a supernal, often colourful and glittering, vertical substance, and (ii) the shadow it casts across man's more limited, and horizontal, consciousness, before emphasizing differences, and without allowing our interest to be deflected by Coleridge's own varying judgements. His mind is from the start saturated in orthodox symbolism, and he rarely gives final allegiance to a vision not so embodied. His most powerful statements of the transcendental are therefore often traditionally religious in outward trappings. These we shall shortly observe. But first, to refresh our minds as to the *Kubla Khan* symbolism underlying alike Coleridge's naturalistic, human, and religious visions, I shall select a few further scattered examples to serve as a more homely approach to the more shattering and super-human revelations.

Pleasing variations are played on vertical symbolisms of domes, vaults, and temples. The poet's 'early youth' was a 'friendly dome': then psychic unity, almost, we may say, the eternity-synthesis, was natural and beneath the 'echoing cloisters pale' he hears, with wonder, of 'guilt' (*To a Young Lady*). Domes may, however, vary: and in *Separation* true love is deemed of higher worth than 'wealth's *glittering fairy-dome of ice*', wherein the phrase-structure strikes a significance expanding beyond its immediate purpose. There is contrast between the 'dazzling charm of outward form' and deep 'inward worth': but, since poetry is mainly engaged in finding images from the one category to express realities in the other, that same 'fairy-dome' may be elsewhere highly charged with the opposing, inward, essence. Domes, often of an expressly inward significance, may also be cosmic, as in Shelley, where sky or other natural phenomena, especially forest-canopies, are given dome-phraseology. In *The Picture* a beyond-sexual integration, to be contrasted with a 'woodland maze', is itself set amid a 'tangle' of 'bush and brake' which is said to

> Soar up and form a melancholy vault
> High o'er me, murmuring like a distant sea.

A mazy 'tangle' blends into a sacred edifice. 'Melancholy' suggests the specifically numinous; and the 'distant sea' is an eternity-symbol corresponding to Shakespeare's use in *Timon* and Wordsworth in his *Immortality Ode*. The sky may be a 'roof' as in *Cymbeline*: in *An Angel Visitant* we have a 'small blue roof of vernal sky' within 'circling hollies', the circular imagination being generally not far off. In *To Nature* the poet builds an 'altar in the fields' with the blue sky as his 'fretted dome' and flower-scent as 'incense', all being offered to 'God'. A short movement in a 'dramatic fragment' called *The Night Scene* presents an interesting maze-dome structure. Earl Henry asserts that he will go by a 'winding passage' to the 'bower' of 'unwavering love' and 'singleness of heart': which is, in its way, the 'friendly dome' of youth's integrity recently noted or the 'watch-tower' of mature integration applied to Wordsworth. Another person, Sandoval, meditating on his exit, compares his passion to a desert 'whirl-blast' such as may 'shape' columns 'from Earth to Heaven' like 'pillars of a temple built by Omnipotence in its own honour'; Omnipotence here corresponding to Kubla Khan himself. But such passionate structures dissolve and fall, the 'mighty columns' prove sand only, and 'lazy snakes trail o'er the level ruins'. We are back among flatness, mazes, the reptilian. Reptiles, as in *Christabel*, *The Ancient Mariner*, and *Psyche* (a tiny but neat poem), are normally to be contrasted with all vertical transcendences: they are, of course, uniquely two-dimensional creatures, as the Biblical account emphasizes. *Fragment* 13 meditates on a city 'awful at midnight' like the 'battlements and crags and towers' which 'Fancy' makes of 'clouds'; the city itself 'silent as the moon' which steeps in 'quiet' light her 'huge temples'. In *Fragment* 6 the moon suffuses Heaven and all nature including 'trees' and 'snake-like stream', whence we pass to the 'broad smooth mountain' (Coleridge's habitual way of blending mountains and domes) which is 'more a thing of Heaven than when distinct', seemingly 'undivided from the universal cloud in which it rises infinite in height'. Our list of sacred structures may be considered as summed in the *Monody on the Death of Chatterton*, where every knell from 'spire or dome' calls the poet, like a mother, to his native eternity.

Altars, temples, and domes are variously naturalistic, psychological, or explicitly religious: but all are equally sacred. *Catullian Hendecasyllables* recounts an 'old Milesian story', wherein we pass from fertile nature and ease over water into a cave, thence through a maze up to a high-set temple and visionary priestess. This seems a peculiarly satisfying example of Coleridge's patterned thinking: it is, however, translated from part of a poem by Friedrich von Matthisson. The choice of the extract remains significant.

Coleridge's specifically religious poetry is normally orthodox. Examples are numerous, and the range wide. The Book of Revelation supplies numerous footnote quotations. Indeed, his religious poetry is distinguished pre-eminently by its apocalyptic tendencies. One of his notes deserves especial attention:

> The Millennium:—in which I suppose that Man will continue to enjoy the highest glory of which his human nature is capable.—That all who in past ages have endeavoured to ameliorate the state of man will rise and enjoy the fruits and flowers, the imperceptible seeds of which they had sown in their former Life: and that the wicked will, during the same period, be suffering the remedies adapted to their several bad habits. I suppose that this period will be followed by the passing away of this Earth and by our entering the state of pure intellect; when all Creation shall rest from its labours.
>
> (Footnote from *Religious Musings*)

This, I think, strikes well the appropriate tone for my next discussions.

The *Ode to the Departing Year*, says Coleridge, addresses that Divine Providence regulating 'into one vast harmony' all temporal events, calamitous though they may appear to mortals. The poet advances with 'no unholy madness', the phrase suggesting the concluding frenzies

of *Kubla Khan*. A chariot—a symbol less important with
Coleridge than with Southey, Shelley, and Keats—is
impregnated with suggestion of victorious evil. 'Death-
fires' dance round the tomb of tyranny. The Departing
Year is now envisioned 'on no earthly shore', in some
eternity where 'memory' sits before the 'cloudy throne' of
divine majesty; and next the Spirit of the Earth interrupts
the wheelings and harping of the blessed with a plea for
retribution to the 'God of Nature'. The agonies of man
cry for justice and assuagement. The poet endures a
nightmare sweat with imagery of death closely resembling
the agonized pantings of birth in *Kubla Khan*:

> And my thick and struggling breath
> Imitates the toil of death!

But he finally 'recentres' his 'immortal mind' (eternal
harmonies rather than historic chaos being felt as the
birth-right of man's intelligence) in 'self-content', cleansed
from all 'vaporous passions that bedim God's Image'.
Notice how, even though most agonizing communal or
national evils are afoot, the very awareness of such as a
God-excluding chaos is, in its way, a spiritual limitation.
Coleridge attempts to integrate temporal chaos into that
harmonious 'eternity' the human mind demands.

In these poems we face the worst, with which no rosy
mountains nor musical ladies can, by themselves, cope.
Rather we are forced to transcendent categories, Biblical
or Miltonic word-music, and crushing, sweeping, indict-
ments of an insensate and brutal civilization. *Fears in
Solitude* ruminates on war-horrors, with dark fears of
invasion. The poet attacks the slave-trade, smug com-
mittees, self-satisfaction, and a febrile and emotionally
castrated Church:

> The sweet words
> Of Christian promise, words that even yet
> Might stem destruction, were they wisely preached,
> Are muttered o'er by men, whose tones proclaim
> How flat and wearisome they feel their trade. . . .

Since imaginative and intellectual virility has left our religion, that life-drained formality turns to a 'juggler's charm' the very 'name of God' and 'Book of Life'. Coleridge, like Pope and Byron, indicts a mock civilization, and implicitly hands over our religious insincerities to the devastating, and deeply righteous, condemnations of Nietzsche. So the 'owlet Atheism' is abroad.

He expands at length on war's obscenity and condemns its sanctioning in education and the press, while nevertheless counselling a *humble* belief in England as a bulwark against tyranny:

> O divine
> And beauteous island! thou hast been my sole
> And most magnificent temple, in the which
> I walk with awe, and sing my stately songs,
> Loving the God that made me!

The poem ends with description of peaceful nature, content, and domestic bliss with wife and child. The disparity between Coleridge's apparent simplicity and innocence and its historic and communal context appears absolute: and yet that surface antinomy—many poems already analysed suggest as much—scarcely tells the whole story. There remains something *within* that responds, however negatively, to the horrors without; and to turn this to the light his poetry travails.

Something dark and Dionysian, like Wordsworth's numinous and mighty forms, like his own more Satanic nature-apprehensions in *Dejection*, broods over, or within, Coleridge's greatest religious utterance. *Religious Musings* introduces us to 'a vision of the Heavenly multitude' with Christ Himself brighter 'than all the Angel-blaze'; for

> the Great
> Invisible (by symbols only seen)

shines more fully from a human figure than from any vast natural splendours; or, we might add, any domed or other architectural elevations. Though to this extent humanist, the mighty music and transcendental approach

K

incorporates the awfulness of divinity. Archangels, the Almighty and His Throne, Heaven, and Hell cluster the page. Christ is defined as 'manifest Godhead' melting those 'floating mists'—a typical image—of 'idolatry' that have 'broke and misshaped the omnipresent Sire', working through 'fear' to 'uncharm' the 'drowsed soul' until it *recollect* (as in *Zapolya*) its native heritage of that 'mystic good' which 'the Eternal dooms for his immortal sons', until the self be annihilated and make 'God its *Identity*'. 'Fear', 'dooms', annihilation: the terrible is definitely incorporated into the immortal hope.

So evil and good interfuse. Praise is accorded all those 'blest' whose vision sees through the transparency of 'the deeds of men' to worship divine 'essence'; who, 'gazing' and 'trembling', are able to 'ascend' beyond 'all visible things' to 'their Father's throne'; who, *with no evil passions within*, realize that nothing is 'deform', since the 'sole operant' is that 'Supreme Fair' in whose sight 'all things are pure'. The synthesis of *Zapolya* is implicit. Such, 'inly armed' with 'celestial courage',

> view o'er their heads
> His waving banners of Omnipotence.

A vast *presence*, as in Wordsworth, is felt, supernatural and transcendent. Now such souls, being pure within and loved of the Creator, necessarily dread not any 'created Might':

> For they are holy things before the Lord
> Aye unprofaned, though Earth should league with Hell;
> God's altar grasping with an eager hand
> Fear, the wild-visag'd, pale, eye-starting wretch,
> Sure-refug'd hears his hot pursuing friends
> Yell at vain distance.

Calmness, a 'soft' and 'solemn' bliss, and 'dreadless awe' are his, while 'Faith's whole armour glitters on his limbs'. 'All things of terrible seeming', as we shall find in *Zapolya*, leave him 'unmoved'. He comes 'kindling with intenser Deity' from the 'celestial Mercy-seat', with a militant purpose filled 'from the renovating wells of Love'. Such are the elect who pass from 'dark passions' and 'thirsty cares' (i.e. passionate cravings) which either (i) vanish or (ii) 'acquire new names, new features', now being themselves

> Enrobed with Light and naturalised in Heaven.

Though sternly orthodox in symbolism the doctrine approaches that of Pope's *Essay on Man*. The dark powers are not necessarily denied: they may, as in Nietzsche's *Zarathustra* and Eliot's *Family Reunion*, become angels. Coleridge has here a most valuable footnote:

> Our evil Passions, under the influence of Religion, become innocent, and may be made to animate our virtue—in the same manner as the thick mist melted by the Sun, increases the light which it had before excluded. In the preceding paragraph, agreeably to this truth, we had allegorically narrated the transfiguration of Fear into holy Awe.

Coleridge's use of mist is always interesting, and must be referred also to the symbolism of *The Ancient Mariner*.

> 'Tis the sublime in man
> Our noontide Majesty, to know ourselves
> Parts and proportions of one wondrous whole!

Whence charity matures. 'Noontide majesty' may be referred to both 'the dread watch-tower of man's absolute self' (see *To William Wordsworth*) and Wordsworth's brooding 'day' in the *Immortality Ode*. Coleridge's emphasis is slightly less naturalistic than Pope's: though both emphasize the infusing 'Supreme Reality', the divine; and to expect otherwise is called 'superstition'. To make one's own 'low self the whole' is erroneous; yet through 'sacred sympathy' the process may be reversed to make 'the whole one Self', all-encompassing, far-reaching as Fancy, unseeking but all-possessing: a state expressed at the conclusion of *France*.

National and international wickedness is given a

horror-struck account, but is nevertheless regarded as
instrumental in the hands of the 'everlasting' 'Lord of
unsleeping Love', who teaches good through evil and
makes 'Truth lovely' through 'brief wrong'. The poet
attempts next a more historic approach, again in the
manner of Pope. 'Imagination' creates a 'host of new
desires' leading to the vices and glories of civilization.
Prominent among these is the 'arched dome', and all
'inventive arts' which first nourished the soul with beauty,
and 'by sensual wants unsensualised the mind', making it
to forget the 'grossness' of its original end while lost in
pleasant activity. Here domes help to symbolize the
cathartic and spiritualizing powers of artistic creation.
So 'warriors, lords, and priests', a Shelleyan list, though
evil, are immediate sources 'of mightier good', while
'necessities' goad 'human thought' to its supreme position.
Evils are given pragmatic justification, while all obviously
outstanding advance-guards of human progress and harmony, such as poets and thinkers, are praised. The creative purpose of revolution is also honoured in terms of
'plastic' art 'moulding' a confusion, and its motive-power
related imagistically to an 'arched romantic rock', recalling
Kubla Khan, a 'sea-breeze', recalling *France*, and sky-
splendours.

The poem progresses in waves; and now, as though
more confident of a final resolution, faces all the un-
acknowledged social and national wickednesses of the
human race. Such demand 'retribution' and 'the Lamb
of God hath opened the fifth seal': a long footnote quoting
from the Book of Revelation. The indictment includes
no single aspect alone of

the abhorréd Form
Whose scarlet robe was stiff with earthly pomp,

but, as Coleridge tells us, 'the union of Religion with
Power and Wealth, wherever it is found'. 'Mitred
atheism' comprehensively sums many of his charges. But
against 'pale Fear' and 'moon-blasted madness when he

yells at midnight'—the intensest Coleridgean negatives—
are set 'pure Faith' and 'meek Piety'—somewhat febrile
phrases that preclude, I think, the highest integration—
waiting to possess the earth, when each heart shall be
'self-governed' and the 'massy gates of Paradise' thrown
wide to 'unearthly melodies'.

Apocalyptic vision now rises above worst evils. We
plunge upward to a 'blest future', thoughts of Father and
Saviour, and the Millennium:

> . . . while as the Thousand Years
> Lead up their mystic dance, the Desert shouts!
> Old Ocean claps his hands! The mighty Dead
> Rise to new life . . .

and Earth, as in Shelley's *Prometheus*, a somewhat similar
prophecy, is 'renovated'. The solid and architectural
imagery of 'massy gates' extends to Heaven's 'Jasper
throne', before which great thinkers now bright as
'Seraphs' (remember our former seraph-intuitions) arrive.
Now poetic 'Fancy' flutters on idle wing. Who, the poet
asks, 'of woman born' may describe that day when the
Sun shall wane 'seized in his mid course', the 'red-eyed
Fiend' be destroyed, and 'Time is no more'? Who
indeed? Unless, perhaps, we turn to *Kubla Khan*. For
here, in orthodox terms, Coleridge is found straining after
that very comprehension his more pagan poem masters
with an easy, unselfconscious, grace:

> Believe thou, O my soul,
> Life is a vision shadowy of Truth;
> And vice and anguish and the wormy grave,
> Shapes of a dream! The veiling clouds retire,
> And lo! the Throne of the redeeming God
> Forth flashing unimaginable day
> Wraps in one blaze earth, heaven, and deepest hell.

The revelation here intended, including feeling of *both life
and death* as 'shadowy' entities of a lesser order than the
expressly 'flashing' Throne, whose blaze yet includes
'deepest hell', corresponds exactly to *Kubla Khan*.

We conclude, too, with a more naturalistic symbolism, addressing spirits who

> hover o'er
> With untired gaze the immeasurable fount
> Ebullient with creative Deity!

Where the cataract of creation, which we have met more than once already, is now shot through with transcendental significance. We next have spirits of 'plastic power' —working in space as the others in time—who organize the all-surging 'grosser and material mass'. The poet would join their 'mystic choir', meanwhile disciplining himself with poetry and religious meditation to breathe the airs of 'omnipresent Love',

> Whose day-spring rises glorious on my soul
> As the great Sun, when he his influence
> Sheds on the frost-bound waters.

We return to our old sun and ice symbolism, denoting the light of reason reflected from purified, and also eternalized, instinct: our 'sunny pleasure-dome with caves of ice'.

The Departing Year and Fears in Solitude face world-agony and attempt through a lyric and philosophic approach a resolution in terms of poetic music and eternal harmony. They avoid simple black-and-white judgements: England's guilt is, for example, emphasized, but possibilities of good-through-evil glimpsed. Religious Musings presses farther, following Pope in recognition of the human dynamic as a fusing medium, using racial progress and the individual good man as central, with the rest a necessary context for creative ascent. The Destiny of Nations plunges even deeper, presenting a single, objectively conceived, personality, Saint Joan, able to bear and transmute the burden of world-evil. Such a dramatic projection alone can approach the synthesis most perfectly accomplished in Zapolya: hence the high place to be accorded dramatic literature and the supreme importance of dramatic action in the New Testament.

We start with a magnificent *power-impregnated* invocation to:—

> Eternal Father! King Omnipotent!
> To the Will Absolute, the One, the Good!
> The I AM, the Word, the Life, the Living God!
>   Such symphony requires best instrument.
> Seize, then, my soul! from Freedom's trophied dome
> The Harp which hangeth high between the Shields
> Of Brutus and Leonidas! With that
> Strong music, that soliciting spell, force back
> Man's free and stirring spirit that lies entranced.
>   For what is Freedom, but the unfettered use
> Of all the powers which God for use had given?
> But chiefly this, him First, him Last to view
> Through meaner powers and secondary things
> Effulgent, as through clouds that veil his blaze.
> For all that meets the bodily sense I deem
> Symbolical, one mighty alphabet
> For infant minds; and we in this low world
> Placed with our backs to bright Reality,
> That we may learn with young unwounded ken
> The substance from its shadow. Infinite Love,
> Whose latence is the plenitude of All,
> Thou with retracted beams, and self-eclipse
> Veiling, revealest thine eternal Sun.

'I am' as a definition of God denotes active being akin to the inward dynamic of human personality; 'king' and 'living' channel pagan power-sources and vital naturalism; 'dome', as usual, is important; Roman and Greek references and the 'strong' *liberating* music preclude enervate conventional religiosity; and 'bright Reality' felt as *behind* and casting a shadow we have met before. A comprehensive humanism and divinity are coactive; with finally both a doctrine and example of *natural* symbolism. In strong contrast Coleridge next attacks that pseudo-science so bitterly denounced in Pope's *Dunciad*, and continues with a short discussion of unstable philosophic theories, and, next, of superstition.

Fancies and superstitions are variously attacked and

respected by Coleridge. Though dark and dangerous, superstitions here 'train up to God' with authentic glimmerings of distant truth, as when

> The Laplander beholds the far-off Sun
> Dart his slant beam on unobeying snows. . . .

Imagery follows telling of savage fancies concerning 'the streamy banners of the North', 'happy spirits', and 'robes of rosy light'. The recurrent snow-light impressionism is emphatic. Now such fancy 'unsensualizes' the mind and 'superstition' with 'unconscious hand' eventually seats 'Reason on her throne'. A powerful passage follows in description of a Greenland superstition involving a 'wizard', dreadful adventure among abysms and 'misshaped prodigies', elemental horrors and wonders, sea and ice, all subjected, however, to faith in some 'Spirit of Good'. Such 'phantasies' are, in their way, wise, teaching reliance on the 'victorious goodness' of God. Power-sources are being respected.

This defence of superstition serves as prologue to our central, and *mythical*, action. It is suggested that 'Beings of higher class than Man' may assist in the creation of kingdoms; and that one such actually helped the warrior-maid, Joan, whose deeds so matched her words that she demands our faith. She grew up in simplicity, maturing in native insight and natural wisdom, while her eye 'spake more than woman's thought'. She is at once like 'an haughty huntress of the woods' and a 'gentle maid': in her masculine and feminine, active and passive, potentialities blend. To her our bad world was a 'place of Tombs', and she touched not its deathly 'pollutions'. She is, however, realistically conceived.

Setting out on a cold night 'urged by the indwelling angel-guide', she ascends a 'steep upland' and comes suddenly on a team of horses 'stiff and cold', their manes all 'hoar with the frozen night-dews'. A man creeps forth:

> his limbs
> The silent frost had eat, scathing like fire.

But his wife and child—'the crisp milk frozen on its innocent lips'—lie dead; exquisitely pictured, mother and child, they lie in frozen immobility, two of Coleridge's favourites, frost and the mother-child relationship, being finely, if tragically, united. The man tells a tale of rapine and slaughter before the 'hovering spirits' of his wife and child welcome him in death. Joan endures again their suffering, her features shoot

> Such strange vivacity as fires the eye
> Of Misery fancy-crazed. . . .

She is in turmoil of thought and emotion. A 'mighty hand was strong upon her'; she returns to the hill-top, in half-unconscious trance 'ghastly as broad-eyed Slumber', desiring escape but subdued by 'an inevitable Presence'. A Voice speaks, choosing her as Christ is chosen.

There follows a fascinating passage on which Coleridge has the following note:

> These are very fine lines, tho' I say it that should not: but, hang me, if I know or ever did know the meaning of them, though my own composition.

The interpretation is simple. The 'tutelary Power' is initiating Joan into mysteries of creation and evil. Just as 'a fresh breeze' 'wakens' a 'merchant-sail' after 'pestful calms'

> With slimy shapes and miscreated life
> Poisoning the vast Pacific,

so over the abyss of primal chaos 'Love rose glittering' with 'gorgeous wings'. The imagery suggests *The Ancient Mariner* directly and, in view of 'glittering' heights or spheres elsewhere, *Kubla Khan* indirectly. Night moaned to see the 'Protoplast' rise (probably like a broad dome-shaped mountain) on 'confusion's charmèd wave', and forthwith

> entered the Profound
> That leads with downward windings to the Cave
> Of Darkness palpable, Desert of Death
> Sunk deep beneath Gehenna's massy roots.

The cave-death association of *Kubla Khan* is explicit.
Notice 'windings'. There she remains a 'dateless age':
but at length, inspired by 'fierce Hate' and 'gloomy Hope',
retraces her steps 'through the uncouth maze' and 'drear
labyrinth' and, while she dare not re-enter the 'diminished
Gulph', summons from chaos a 'hideous fronted brood',
letting loose horrors on earth and wickedness in men;
with *fear*, origin of cruelty; and sickness. The winding
troubles and cavernous glooms of *Kubla Khan* are finely
extended.

The Maid, however, faced by ultimate evil, exults in
the glory of God-witnessing martyrdoms, and asserts
triumph:

> O ye spirits of God,
> Hover around my mortal agonies!

She hears a 'faint melody', such as soothes 'an agèd Hermit
in his holy dream' to 'foretell and solace death':

> and now they rise
> Louder, as when with harp and mingled voice
> The white-robed multitude of slaughtered saints
> At Heaven's wide-open'd portals gratulant
> Receive some martyred patriot. The harmony
> Entranced the Maid, till each suspended sense
> Brief slumber seized, and confused ecstasy.

This, set directly against our recent cavernous and deathly
labyrinths and abysms, corresponds, as do all Heavenly
descriptions, to the dome in *Kubla Khan*. That is why an
early text proceeds *immediately* with

> But lo! no more was seen the ice-pil'd mount
> And meteor-lighted dome.

The 'meteor' throws back to our Laplander passage. The
Heaven-dome equation (with ice, as in *Kubla Khan*, and
underfeeling of our many other *white* structures, mountains or otherwise) could scarcely be more vivid. Characteristically Coleridge altered the image, continuing with
the vision 'thinning' through 'mist' until

> an Isle appeared,
> Its high, o'er-hanging, white, broad-breasted cliffs,
> Glassed on the subject ocean.

Which returns us to much the same thing. As so often, the bright structure lifts above water, here specifically 'subject'. 'Broad-breasted' hints a giant, human, figure, which we shall meet again.

Next appears a 'fair Form', olive-crowned and emblematic of Peace. She is, however, 'wan' of cheek, with an 'anxious' pleasure in 'her faint eye' as a 'pale convalescent' having 'newly left a couch of pain', though destined one day to rule the world. She resembles Moneta, just as the Maid's earlier trance and agony of psychic rebirth resembled Keats himself as dramatized in *Hyperion*. Black clouds and 'reddening shapes' appear; warrior-hosts battle in air and let fall blood-drops on earth; stains of 'ominous light' limn 'hideous features' in the sky. Peace bows her head. The Maid contemplates the horrors of destruction. A paragraph returns to a bitter war-diagnosis that might be compared with that in Mr. Francis Berry's *The Iron Christ*. The Maid sees a pestilential, and then a brilliant, cloud-formation, while from that last springs a semi-divine being:

> And soon from forth its bursting sides emerged
> A dazzling form, broad-bosomed, bold of eye,
> And wild her hair, save where with laurels bound.
> Not more majestic stood the healing God,
> When from his bow the arrow sped that slew
> Huge Python. Shriek'd Ambition's giant throng,
> And with them hissed the locust-fiends that crawled
> And glittered in Corruption's slimy track.

The form is feminine, yet compared with Apollo: it is, in fact, super-sexual, and should be referred to Coleridge's seraph types already noticed. The Maid herself, as we have seen, was imagined somewhat similarly. 'Broad-bosomed' throws back to the 'broad-breasted' paradise-image earlier: a similar super-sexual being recurs in Shelley's *Witch of Atlas*. Coleridge's figure rises above the reptilian evils on their 'slimy track', flatness again being emphasized. The figure symbolizes, like Mr. Berry's Iron Christ, the superman perfection to which war-agonies are preparatory. Joan is addressed by the 'heavenly Vision' as 'Maiden beloved and Delegate of Heaven' and commanded to save her country. A mystic nationalism is emphatic.

Final praise is offered to that divine energy inspiring *alike* prophet and all evilly diseased and man-infecting enthusiasts. This conclusion aims to clasp the turbulent and paradoxical substances into one harmonious whole. But the synthesis depends mainly on use of a central, dramatic, and heroic, person. Our subjective, experiencing selves are more involved: only so can worst conflicts of *power* and *love* be, unless highly symbolically, resolved. Before passing to Coleridge's dramatic work we might remember the heroic and pagan emphasis in this the most powerful of Coleridge's religious poems: the original references to Leonidas and Brutus and the phrase 'strong music'; the glittering ice-dome; the 'broad-breasted' cliff and 'broad-bosomed' Apollo-form; the bisexual union of strength and gentleness in both heroine and divine-messenger. Such intuitions stand out from a bleakness and horror that makes a queer fragmentary addition at the poem's conclusion strangely organic:

> And first a landscape rose
> More wild and waste and desolate than where
> The white bear, drifting on a field of ice,
> Howls to her sundered cubs with piteous rage
> And savage agony.

Our second, and a truly terrible, image of maternal, ice-tormented, pain.

We have examined poems which expand the main elements briefly compacted in *Kubla Khan*, and the process has exhausted all Coleridge's minor poetry of importance. Woods, chasms, rivers, labyrinths, caves, mountains, ladies of song, music, monarchs, glittering dome-like

structures, and other transcendental symbolisms have been
continually in evidence. 'Ice' recurs frequently. The
organic coherence of Coleridge's impressionism is best
seen when, as we have observed, he follows a description
of Heavenly hosts by a reference without further explanation to 'the ice-piled mount and meteor-lighted dome'
which he considers already before us. True, he deleted
the image in a later version; but *Kubla Khan* itself remained unknown for nearly twenty years and was only
finally published at the instigation of Lord Byron. In
it the author saw no '*poetic* merit'. We have already
noticed an amusing footnote showing that Coleridge wa
far from understanding his own symbolisms.

III

The additional complexity and power of synthesis
enjoyed by *The Destiny of Nations* over other poems
attempting to transmute widest evils into a harmony was,
partly at least, due to its semi-dramatic nature. That was,
moreover, an especially *inclusive* poem, ranging widely
across all Coleridge's favourite territories. It thus forms
a neat introduction to his two great plays. In these we
find a comparable emotional and spiritual drive with, also,
a very similar use of symbolism to the work hitherto
discussed, with a particularly interesting emphasis on
(i) heroic women, recalling Joan in *The Destiny of Nations*,
and (ii) caves. We scarcely expect elaborate dome-
formations, since all such greater art-forms are themselves
the eternalizing structure symbolized elsewhere by such
visual modellings: but certain closely related essences,
such as temples and music, recur. Coleridge is dramatizing not merely interesting or exciting stories, but rather
all ultimate problems of human destiny.

Remorse is a strangely iridescent creation, with penetra-
tions idealistic and satanic, sinking shafts into subterranean darkness or exploring gleams that slant swiftly
upward to heavenly grace.

Occasionally the accent is ominous and dull:

> I have seem'd to hear
> A low dead thunder mutter thro' the night,
> As 'twere a giant angry in his sleep.
>
> (IV. ii. 95)

Or it may be icy, as in *The Duchess of Malfi*, as when uttermost obedience is phrased in terms of climbing an 'ice-glazed precipice' (II. i. 18). Such is, in Coleridge, as likely to suggest the paradisal as the satanic, and has no deeply evil impregnation here. But such impressionism may also give

> Oh cold—cold—cold! shot through with icy cold!
>
> (II. i. 123)

or

> Heart-chilling Superstition! thou can'st glaze
> Ev'n Pity's eye with her own frozen tear.
>
> (IV. ii. 1)

There is little warmth. The impressionistic atmosphere is often shadowed. Alhadra meditates revenge in wild moonlit scenery at midnight when the 'screech-owl' is the 'sole eye' of the midnight world (IV. iii. 6). Moonlight is continual and dominating. Though many happy nature-images occur, owls, wolves, and ravens are almost as organic here as eagles and leopards in *Zapolya*. The sun is, significantly, unemphasized:

> A rim of the sun lies yet upon the sea
> And now 'tis gone.   (III. ii. 185)

Moreover, the people, good or bad, are in half-darkness. The hero and heroine follow against all reason a gleaming hope concerned respectively and reciprocally with the other's (i) faith and (ii) life. A 'dim power' guides Teresa (III. ii. 161). The villain is only half-wicked and deeply baffled by himself and the plot. The action shows a steady working-out of deceptions, moon-struck crime is dissolved into a tragic, yet not dishonourable, awakening, hopes are fulfilled, and heroic strength, at the last, treads the scene unchained.

But from the start evil is countered by fleeting brightnesses. Alvar tells how, when he and Teresa parted, 'purple' dawn from the 'kindling east' blended with her blushes, and 'suffused the tear-drops there with rosy light':

> There seemed a glory round us, and Teresa
> The angel of the vision.   (i. i. 50–5)

Coleridge's recurring intuition of the angelic and visionary in association with some lady or other is lively here. So 'night after night' Teresa has visited Alvar's sleep either as a 'saintly sufferer' or 'saint in glory' (i. i. 82). Such intuitions relate variously to the Abyssinian maid of *Kubla Khan* and the dreams in *Zapolya*. Teresa, expanding delicate and fervent intuitions concerning love's truth in death, dreams of a bowery paradise; and adds a description of a 'crazy Moorish maid' who played her dead lover's favourite tunes on 'her lute' while 'listening' to the 'shadow' she herself creates (i. ii. 30–5). Reflections of both *Kubla Khan* and an 'idiot boy' to be noticed shortly are apparent. Coleridge's subtle, quivering, apprehensions of positive vision make love at once a 'timorous and tender flower' (i. ii. 83), yet dauntless and finally victorious. Nor are the emotions selfish. Teresa forgives her lover's supposed murderer, saying how Alvar's 'spirit ever at the throne of God asks mercy for thee' (v. i. 69–70). Alvar, who believes in the 'sacred source of penitent tears' (v. i. 97), would release his brother from criminal unreality:

> Let me recall him to his nobler nature,
> That he may wake us from a dream of murder.
>   (v. i. 94–5)

Here the poetic will is aiming to dispel the nightmare mockery of human evil, with an implied metaphysic akin to that of *Macbeth*.

Ordonio is a remarkable study. He is no simple Machiavellian (in the popular sense), no Iago. Bosola is, perhaps, his nearest relative: yet he also touches a

moonstruck insanity and trance-like paralysis resembling
that of Webster's Ferdinand and Cardinal in their final appearances. His being is continually lighted with unearthly
illuminations. He has a 'proud forbidding eye' and 'dark
brow' (i. ii. 81), but is from the start unstably poised in his
dangerous course and most susceptible to verbal shock
(i. ii. 143–7). He can address an accomplice with:

> And you kill'd him?
> Oh blood hounds! may eternal wrath flame round you!
> He was his maker's image undefac'd.   (ii. i. 118)

His ethical thinking, whether in support of good or evil,
penetrates both metaphysically and mystically as he
mutters (thinking of himself) about 'this unutterable dying
away', this 'sickness of the heart' (ii. i. 126–7). Like the
Ancient Mariner and Sweeney in Eliot's play he relieves
his burdened nature by a confession purporting, as with
Sweeney, to relate to someone else, which is, however,
here ironically used to set the stage for the murder of his
interlocutor. The self-diagnosis is trenchant:

> . . . All men seemed mad to him!
> Nature had made him for some other planet,
> And pressed his soul into a human shape
> By accident or malice. In this world
> He found no fit companion.   (iv. i. 105)

He continues in terms of 'phantom thoughts', unchecked
imaginations, and mysterious 'shadows', and records how
he first uttered and next gave 'substance and reality' to a
fancy 'wilder than the rest'; that is, crime. Thereafter he,
like Sweeney, must conform painfully to 'living purposes'
and 'occupations' and 'semblances of ordinary men' (iv. i.
112–38). The disclosure is of wide significance, suiting
human guilt in general. The setting is of wild gloom, and
with great dramatic power the narrative works up to an
avowal of its autobiographical nature and the subsequent
murder.

Ordonio's criminal instincts are closely involved in
metaphysical speculation:

Ordonio: Say I had laid a body in the sun.
            Well! in a month there swarm forth from the corse
            A thousand, nay ten thousand, sentient beings
            In place of that one man.—Say I had killed him!
                              (Teresa starts and stops listening.)
            Yet who shall tell me, that each one and all
            Of these ten thousand lives is not as happy
            As that one life, which being pushed aside,
            Made room for these unnumbered—
Valdez: O mere madness!
                                    (III. ii. 107)

Such strange unbalanced clarity of perception resembles
Hieronimo's thoughts on the unreason of paternal love in
one of those amazing additions to *The Spanish Tragedy*,
which include, too, an imagined *painting* of a past crime
paralleled by the central use of such a picture in *Remorse*.
Ordonio thinks on death:

> There, where Ordonio likewise would fain lie!
> In the sleep-compelling earth, in un-pierc'd darkness!
> For while we live—
> An inward day that never, never sets,
> Glares round the soul, and mocks the closing eyelids!
>   (III. ii. 122)

'Un-pierc'd darkness': *Kubla Khan's* measureless, subterranean caverns of death. Reminiscence of *Macbeth*
grows patent:

> Over his rocky grave the fir-grove sighs
> A lulling ceaseless dirge! 'Tis well with him.
>   (III. ii. 127)

Though he sneers at 'moist-eyed Penitence' (III. ii. 104)
Ordonio is, like the Ancient Mariner, an 'inly-tortured
man' with 'a frightful glitter' in his 'eye' (v. i. 117–18).
In the last scene, burdened with crimes past and pre-
meditated, he reasons almost kindly with his powerless
victim. He can often rise impersonally above himself:
life, he says, is a 'pool amid a storm of rain', and from time
to time one bubble bursts another—that is all (v. i. 112).

L.

And yet he boasts of never having willingly inflicted
'faintness, cold, and hunger' on anyone (v. i. 121–6).
Never was a first-class villain so sincere in metaphysical
justification. Yet Alvar, though in his power, bravely
charges Ordonio with self-deception, asserting that such
superficial cynicisms have brought their possessor no
peace; and Ordonio, moved, murmurs vacantly Alvar's
phrase of salvation. Soon after he grows wild with
remorse at Isidore's murder, agonized by the typical
Coleridgean thought of widow and children:

> Not all the blessings of an host of angels
> Can blow away a desolate widow's curse!
>
> (v. i. 173)

and

> Heap it like coals of fire upon my heart,
> And shoot it hissing through my brain!
>
> (v. i. 180)

Recognizing his supposedly murdered, but forgiving,
brother he cries: 'Touch me not! Touch not pollution
Alvar! I will die' (v. i. 203). He is distracted, and kneels.
Unable longer to bear his *lonely* agony he prays, and
indeed longs, for 'Eternal Justice' to prepare his punishment 'in the obscure world' (v. i. 226). The conception
is daring and awe-inspiring: in him you sense layers of
consciousness such as those which Wordsworth more
uncomprisingly projects through Oswald. Ordonio is
a nightmare figure, dreaming away his existence into
horrors, yet scarcely daring to awake.

He holds, however, no monopoly in speculative intelligence. Alvar can counter him in his own especial manner:

> *Alvar:*   Yon insect on the wall,
> Which moves this way and that its hundred limbs,
> Were it a toy of mere mechanic craft,
> It were an infinitely curious thing!
> But it has life, Ordonio! life, enjoyment!
> And by the power of its miraculous will
> Wields all the complex movements of its frame
> Unerringly to pleasurable ends!

Saw I that insect on this goblet's brim
I would remove it with an anxious pity!
Ordonio: What meanest thou?
Alvar: There's poison in the wine.
Ordonio: Thou hast guessed right; there's poison in the wine.
(v. i. 127)

How quietly tense, yet with what feeling for dark currents
beneath, the dialogue murmurs. Alvar speaks, too, a
philosophical reading of the whole action:

Of this be certain:
Time, as he courses onward, still unrolls
The volume of concealment. In the future,
As in the optician's glassy cylinder,
The indistinguishable blots and colours
Of the dim past collect and shape themselves,
Up-starting in their own completed image
To scare or to reward.   (II. ii. 8)

The play dramatizes a working-out of complexities, a
lifting of shadows. The plot is crammed with deceptions.
The hero and heroine are continually and variously mistaken concerning each other. The villain and his accomplice are both mistaken in different ways concerning their
own crimes. Indeed, a deep truth, such as is driven home
differently in *Macbeth*, is hinted by Ordonio's only actual
murder being perpetrated against his supposedly traitor-
ous accomplice in a crime which has never really existed:
a neat, if vicious, circle, going to the very heart of evil felt
as a symbolization of an unnecessarily guilty soul-state.
The complexities are baffling: these the play works not
so much to explain as to *unravel*. Finally, of course, the
clearest language for such profundities will be intensely
symbolic: and it is so here.

The human action interlocks with some fascinating
atmospheric effects. Certain primary examples I shall
now observe, in which correspondences to *Kubla Khan*
may be noticed.

Ordonio and his accomplice Isidore converse in 'a wild

and mountainous country', with, according to the direction in Coleridge's earlier version, *Osorio*, a view of 'a
house, which stands under the brow of a slate rock. . . .'
Isidore describes a Moorish magician he considers well
suited to Ordonio's plots; one who has already, when
questioned as to his identity, answered:

> Say to the Lord Ordonio,
> He that can bring the dead to life again.
> (II. i. 162)

The wizard is Alvar, the hero, in disguise, and his employ-
ment is to prove directly unfortunate for Ordonio: therefore his being given a paradise-setting is not inappropriate.
You approach his resort by following a meandering
brooklet, tracing its course 'backward' (this points on
to Shelley) and entering, through a narrow opening, a
'green dell' surrounded by 'high off-sloping hills' and
called 'The Giant's Cradle'. There is a lake wherein trees
are reflected, so that 'a kind of faery forest' grows 'down
in the water'. A 'puny cataract' flows in at one end,

> And there, a curious sight! you see its shadow
> For ever curling, like a wreath of smoke,
> Up through the foliage of those faery trees.
> (II. i. 167–80)

Many *Kubla Khan* elements are present: a mazy river,
forests, mountains, cataract, and a mysterious shadow.
Especially interesting is the image of watery violence
transmuted into ascending mist, which rises to a 'faery'
height: to which the work of Byron and Shelley contains
valuable analogies. Here there is no 'dome': but the use
of a mountain-surrounded, and therefore circular, valley
enables the poet very neatly to subordinate his river,
as it were, to a circular height; and as in *Kubla Khan*
a vast, human, personality is half-felt dominating the
whole business in 'Giant's Cradle'. Now, as though
himself caught in the fascinating web of this recurring
symbolism, Coleridge adds in *Remorse* a passage (II. i.
182–91) not found in *Osorio*. It follows immediately on

our last passage, though dialogue replaces description.
It adds suggestion, however indirect, of two *Kubla Khan*
elements so far omitted, (i) vast architecture, and (ii) a
smaller human and musical figure, to correspond to the
Abyssinian maiden. Ordonio thinks they are overheard.
He guiltily senses a presence above 'where the smooth
high wall of slate rock *glitters*'. Isidore replies:

> 'Neath those tall stones, which propping each the other,
> Form a mock portal with their pointed arch?

A brilliant architecture is indirectly being composed.
There, says Isidore, sits only a poor 'Idiot Boy'. Here we
should recall (i) Wordsworth's *Idiot Boy*, and (ii) the 'crazy'
Moorish maid and her wistful music in a speech of Teresa's
already noticed; whence a reference of this 'Idiot Boy' to
the Abyssinian Maid of *Kubla Khan* becomes reasonable.
His significance is semi-divine, yet wistful. He 'sits in the
sun, and twirls a Bough about'. He is in tears:

> And so he sits, swaying his cone-like head,
> And staring at his bough from morn to sun-set,
> See-saws his voice in inarticulate noises.

High on the 'glittering rock', at once in sunshine and in
tears, his head 'cone-like'—or dome-like?—he is a symbol
of mourning. The bough is nature. Remember the guilty
dialogue he over-watches. In his simplicity he sits murmuring as a god mourning wistfully over the agonies of
the natural creation. This Idiot Boy is, indeed, that
very power Ordonio is shortly to feel rising against him
from without and, still more potently, from within. By
a dramatic irony as subtle as that when Macbeth is com-
forted by his deepest accuser—also a child with a tree in
his hand—Ordonio is relieved by Isidore's explanation.
The boy's nonsensical music might also be compared
with Feste's final song in *Twelfth Night*.

Nature-settings vary. The play starts by the 'sea-shore'
(I. i) and the wizard's cottage at II. ii has 'flowers and
plants'. But a more elaborate and gloomy direction occurs
at IV. i:

A cavern dark except where a gleam of moonlight is seen on one side at the further end of it; supposed to be cast on it from a crevice in a part of the cavern out of sight. Isidore alone, an extinguished torch in his hand.

Herein is acted a miniature drama of intensest fear, cross-purposes, and crime. Isidore goes to the chasm edge off-stage and returns paralysed with horror:

> A hellish pit! The very same I dreamt of!
> I was just in—and those damn'd fingers of ice
> Which clutched my hair up! Ha! what's that—it mov'd.
>
> (IV. i. 13)

Ordonio enters 'with a torch'. The poetry plays variations on melodramatic horror concerning the awful chasm, with a conversation satanically half-lighted by the torch-flame round which the cold breath makes 'as many colours' as clouds round a moon (IV. i. 23–6). The chasm has a 'jutting' stone and a 'long lank weed' that 'nods and drips' (IV. i. 17–19). Isidore tells how waterdrops extinguished his torch; how he stepped to the brink; mistook 'moonshine' for 'substance', his foot hanging above the 'void'; while 'fear' itself, or some strange 'Being', uncannily preserved him, acting as an *inhibition*:

> An arm of frost above and from behind me
> Pluck'd up and snatch'd me backward. Merciful Heaven!
>
> (IV. i. 27–40)

Here, as so often in Coleridge, a poignant dramatic phrase may be understood on many levels. His symbolisms are at once objective and inward with an inwardness that expands inexhaustibly. Yet the realism is nightmarishly tense:

> If every atom of a dead man's flesh
> Should creep, each one with a particular life,
> Yet all as cold as ever—'twas just so!
> Or had it drizzled needle-points of frost
> Upon a feverish head made suddenly bald. . . .
>
> (IV. i. 45)

Fear and cold nowhere else in Coleridge come together
with so crushing an impact. All this, says Isidore, was
forecast by a recent nightmare in which he saw this same
fearful chasm. It is a place that 'collects the guilt and
crowds it round the heart' (IV. i. 96), and it is here that
Ordonio tells his life-story and drives it to the assertion
of Isidore's treachery leading to their fight and Isidore's
murder in the very spot that raised his frenzied horror.
This is Ordonio's only *actual* murder.

The darker, more haunted, nature-imagery of *Kubla
Khan* and other short poems is thus expanded and welded
into a dramatic purpose. We have, however, frequently
found nature blending into transcendent architectures as
in our recently discussed 'glittering' hill-side and such a
phrase as 'I saw the blessed arch of the whole heaven'
(I. ii. 233). At an extreme this intuition will project itself
through sacred buildings and music; and we have one,
quite central, scene in *Remorse* where this occurs.

Alvar, disguised as the Moorish magician, stages a
surprise for Ordonio in terms of the very wizardry
Ordonio is arranging to impress Teresa. The dramatic
intention resembles, though with a yet finer subtlety and
irony, that found in *The Spanish Tragedy* and *Hamlet*: to
work spectacularly on a guilty conscience. The setting
(III. i) is:

> A Hall of Armory, with an Altar at the back of the stage.
> Soft music from an instrument of glass or steel.

Military and sacred impressions coalesce: the attempt is
intermittent and discontinuous in *Remorse*, but will suc-
ceed proudly and on every level in *Zapolya*. Notice, too,
the mechanical impressionism setting the stage for transcendental powers. We open with reminiscence of Alvar,
supposed dead, who loved 'sad music' from childhood
(III. i. 2–8) and learned notes taught, like Coleridge's own
poem *Kubla Khan*, 'in a dream'. References follow to
wizardry and the supernatural. A 'strain of music' is
heard, and Alvar proceeds to a terrific invocation calling

up 'the departed' in terms of 'Paradise', 'dizzy' speed, and circles.   'What ear unstunn'd', he asks,

> What sense unmadden'd, might bear up against
> The rushing of your congregated wings?
>
> [*Music.*
> Even now your living wheel turns o'er my head!
>
> (III. i. 47)

We may call it an invocation to 'eternity', falling into line with the doctrine and main eternity-symbol ('wheel') of Pope's *Essay on Man* and similar explorations in Shelley (e.g. in particular a certain passage in Act IV of *Prometheus* and much of *The Triumph of Life*, the latter especially recalled, as is, too, Pope's *Essay*, by 'unstunn'd'). There follows 'music expressive of the movements and images that follow'. These suggest nature: it is a *descent* from eternity to our world. Height-symbols in nature serve, however, as a transition. We watch the action of eternity on nature, dragging it agonizedly up, as in *The Triumph of Life*. So these spirits of eternity 'toss high' the 'desert sands' (compare the sky-aspiring sand-pillars of an earlier poem) till they 'roar and *whiten*', resembling water and making a 'sweet appearance, but a dread illusion to the parch'd caravan' by night. There is more:

> And ye upbuild on the becalmed waves
> That whirling pillar, which from Earth to Heaven
> Stands vast, and moves in blackness!

It is specifically an earth-and-heaven structure. Or, descending farther, they 'split the ice mount' (i.e. iceberg) and with huge fragments make sea-tempest with 'sudden gulphs' to 'suck down' 'some Lapland wizard's skiff'; later to dance 'round and round the whirlpool's marge' awaiting the soul emerging from the 'blue-swoln corse' to join the 'mighty' armies of death. In Wordsworth often, in Shelley's *West Wind* and *Triumph of Life*, and in Keats continually, eternity is, from a mortal viewpoint, darkly toned. It is so here (III. i. 50–62). Next mysterious sounds are worked from the altar and there is a religious and penitential chant. Conversation grows more tense, Ordonio thinking of his brother in Heaven; his disguised brother meanwhile working into his soul with description of its guilt; and others fearful of 'unholy fancies', 'hidden Powers', 'lawless' mystery, and a seemingly 'unholy rite'. The whole rises to a crescendo, the music increasing and finally the altar incense blazing to illumine a picture of Alvar's murder. No wonder Ordonio, an extremely sensitive criminal, is disturbed. The trick that Hamlet played on Claudius, a far tougher reprobate, was a flea-bite in comparison: it needs a later poetry to wring the maximum *aesthetic* intensity from such a scene. This Coleridge masters magnificently with a truly superb orchestration. The weighted significance of the altar as a sacred symbol is underlined by the following scene (iii. ii) being set in the 'interior of a Chapel, with painted windows', wherein Teresa compares the light from the 'sun's bright orb' pushing through the 'gorgeous' colours to her own 'fancy' and 'wishful hope' which, though coloured, glow likewise from some authentic, if nameless, source (iii. ii. 26–31). It is, of course, right that the sun here should be ecclesiastically dimmed to contrast with its use in *Zapolya*.

Our two dominating scenes of (i) sepulchral nature (the cavern) with murder, and (ii) altar, music, and divine powers, present aspects of *Kubla Khan*. Though other nature-scenes and numerous normal nature-thoughts are, of course, to be expected, we have here a neat enough opposition. Yet, remembering that passage where a whole *Kubla Khan* mechanism was exploited mainly in terms of *nature*, we may ask: to what extent is evil in *Remorse* felt as, imaginatively, a nature-force, with good as transcendental and divine? There is no precise answer. Our eternity-speech, though given a ritual-and-altar setting, was as naturalistically cosmic as transcendental. It was, however, in the sepulchral cave that Ordonio made his autobiographical statement, and we may delicately refer his evil-instincts to that abysmal background of nodding

weed, dripping water, and gloomy chasm. In an early
soliloquy he puts his own, and our, problem neatly:

> What have I done but that which nature destined,
> Or the blind elements stirred up within me?
> If good were meant, why were we made these beings?
> And if not meant—   (ii. i. 130)

The break-off opens more abysmal horror than could
any possible conclusion. For an answer we must go to
Alhadra's magnificent:

> Know you not
> What nature makes you mourn she bids you heal?
> Great evils ask great Passions to redress them. . . .
>   (i. ii. 228)

Alhadra, the Moorish woman, is, indeed, the play's only
active force. We may recall Pope's comment on Addison
as one to 'set the passions on the side of truth' (*Epistle to
Augustus*, 218) together with his implicit solution of this
problem, in the *Essay on Man*, in terms of a practical
psychology. Alvar, the play's hero, is almost as speculative a type—in spite of many attempts to endue him with
heroism—as Ordonio, and the part he plays of disguise
and pretended wizardry, though in fact most dangerous,
is not dramatically heroic. The final solution is, I think,
at least equally embodied in Alhadra, who bears to Alvar
something of the relation of Fortinbras to Hamlet.

The Moors here, conceived as a fiery yet downtrodden
race, are important. That Alvar, the idealized hero,
should have to disguise himself as a Moor—he is said
to look fine in the disguise—throughout the action has
a subtle, anti-Christian significance. A stage direction
(iv. ii) reads:

> The interior court of a Saracenic or Gothic Castle, with the
> iron gate of a dungeon visible.

That more colourful essence so continually in literature
projected by an oriental toning (as in the whole conception
of *Kubla Khan* and its Abyssinian maid) is here vital. The

Moors, suffering under persecution from the Inquisition, are felt as noble, passionate, and active forces in a civilization mentally twisted and giving birth to such persons as Ordonio and the Inquisitor. We have a contrast of civilizations, and that contrast may be felt to widen from the particular and historic instance to something more generalized and modern. There is clear contemporary satire. Alvar in prison meditates on civilization's cruelty. This place was constructed by his own forefathers 'for man', the ironic effect of 'love' and 'wisdom' (i.e. society's *pretence*) towards each offending 'brother'. Crime, he thinks, is nursed by 'ignorance' and 'poverty' till energies 'roll back' on the heart, and, corrupting, become 'poison'. The criminal diagnosis, as so often, is trenchant: so the prisoned evil-doer

> lies
> Circled with evil, till his very soul
> Unmoulds its essence, hopelessly deformed
> By sights of evermore deformity!   (v. i. 1–19)

This indictment is clearly directed against a false social order, and naturally to be alined with the heroine's rejection of religious orthodoxy:

> She hath no faith in Holy Church, 'tis true:
> Her lover trained her in some newer nonsense!
> (ii. i. 35)

This is significant: Coleridge's imagination is pressing towards some less traditional and more vitally positive faith. Now anti-Christian sentiment is powerful in Alhadra, the Moorish woman. She is outspoken, as ir

> These fell inquisitors! These sons of blood!
> (i. ii. 186)

and

> Christians never pardon—'tis their faith.
> (i. ii. 200)

She tells a terrible tale of suffering with her child in prison (i. ii. 205–25). The agony is piled on, and,

remembering Coleridge's extreme sensitiveness to the
mother-and-child relationship, we need not be surprised
to find Alhadra accorded a vigorous dramatic sympathy.
Indeed, she alone suffers both unjustly and irrevocably:
it is her husband Ordonio murders in the cavern. She
gathers her compatriots for revenge, emphasizing that
the crime was committed by a Christian (iv. iii. 43). She
harangues these 'warriors of Mahomet' in terms of honour
(iv. iii. 28–30), blazing an heroic aristocracy:

> And would ye work it
> In the slave's garb? Curse on those Christian robes!
> They are spell-blasted: and whoever wears them,
> His arm shrinks wither'd, his heart melts away,
> And his bones soften.   (iv. iii. 30)

Which is emphatic enough. Whatever his confessed
beliefs and religious acceptances, Coleridge's genius when
given to full-length and complex dramatic creation obeys
a poetic law functioning similarly in Shakespeare, Byron,
and Nietzsche, and his designing here implicitly charges
our religious heritage with a certain decadence, a loss
of contact with power-sources and heroic virility; with
final lack of courage. Yet desecration of human ties is
also involved, and Alhadra refers again and again to the
wronging of her 'babes'.

So, in the final scene, when Ordonio's perverted and
sickly criminality changes to a recognition and remorse
almost equally nightmarish and disturbing, the entrance
of Alhadra and her Moors lets in fresh air and simultaneously splashes our variously dim and lovely, abysmal
and transcendental, world with the strong colour of human
action: she personifies the more virile essences of *The
Destiny of Nations*. Alhadra slays Ordonio and, taking the
stage, as it were, by sovereign right, addresses her followers:

> I thank thee, Heaven! thou hast ordained it wisely,
> That still extremes bring their own cure. That point
> In misery, which makes the oppressed Man
> Regardless of his own life, makes him too

Lord of the Oppressor's—knew I an hundred men
Despairing, but not palsied by despair,
This arm should shake the Kingdoms of the World;
The deep foundations of iniquity
Should sink away, earth groaning from beneath them;
The strongholds of the cruel men should fall,
Their Temples and their Mountainous Towers should fall;
Till Desolation seemed a beautiful thing,
And all that were and had the Spirit of Life,
Sang a new song to her who had gone forth,
Conquering and still to conquer!   (v. i. 265)

Not only the Elizabethans could write dramatic poetry.
We may feel 'temples' and 'mountainous towers', that is,
dome-symbolisms, besides deep, cavernous, 'foundations',
all hitherto most important, now melted into the one fiery
humanism. The finest human poetry often has to fight
against such symbolisms, attacking normal intuitions of
good and evil, the divine and natural, in their terrifying
vertical opposition; as in Flecker's *Hassan*, where the
golden wisdom is opposed to (i) throned whiteness and
(ii) cavernous impenetrability.

In comparison Alvar's best moralizing is a poor thing.
It is an old difficulty. Intellectually we respond to Alvar's
early remark to Alhadra:

I sought the guilty,
And what I sought I found: but ere the spear
Flew from my hand, there rose an angel form
Betwixt me and my aim. With baffled purpose
To the Avenger I leave vengeance, and depart!
(ii. ii. 15)

Can such Christian sentiments be properly blended with
an Alhadra's passionate power? Teresa has a speech
describing Alvar in terms that seem to do so, referring to
his 'kingly forehead', smiles, the 'spiritual and almost
heavenly light in his commanding eye', wherein he is
'heroic' with a 'native heraldry' and friend both to men
and his own 'guardian angel' (iv. ii. 50–6). This is, however, merely epithetical. Alvar is conceived as a figure of

ideal nobility, but he is, like Hamlet, too deeply immersed
in a world of intellectual and spiritual complexity to
strike convincingly the heroic attitude that, on a lower
plane, springs to flaming life in Alhadra. However,
Teresa's description points truly towards the synthesis
achieved in *Zapolya*: wherein the agonized oppositions of
Remorse are resolved in a level, at once more horizontal
and more monistic, reading of human destiny.

In *Zapolya* Coleridge creates with a splendour touched
elsewhere only in *Kubla Khan* and the *Hymn before Sunrise*. The thought and the persons created, indeed the
whole action, is splendid. We are beyond fears, and
freezing purity and horror alike are replaced by golden
warmth. The transmutation of evil, and especially war-
associated, energies towards which the poetry of *Religious
Musings* and *The Destiny of Nations* labours is here
superbly accomplished.

The style corresponds: close-packed, weighted, manly,
and full-throated:

> Was it for this, Illyrians! that I forded
> Your thaw-swoln torrents, when the shouldering ice
> Fought with the foe, and stained its jagged points
> With gore from wounds I felt not?
>
> (Prelude, i. 152)

Thus has 'Victory' with 'firm-footed Peace' as a goddess, been brought to earth. Courage is everywhere superb.
Close-knotted thought is woven with abstract personification into blank-verse movements of a Shakespearian
confidence:

> Mark how the scorpion, falsehood,
> Coils round in its own perplexity, and fixes
> Its sting in its own head.   (Pre. i. 348)

Again,

> I had a glimpse
> Of some fierce shape; and but that Fancy often
> Is Nature's intermeddler, and cries halves
> With the outward sight, I should believe I saw it
> Bear off some human prey.   (ii. i. 161)

and

> O surer than Suspicion's hundred eyes
> Is that fine sense, which to the pure in heart,
> By mere oppugnancy of their own goodness,
> Reveals the approach of evil.   (iv. i. 78)

So vivid may be the poetic condensation.

There is, too, a dialogue on political affairs as penetrating as those in *Troilus and Cressida*. The loyal Raab Kiuprili argues with Emerick who defends his usurpation by adducing popular acclamation. Raab Kiuprili answers acutely that any authority with the magic power of convening multitudes will likewise be able to sway their choice. The argument works up to a magnificent, and magnificently phrased, defence of constitutional monarchy, in terms of a river, mighty yet controlled, gliding its 'majestic channel' (Pre. i. 366); to support and serve which is the 'true patriot's glory' (Pre. i. 367). There is sense of a great purpose, to which indeed this whole play's action is ancillary, working through human customs and systems, so that the rightful heir is God-ordained and God-guarded. Yet there is no simple thesis. Consider Emerick's argument for worth rather than birth:

> Whence sprang the name of Emperor? Was it not
> By Nature's fiat? In the storm of triumph,
> 'Mid warriors' shouts, did her oracular voice
> Make itself heard: Let the commanding spirit
> Possess the station of command!   (Pre. i. 321)

That essential authority blazing poetically from the clarion-tongued speech of *Zapolya* shadows a mighty controlling force which might well be supposed to express itself through nature rather than law. Certainly, were the hero not qualified on both counts, this play would have none of him. Andreas is therefore even worthier by 'virtue' than by 'birth' (iv. i. 348–9). As Raab Kiuprili says with an argument precisely similar to his antagonist's later on, no hereditary honours outweigh true worth:

Raab Kiuprili: The longest line that ever tracing herald
                 Or found or feigned, placed by a beggar's soul
                 Hath but a mushroom's date in the comparison:
                 And with the soul, the conscience is coeval,
                 Yea, the soul's essence.
Emerick: Conscience, good my lord,
                 Is but the pulse of reason. . . .
                                             (Pre. i. 298)

How firmly that last remark integrates an abstraction into
vitally physical categories, as so often in *Troilus and
Cressida*. As for himself, Raab Kiuprili feels that to be a
'kingdom's bulwark' and a 'king's glory', yet loved by
both, is 'more than to be king' (Pre. i. 402). Nobility of
thought is continual. So this argument serves at the
start to introduce, through controversy, essences equally,
and with no opposition, valid in the later action; and we
need search for no precise political doctrines from a work
offering something of an infinitely greater value. This
'something' I shall now inspect in successive reference to
(i) nature, (ii) humanity, and (iii) the divine; which are,
however, felt as all but identical.

   Though we find a few touches of freezing cold—
mostly in a speech of the Prelude already quoted—and
others of ominous gloom, the dominating nature tone is
warm and happy. The sky is 'bright blue ether' (i. i. 50).
'A spring morning' has its 'wild gladsome minstrelsy of
birds' and its 'bright jewelry of flowers and dewdrops',
each drop an 'orb of glory' (i. i. 32–7). Jewellery, which
often supports poetic intuitions of the humanly artistic
and religious, is here blended with nature. Girls are
'roses' and their modesty as dewdrops thereon (i. i. 140;
150–3). The human-nature comparison is frequent,
the 'may of life' (iii. i. 235) being a typical phrase. A king
may call forth 'all deservings' to the 'broad daylight and
fostering breeze of glory' (Pre. i. 266): human qualities
are a growth and sovereign favour their sun. Human
virtues are nature-born: 'great Nature hath endowed thee
with her best gifts' (i. i. 410). This is, precisely, the

'great creating Nature' of *The Winter's Tale* and *Cymbeline*; a phrase wherein no nature-divine antinomy is felt or even conceivable. So the hero, embracing Raab Kiuprili, lets his own 'youth' 'climb round' him as 'a vine around its elm'; as his 'fruitage' (iv. i. 363–5). When Andreas senses and, by innate aristocracy, witnesses, his royal origin, his passionate excitement is compared to the 'groundswell of a teeming instinct' which will later rise over placid, mirroring, waters (i. i. 375–8). Instinct is a voice from God. Innocence enjoys 'Nature's wisdom' (iv. i. 73). Andreas, feeling his high destiny, cries to the 'blest Spirits' of his parents to 'hover' over him:

> . . . like a flower that coils forth from a ruin,
> I feel and seek the light I cannot see!
>
> (i. i. 323)

Action is an organic, nature-rooted, process, and the plot devised to reveal its blossoming into victory, recognition, and joyful power.

Setting varies from palatial magnificence to a nature of pastoral pleasantness or rugged strength. We are within a *circle* of mountains (Pre. i. 359). Mountains, forests, and caves are important. The animals are picturesque and many powerful: the crocodile, hyena, 'milk-white hind', lion, tiger, 'royal leopard', falcon, eagle. An oak-tree plays a central part, the baby Andreas being placed beneath it. So does a wood and cave:

> A savage wood. At one side a cavern, overhung with ivy.
>
> (Direction to ii. i)

This 'savage place' (ii. i. 90) is the scene in turn of tragedy, fears, courage, oracular truth, and recognition. It, equally with the 'savage place' in *Kubla Khan*, is strongly associated, through the plot itself, with child-origins, almost with birth: both are haunted. The cave in *Cymbeline* accompanied by sun-worship may be remembered: this is, too, a sun-kissed, sun-warmed, play. In it nature is at once strong and kindly, rough and kingly.

There is emphasis on courage, in strong contrast to

M

Coleridge's emphatic earlier fears. Raab Kiuprili, in a
passage already quoted, boldly confronts the angry mob
with record of his own courage felt as creative of peace.
The play shows a *peace-serving* warfare (Pre. i. 387–94),
a creative heroism, a courage passionate yet humble.
Cowardice comes in for ridicule. 'Hectoring sparks' are
always 'cowards' (I. i. 119–20). Again

> Should'st thou but dream thou'rt valiant, cross thyself!
> And ache all over at the dangerous fancy!
>
> (III. i. 142)

The valuation is Shakespearian, and Laska, of whom
this is spoken, resembles Parolles and Cloten. He is,
however, as lonely in the play as Shakespeare's cowards,
all the rest, tyrant included, being reasonably noble.
Andreas, the hero, is a fine study in bravery. This, by
itself, evidences his royalty: by 'each noble deed, achieved
or suffered', action and passivity both involved, he solves
the 'riddle' of his birth (I. i. 416). Remembering the
mysterious birth-symbol in *Kubla Khan* and a phrase in
Wordsworth's *Immortality Ode* where man's prenatal
existence is called an 'imperial palace', we may read a
generalized significance into such phrases; indeed, into
the whole action, wherein Andreas searches out and wins
his own royal destiny. The one essential is courage: he
welcomes it, willing to inherit 'danger' as a 'birth-right'
(I. i. 329–30). He is tested against a typically Coleridgean
horror of supernatural, satanic danger, concerned with
(i) the war-wolf—remember Coleridge's horror of war-
evil, and (ii) the haunted cave. At first, though warned
of demons, he is bold enough.

> Or, if avengers more than human haunt there
> Take they what shape they list, savage or heavenly,
> They shall make answer to me, though my heart's blood
> Should be the spell to bind them. Blood calls for blood!
>
> (I. i. 442)

He is, however, no paragon of impossible courage. He
approaches the supposedly haunted cave and boldly, yet

half fearfully, twice summons with his horn whatever
spirits may be there:

> Still silent? Is the monster gorged? Heaven shield me!
> Thou, faithful spear! be both my torch and guide.
>
> (ii. i. 180)

When at last answered, his boar-spear 'trembles like a
reed' (ii. i. 188). His courage is less apathy than victory.

The heroine, Glycine, shows an equal courage under
precisely similar conditions. The softer, more feminine
and family, values receive a fine emphasis. Andreas in
blazing verse asserts devotion both to his supposedly dead
mother and to Glycine. This fo. Glycine:

> May heaven and thine own virtues, high-born lady,
> Be as a shield of fire, far, far aloof
> To scare all evil from thee! Yet, if fate
> Hath destined thee one doubtful hour of danger,
> From the uttermost region of the earth, methinks,
> Swift as a spirit invoked, I should be with thee!
>
> (i. i. 423)

He feels angelic in strength and valour. As for his mother,
the main action concerns his daring devotion to her
memory:

> What! had I a mother?
> And left her bleeding, dying? Bought I vile life
> With the desertion of a dying mother?
>
> (i. i. 368)

He expatiates on her tears, tones of voice, prayers, and all
the motherhood once expended which he has never repaid
by 'lisping a mother's name' (i. i. 430–7). So he will visit
the woodland cave, 'the spot, where she lay bleeding'
(i. i. 439):

> No more shall beast of ravine
> Affront with baser spoil that sacred forest!
>
> (i. i. 440)

The word 'mother' is a 'sacred name'—the thought is
basic to his heroic quest—and, again, when found he
addresses Zapolya as 'heroic mother' (iv. i. 359–60). Both

Zapolya and Glycine are heroic, Glycine visiting the cave
in search of Andreas, and later (IV. i. 146) proving a warrior in Andreas's defence. The play's prevailing blend
of sexual principles, masculine and feminine, courage and
gentleness, felt in the chivalric tone throughout, is
summed in Andreas's line to Glycine:

> Thou sword that leap'st forth from a bed of roses:
> Thou falcon-hearted dove. . . .   (IV. i. 375)

This compresses the whole play's meaning, which is
supported, too, by the noble and determining actions of a
third woman, Sarolta. The balancing of mother against
lover with respect to Andreas is subtle: a phrase such as
'eyes fair as thine' (I. i. 430) suggests an inclusion often
omitted in heroic delineation, Andreas letting no sexual-
romantic powers foreclose his filial love. Thoughts of
motherhood dominate Andreas. He is himself an
emotional force, and 'hot tears' spring readily to his
eyes (I. i. 421).

The people are felt as superb creatures. Raab Kiuprili
is a 'majestic form' (IV. i. 181) and even Emerick appears
truly royal. A trumpet-blast announces that the 'tyrant's
pawing courser' is near. A volley of trumpets follows:

> Hark! Now the king comes forth!
> For ever 'midst this crash of horns and clarions
> He mounts his steed, which proudly rears an-end,
> While he looks round at ease, and scans the crowd,
> Vain of his stately form and horsemanship!
>   (IV. i. 57)

Those more noble are as a race of supermen and lines like

> She hath not yet the glory round her head,
> Nor those strong eagle wings,   (I. i. 398)

fall naturally into place. Andreas especially is a 'precious
bark' which is 'freighted with all our treasures' (IV. i. 382).
He expresses an infinite worth within the specifically
human, which blends into ethical and divine categories;
he is both 'a sworded virtue' (IV. i. 115) and 'thou blest

one' (III. i. 303). The people see each other, through love, as semi-divine:

> Deep love, the godlike in us, still believes
> Its objects as immortal as itself.
>
> (1. i. 386)

Zapolya is a 'star-bright queen' (III. i. 327). Emerick the tyrant, desiring Sarolta, regards 'those lips, those angel eyes, that regal forehead' as the 'natural thrones' of 'joy, love, and beauty' (III. i. 264–5). Royalty and divinity are naturally here alternative. 'Angel' is typical: Zapolya often in her 'dreams' has done worship to Old Bathory as to 'an angel' (IV. i. 106–7). Even Laska, when meditating on his hopes of advance, sees himself 'like Hercules', with a goddess on either side (III. i. 64–5). Andreas compares his own strength to that of 'the gods' (IV. i. 177). Raab Kiuprili

> . . . looked as if he were some god disguised
> In an old warrior's venerable shape
> To guard and guide my mother.   (III. i. 84)

The 'royal court' where Sarolta shines seems to lesser people like an 'earthly heaven' and 'seat of gods' (I. i. 43–5): Andreas, on first seeing her, addresses her as a 'shape from Heaven' (I. i. 308). Yet any human sanctity, especially those concerned with allegiance or the family, creates the divinity on earth: so her husband's wish alone can, if we are to trust a phrase, make a place almost as 'sacred' (I. i. 37) to Sarolta, as the scene of his mother's supposed death to Andreas; while Andreas's own love for Glycine is 'religion' (IV. i. 196).

The divine is everywhere, but the toning is not quite orthodox. There are certain references to baptism and monks and phrases such as 'sainted lord' (II. i. 44) and 'saints protect me' (II. i. 109). These are, however, for Coleridge, very thinly scattered. Yet we face no crude paganism, but rather a 'nobler faith' (I. i. 457) than any superstitious fears, a phrase neatly blending religious with human, almost warrior, values. Indeed, the divine is

closely *enlocked* with the human action; is felt pushing
through, helping, guiding, yet without any strong distinction between its own, and nature's, energies. It is
definitely kind, and 'blest Heaven' (I. i. 319) and 'comes
she from Heaven to bless us?' (IV. i. 339) are typical phrases;
though Heaven's 'justice' cannot, like man's, be bought
(Pre. i. 112). After her first fears Zapolya sees Glycine
as an 'Angel of Mercy' (II. i. 124). Elsewhere Heaven is
said to 'overrule' a wicked purpose and send an 'angel',
in human shape of course, since there is nothing strictly
supernatural in the action, to save innocence (IV. i. 380).
A child's innocence is 'as a prophet's prayer, strong and
prevailing' (Pre. i. 497); a simile relating to Wordsworth's equation (adversely criticized by Coleridge as
absurdly irrational) of child with 'prophet' and 'seer' in
the *Immortality Ode*. There is, too, a 'prayer' in Glycine's
uplifted eyes that 'seeks high Heaven' (I. i. 315–16).
Prayer is not vain: indeed, Heaven is deliberately at work
unravelling human troubles. Casimir—a little fearfully—
recognizes his long-lost father as 'Heaven's immediate
minister' (IV. i. 262); Raab Kiuprili blames himself for not
trusting the purposes of 'righteous Heaven' (II. i. 137),
and later trusts to 'Heaven alone' since it only may save
him (IV. i. 220). 'O sleepless eye of Heaven!' says
Sarolta, welcoming her own rescue by Andreas, whom she
calls a 'blessed spirit' (III. i. 296). The people feel
Heaven's nearness and insistent voice: 'the light hath
flashed from Heaven and I must follow it' (III. i. 325).
Usually the tone is bright, but a weightier accent may
sound as in

> Pardon, O thou that portion'st out our sufferance
> And fill'st again the widow's empty cruse!   (II. i. 131)

where personal deity, Biblical reminiscence, and a certain
affinity to the more solemn poetic philosophies of *King
Lear* and *Cymbeline*, all stand out slightly from the prevailing buoyancy. Heaven here all but impels human
nature: Glycine is said to have worked 'with Heaven-

guarded instinct' (IV. i. 193). Andreas's mother tells him the 'eclipse' is passing from the 'full orb of his destiny', but nevertheless commands patience:

> '. . . Leave then to Heaven
> The work of Heaven: and with a silent spirit
> Sympathise with the powers which work in silence!'
> Thus spake she, and she looked as she were then
> Fresh from some heavenly vision!   (III. i. 100)

As so often, one feels a generalized significance potential in the superb phrases; the play explicates a reading of life in its totality, dramatically condensed, and deliberately given an action suiting the central intuition of an eternal and kindly purpose prevailing over superstitious fear and injustice; and must be widely related to such poems as *Religious Musings* and *The Destiny of Nations*. Andreas is here told he cannot 'hasten' the victory. The happy conclusion is met with reverence: such 'awful' scenes, we are told, 'with flashing light force wisdom on us all' (IV. i. 389). The analogy to Shakespeare's final plays is obvious.

In such a work by such a poet we expect dreams and visions. Raab Kiuprili and Zapolya discuss (II. i) the former's dream and his expression of pain during its passage. Yet he suffered in terms of strong, if thwarted, action, and the dream's content refers distantly and indirectly to the play's approaching resolution. Zapolya's own repeated dreams presenting 'in clear vision' the cave and wood are 'signs' in which 'Heaven's especial hand' is at work (II. i. 45–54). On the return of these two to the cave the action eventually pivots. So, though starting with the lovely 'Is Heaven's last mercy fled? Is sleep grown treacherous?' (II. i. 3), the scene swiftly builds a sense of sleep and dream as a meeting-place of the divine and human.

The play blazes. Light-impressions start up everywhere. Andreas's spear is both his 'torch and guide' (II. i. 181); his sword 'shoots lightnings' (III. i. 332) and falls like Heaven's 'lightnings' (III. i. 356) on Emerick.

Divine light is, as it were, entwined with human actions
and their material symbols. Light is felt 'streaming' from
Andreas's own native 'honour' to guide him towards his
own desire (i. i. 418): a compact miniature of this play's
peculiarly subtle yet monistic statement. Humanity is
guarded by both its own intrinsic worth and Heavenly
watchers. 'May every star', prays Bathory, be as an
'angel's eye' to 'watch and guard' her love (iii. i. 212).
Zapolya's 'light' of faith kindles Raab Kiuprili's (ii. i.
41–2). The action is, indeed, concerned to transmute
Hope's 'brief flash' (ii. i. 147)—remember the pathetic
references to 'hope' throughout Coleridge's other work—
to the 'oil of gladness glittering on the water of an ebbing
grief' (i. i. 173); which depends on the 'orb' of Andreas's
destiny developing from eclipse to a 'victor Crescent'
(iii. i. 96–100). The impressionism is strangely concrete,
and even gives us 'At thy first step, thou tread'st upon the
light . . .' (ii. i. 186). It is one aspect of what might be
called the play's 'golden' humanism; and gold itself is
vivid. Gold or jewelled objects are prominent in actuality
or metaphor: Laska's purse as a 'golden goddess' (iii. i.
67), a 'golden casket' (i. i. 360), the baby Andreas with a
'jewel' bound on his arm (i. i. 449), thoughts of a man
delving 'for hidden gold' (ii. i. 216). Love and duty is as
a 'golden chain' (iv. i. 395), and the association is definitely sacred when we hear of trophies 'valiantly wrested
from a valiant foe' which, though 'love's natural offerings
to a rightful king' (allegiance at iv. i. 362 is explicitly one
with 'sublimest friendship'), will become a usurper like

> . . . gold plucked from the images of gods
> Upon a sacriligious robber's back.
>
> (Pre. i. 166)

All worth, heroism, and sanctity are summed in the 'helm
and breastplate both inlaid with gold' (iii. i. 88) in search
of which Andreas visits the palace chapel.

The chapel is interesting. Rough and wild nature-
settings alternate with civilization's architecture: each has

its own splendour and its own sanctity. The Prelude
starts before a 'Palace with a magnificent colonnade', and
the direction at III. i. 2 1 3 is 'a splendid bed-chamber hung
with tapestry'. Our visionary humanism, the sense of the
temporal embodying the eternal, readily allows a certain
reserved emphasis on the plastic and architectural, though
with no denial of nature's other magnificence. The chapel
is up a 'flight of stairs', and the 'low arched oratory'
opposite a 'silver lamp' (III. i. 193–6).

The balance of nature against architectural and
statuesque sanctity relates directly to *Kubla Khan*, though
we shall find no such *opposition* as that in *Remorse*. Coleridge's early poem and this, his greatest full-length work,
are, however, strikingly matched. Both speak, and they
alone, with the same superb, full-voiced, clarion confidence. Moreover, minor reminiscences occur: as when
'Death's lengthening *shadow*' is cast by 'Life's setting sun'
(II. i. 26); or Andreas, agonized by thought of his lost
mother, swears that she cannot die—wherein a universal
human emotion may be felt—and wishes to be dissolved
into waters that 'pierce into the secret depths of earth' and
'find their way in darkness' (I. i. 380) to seek her; or when
such a phrase as 'thenceforth must darkling flow, and
sink in darkness' (II. i. 187) may be felt as a threat of death,
a human being imagined as a river treading on 'light' and
death as an underground channel. Such fleeting minia-
tures recall *Kubla Khan*. Moreover, the mystery of birth,
so vivid there, is likewise dramatically exciting, almost
central, here. Andreas, questioned on his birthplace,
answers:

> Deluding spirits! Do ye mock me?
> Question the Night! Bid Darkness tell its birth-place?
> (II. i. 208)

Put mankind for Andreas, and the question and answer
both sink deep into problems of the natal or prenatal
mystery raised by Wordsworth's *Immortality Ode* and
Shelley's *Witch of Atlas*. The rugged nature-setting

throughout, the mountain slopes, and especially the forest and haunted cave, witness that *Zapolya* is of the same imaginative *genre* as *Kubla Khan*.

But we need not stop among natural phenomena. The main persons and their thoughts have all what might be called architectural stability: their actions, personalities, and blank-verse utterances are emotionally strangely four-square, both earth-planted and sky-reaching. A certain weight and mass is apparent. A cloud-description is imagistically symptomatic:

> . . . the cross winds waywardly
> Chase the fantastic masses of the clouds.
>
> (IV. i. 41)

'Masses.' Again, 'yonder mass' is made to wear the 'shape' (cp. the 'fierce shape' of II. i. 162) of a 'huge ram' butting: and after more comparisons becomes 'a monster couchant on a rocky shelf' and then

> Mark, too, the edges of the lurid mass—
> Restless, as if some idly-vexing Sprite
> On swift wing coasting by, with tetchy hand
> Pluck'd at the ringlets of the vaporous Fleece.
>
> (IV. i. 50)

Again,

> 'Twas as a vision blazoned on a cloud
> By lightning, shaped into a *passionate scheme*
> *Of life and death*!   (IV. i. 166)

The last phrase might serve as a definition of the life-death symbolism of *Kubla Khan*, wherein the Dome's shadow falls midway between the river's origin and disappearance. Imagery of the statuesque or architectural occurs. Civil rage shakes the 'pillars of Illyria' (I. i. 303), and one's native country's 'cause' is an 'ark all sacred' (IV. i. 86). Such blend into a sense of human sanctity statuesquely conceived. Andreas kneels, saying 'I am rooted to the earth' (I. i. 313). He calls himself a 'stone' (I. i. 353) and is compared to a 'fragment' thrown out by

COLERIDGE'S DIVINE COMEDY

earthquake and 'mysteriously inscribed by nature' (I. i. 307). That is, while yet unknown, he is imprinted with self-evident nobility. The poetry feels him as weighty, artistically significant, a projection of eternal values:

> So looks the statue, in our hall, o' the god,
> The shaft just flown that killed the serpent.
>
> (I. i. 258)

In this play of transcendental humanism Andreas himself almost corresponds to the dome in *Kubla Khan* as well as to the Apollo-figure in *The Destiny of Nations*, and is accordingly, at times, eternalized. Conversely, we may, in retrospect, see a new point in the dominating part played by an oriental potentate in the earlier poem, its transcendence being blended with a feeling for human, almost essentially pagan, power. Such power is in Andreas's upward and passionate aspiration. A lovely passage, compacting the main contrasts of *Kubla Khan* and strangely resembling descriptions of the royal boys in *Cymbeline* and Ludolf in Keats's *Otho the Great*, finely condenses the doctrine of Nietzsche's *Zarathustra*:

> Hush, Glycine!
> It is the ground-swell of a teeming instinct:
> Let it but lift itself to air and sunshine,
> And it will find a mirror in the waters
> It now makes boil above it. Check him not!
>
> (I. i. 374)

Two psychic states ('instinct' and one more spiritual) are contrasted in terms of vertical position in direct relation to water: 'ground-swell' and 'boil' remind us of the violently gushing cataract, swirling river, and 'waves' of *Kubla Khan*; while 'lift itself to air and sunshine', together with the thought of *reflection* from above, as clearly suggest the 'sunny' dome built 'in air' and its 'shadow' on the waves. Moreover, Andreas feels his life's spiritual urge as, metaphorically, a *temple-building* quest. At the play's heart he addresses the mysterious voice issuing from the cave:

Those *piled* thoughts, *built* up in solitude,
Year following year, that pressed upon my heart
As on the altar of some unknown God,
Then, as if touched by fire from heaven descending,
Blazed up within me at a father's name—
Do they desert me now?—at my last trial?
Voice of command! And thou, O hidden light!
I have obeyed! Declare yet by what name
I dare invoke you! Tell what sacrifice
Will make you gracious.

And from within Raab Kiuprili answers:

Patience! Truth! Obedience!
Be thy whole soul transparent! So the Light
Thou seek'st may enshrine itself within thee.

(II. i. 190)

That is a statement of uttermost wisdom answering Coleridge's tortured life-work. Andreas is a human universal.
He dares supernatural fears to penetrate his own origin
and destiny and redeem his mother's pain; and next
passes through a kind of preliminary *initiation*, with Raab
Kiuprili as the high priest and the cave as an oracular
setting. The plot-realism is shot through with transcendental meaning, and we need call on no further quotations to establish the play's kinship with its precursor in
miniature, *Kubla Khan*. All such symbolisms are, however, here subdued *within* the more horizontal humanism.

The effective richness of everything here is interestingly reflected into Glycine's lovely song in II. i. She
naturally challenges comparison with Coleridge's many
musical ladies, including the 'Abyssinian maid'. Like
her, she sings of height. A 'sunny shaft' slants 'from sky
to earth' from heaven to nature, linking the two. In it
is poised a bird 'enchanted', symbolizing directly the
quality of our play:

He sank, he rose, he twinkled, he trolled
    Within that shaft of sunny mist;
His eyes of fire, his beak of gold,
    All else of amethyst!

He sings the transience of love, flowers, and dew-drops, but ends

> Sweet month of May,
> We must away;
> Far, far away!
> To-day! to-day!

The rich metal-imagery denotes, as so often, a supernal, not precisely natural, state: yet it is a 'bird', in sunlight. It sings of mortal transience, yet calls us to a far quest not in the distant future but 'to-day'. The song beautifully captures an intuition of the almost super-sexual yet not unsexual—something also given gold-impressionism in Flecker's 'Samarkand' conclusion to *Hassan* and Yeats's artificial golden singing birds in his two *Byzantium* poems. So Glycine sings of eternity incarnate as she approaches the mysterious cave.

Zapolya plays subtly on sounds and music. The militaristic opening has its 'drums'. Early in the Prelude the former king's death is announced by a tolling bell and a black flag; an event which the rest of the action aims, as it were, to redeem. So other sounds are brighter. Directly after there is a funereal music, changing to triumphant music for the usurper, Emerick. But music is really too aesthetic for the specifically heroic theme. Andreas must return with sounds of 'trump and timbril-clang and popular shout' (Pre. i. 539). Emerick's approach is announced by horns; and, indeed, trumpets and hunting horns dominate powerfully. The main action is set in a hunting atmosphere, which assists, as once in *Cymbeline*, the impact of a manly, yet humanly non-destructive, heroism. Moreover, the war-wolf, superstitiously felt lurking behind the action, may (in spite of the word's derivation and more normal spelling) be allowed to symbolize Coleridge's abhorrence of the worst in warfare: as a scapegoat he therein embodies and disposes of it. The play, therefore, moves from a military start to a hunting world, and horns are the audible symbols of its direction. They speak at crucial moments: when Andreas, armed with a boar-spear, approaches the cave, he summons, again and again, the unknown spirit with his horn. Later, more horns powerfully serve a purpose similar to that in *Measure for Measure* and *King Lear*, where such sounds are used to summon, as it were, the whole play's action to a final judgement. Here stage-direction of horns and tense conversation concerning the nearing hunt are definitely related to a supernatural judgement (IV. i. 201–15): the horns are also accompanied by 'distant thunder'. The blend of realism and symbolical suggestion is Shakespearian. We might compare John Masefield's *Nan*; and, too, *A Midsummer Night's Dream*, where Theseus, the play's saving, because comprehensively humanistic, force, enters, at dawn, to speak striking lines on hunting and wake the lovers with a huntsman's music. A 'may-pole dance' (I. i. 53) is here natural as in *A Midsummer Night's Dream*. And when persons with 'hunting spears' cross the stage singing to 'lively and irregular music' (IV. i. 146) we have something of the whole play's atmosphere neatly, and richly, compacted.

I have emphasized the main impressionistic directions, but the action and human interest would stand a fuller analysis. The conclusion is one of recognition, repentance where necessary, and forgiveness. All negatives dissolve into a final peace and strength. There are not here the vivid conflicts and impressionistic variation of *Remorse*; nor the close realism and communal subtlety of Byron's greater plays: but, in its own way, *Zapolya* may, not without honour, be compared with Shakespeare's final manner. These lines from *Cymbeline* set its tone:

> O divine Nature! how thyself thou blazonest
> In these two princely boys.

The blend of instinct with sanctity and of power with grace to make a golden humanism matches Nietzsche's highest intuition in *Zarathustra*. That 'angelic strength' which Coleridge noted in *Antony and Cleopatra* characterizes *Zapolya*, wherein the splendid audacities of *Kubla*

Khan are expanded into a dramatic poetry of a kindred lion magnificence.

These plays should be considered together. *Zapolya* bears to *Remorse* a relation closely similar to that of Byron's *Sardanapalus* to his *Marino Faliero*. With both poets a sun-play balances a moon-play; and in both, though the earlier work is more dramatically intense with sharper conflicts and consequently a more, at first sight, gripping plot, the two later works point resolutions not unsimilar and of extreme importance. The violent ethical antinomy of *Remorse* receives a synthesis in *Zapolya*. This is especially clear in reference to the cave-symbol. In both plays, persons are forced to the cave concerned by dreams. In *Remorse* the cave is sepulchral, gruesome, associated with a nightmare, a setting for a criminal's account of his own perverted progress and, next, for actual murder. Now in *Zapolya* the cave is, first, fearsome, supposed haunted by demons, but, faced with courage, proves instead oracular, the life it contains being not at all demonic but rather the hero's own mother and his, and her, ancient preserver; and the way is next clear to establishing the hero's own royal heritage. Put cave=the subconscious life (a very usual, almost automatic, equation in poets of the period), and you have a powerful doctrine precisely correspondent with that gradually worked out in Nietzsche's *Zarathustra*. The subconscious self may variously (i) tempt to crime, (ii) repel by its mysterious fearsomeness, and (iii) prove oracular and the way to spiritual royalty. To what extent the choice is our own I cannot discuss here: but the cave, i.e. the subconscious life, is, I think, to be regarded as a constant. Now, just as the deepest evil in *Remorse* becomes good in *Zapolya*, so its transcendent ethical judgement (in terms of altar, incense, sacred music, and many cosmic circularities and terrible eternities) is softened, humanized in the later play. Altar-images are now felt *within* the hero's soul, as it were; or altar and incense are used casually and metaphorically in service to

the recurring sense of divinity as a flashing, revealing, yet
kindly force. There is, as in *Remorse*, a chapel, but its
purpose is solely to provide the hero with golden helm and
armour: the transcendental is one with the pagan heroism
formerly projected in Alhadra. The fears and gleaming,
insubstantial, though finally justified, hopes in *Remorse*
become a passionate ardour and clear sense of purpose,
human and divine, in *Zapolya*. The action of both works
to recapture a *lost* splendour. This is emphasized in *Remorse* but becomes all-important in *Zapolya*, where the
hero fights to redeem his mother's sacrificial pain and re-
win his lost, but royal, destiny; to re-inherit

> the glories he hath known
> And that imperial palace whence he came.

The meanings in *Zapolya* are never to be limited to the
supposed fiction.

My last quotation, from Wordsworth's *Immortality
Ode*, may return us to *Kubla Khan*. That early poem
clasps firmly not only all Coleridge's minor poems, but his
two major works also. Though in splendour of statement
and golden resonance it draws level with *Zapolya*, its
tonings include the satanic mysteries and cavernous dark-
nesses of *Remorse*. Its radiance is, as with *Zapolya*,
humanistic: not only is the 'sunny dome' precisely the
soul-state there projected, but it remains dominated by
Kubla, an oriental monarch. Like *Zapolya*, it includes,
without quavering, warfare. Critical opinion has selected
Kubla Khan from out a mass of similar poems for especial
attention. Why? Partly because of its amazing compres-
sion and multi-directional radiations; but also for its
expression of a divine transcendence in terms of those
colourful and barbaric power-sources for which our
civilization craves divine recognition. Hence the poem's
impact of delighted, almost unholy, surprise: in one swift
poetic action stamping all the pulses and impulses of human
life with apocalyptic sanction.

III

THE NAKED SERAPH: AN ESSAY ON SHELLEY

I

THOUGH he never shows Byron's interest in historic detail, and is usually averse from the weighty rondures and plastic forms of Milton and Keats, Shelley's deficiency in description of human works could be over-emphasized. In his earliest and latest poetry, for example, he powerfully visualizes the Miltonic and Keatsian chariot. Indeed, his first style is strangely Miltonic in imagistic modelling. Moreover, he has many temples, pyramids, and, especially, domes. They recur with emphatic reiteration and clearly blend into his other height impressions. These domes are of three sorts: (i) architectural, (ii) arboreal—opaque frondage being often considered as a 'dome', a similitude the less extravagant when we remember the relation of cathedral design to sacred groves and poems of Wordsworth, Coleridge, and Keats associating woodland with religious awe; and (iii) cosmic, the sky by day or night being often a 'dome'. These elevations normally lift, as in Coleridge, above water, either river or sea; and the eternity-time contrast is usually explicit. Shelley's work is clarified by our readiness to identify ourselves with his upper centres of vision, which are often above his trees, among his mountain-peaks, clouds, and domes. He tends to write of the eternity-time conflict from the viewpoint not of time, but eternity; though his eternity is generally dynamic. His lower elements of sea and river are caught up, whirled into the vortex of an indomitable aspiration blending the height of Coleridge's dome with the motion of Coleridge's river. Though we face new complexities, our old axes of reference hold good.

N

The early *Queen Mab* has exquisite pieces, especially in the varied linear pauses and unrhymed repose of the more lyrical parts, recalling Collins's *Ode to Evening*. These are classical and statuesque. There is a breathing solidity in the images, with an equally magical sense of natural life. It is an initiation poem, with immortal disclosures. Death is firmly imagined before these start to burn from the Fairy revelation. It is a 'gloomy Power' of 'tainted sepulchres':

> Must then that peerless form
> Which love and admiration cannot view
> Without a beating heart, those azure veins
> Which steal like streams along a field of snow,
> That lovely outline, which is fair
> As breathing marble, perish? (I. 9)

Must this give place to 'putrefaction'; or is it a sleep waiting for some 'roseate' morning? Observe how concrete the poetic exposition, with neat reminders of Shakespeare's final plays. At the start, Shelley is, as it were, at the end of his journey.

> Her dewy eyes are closed,
> And on their lids, whose texture fine
> Scarce hides the dark blue orbs beneath,
> The baby Sleep is pillowed:
> Her golden tresses shade
> The bosom's stainless pride,
> Curling like tendrils of the parasite
> Around a marble column. (I. 37)

See the classic outlines, the sculptural and tactile possession, the artistic repose. 'Baby Sleep' points on to *The Revolt of Islam* and *Prometheus* and back to Shakespeare. Such 'glowing limbs' (I. 32) are to be Shelley's continual delight, often with a sense of human nakedness in spiritualized loveliness, or the spirit stripped of its body in new naked freedom (cp. Browning's 'immortal nakedness' in *The Ring and the Book*). Ianthe's soul is thus seen to rise

> All beautiful in naked purity,
> The perfect semblance of its bodily frame. (I. 132)

It is a human essence which 'wantons in endless being'
(I. 151). So the Fairy Queen rends for us 'the veil of
mortal frailty' (I. 181). But the human vision is closely
related to nature's magic life and cosmic vastness. This
gospel is deliberately referred to human death:

> Spirit of Nature! here!
> In this interminable wilderness
> Of worlds, at whose immensity
> Even soaring fancy staggers,
> Here is thy fitting temple.
> Yet not the slightest leaf
> That quivers to the passing breeze
> Is less instinct with thee:
> Yet not the meanest worm
> That lurks in graves and fattens on the dead
> Less shares thy eternal breath.   (I. 264)

As in Wordsworth, man's mind is felt mystically inter-
linked with natural and cosmic law. All meanest human
feelings are part of it:

> . . . the weak touch
> That moves the finest nerve,
> And in one human brain,
> Causes the faintest thought, becomes a link
> In the great chain of Nature.   (II. 104)

Not an atom of earth (II. 212) but 'once was living man'
(a thought found, too, in Byron's *Sardanapalus*). The
'fragile blade of grass' (II. 227) that springs up at morning
and perishes at noon (note the New Testament reminiscence) is 'an unbounded world' (like Blake's grain of
sand). Invisible atoms of the atmosphere 'think, feel, and
live like man', with 'affections' and 'antipathies' and a
'moral state'; their 'minutest throb' obeying law as 'fixed'
as that governing the 'rolling' planets and suns (II. 231–
43). The 'meanest worm' has 'spirit, thought, and love'
(IV. 96): an amazing doctrine, but asserted by the most
revered documents of our race. What seems 'unlinked
contingency and chance' (VI. 170) obeys a righteous law:
as in Pope's *Essay on Man*, or 'not a sparrow falls to

the ground . . .' and 'the very hairs of your head are numbered. . . .' A life-spirit that knows no cessation burns in life and in death, the latter a sleep only, as a child's slumber in the 'dim newness' (vi. 153) of its being.

We find, too, images of solid, human, fabrication. 'Orbs' and planetary circlings (ii. 243), as well as thoughts of nature's 'temple' (i. 268), are a transition, and indeed such universal machinery accompanies the metaphysical and geometrical imagination often. That 'Spirit of Nature' which infuses alike the 'mighty spheres' and a 'faint April sun-gleam' works towards some flawless conclusion of 'perfect symmetry' (iii. 226–40). There is much talk of the Fairy Queen's chariot:

> From her celestial car
> The Fairy Queen descended,
> And thrice she waved her wand
> Circled with wreaths of amaranth:
> Her thin and misty form
> Moved with the moving air,
> And the clear silver tones,
> As thus she spoke, were such
> As are unheard by all but gifted ear.   (i. 105)

Notice the solidifying of a spiritual essence in 'car', 'wand', 'circled', 'silver', and how a transverse technique subtly increases the general impression of realism in 'thin and misty form' and 'moving air'. When her car moves, the atmosphere flies in 'flaming sparkles' struck by those 'celestial hoofs', and a 'line of lightning' is traced by its 'burning wheels' (i. 212–17): there is a Dantesque, metaphysical impact. Here is another fine image:

> For birth and life and death, and that strange state
> Before the naked soul has found its home,
> All tend to perfect happiness, and urge
> The restless wheels of being on their way,
> Whose flashing spokes, instinct with infinite life,
> Bicker and burn to gain their destined goal. . . .
>
> (ix. 149)

The circular and mechanical impressionism resembles

that in Milton's *Nativity Ode*: there are, too, other sorts
of weighty suggestion, all but Miltonic. There are many
images of buildings: 'Palmyra's ruined palaces' (II. 110),
Pyramids (II. 127), Salem's 'thousand golden domes'
(II. 138). There is the 'fair oak' whose 'leafy dome'
makes a 'temple' for vows of love (VI. 209). The architectural, natural, and vital are often significantly fused.
'Darksome rocks' have icicles forming into 'white and
glittering spires', and a 'castled steep' with an idle banner
becomes a 'metaphor of peace' (IV. 10–15). A mountain
is felt both as a 'pillar' and, as in Wordsworth, a spiritual
substance:

> the block
> That for uncounted ages has remained
> The moveless pillar of a mountain's weight
> Is active, living, spirit.   (IV. 140)

Again, 'yon glare that fires the arch of Heaven' is a fine
phrase with a parallel in the similar poetic solidities of
Cymbeline (IV. 33). Heaven's dark 'blue vault' (I. 209) is
'studded' with stars. When the 'sun's broad orb' rests on
'the burnished wave', and 'lines of purple gold' hang over
its 'sphere', while clouds turn to 'rocks of jet' crowned by
a 'diamond wreath' to make sky 'islands' in a 'dark blue
sea' and build a 'Fairy's fane' (II. 1–21), we are close to
that spiritualized architecture which we associate with
Kubla Khan: wherein a dome structure rises over natural
fecundity, to establish an archetypal symbolism covering
the whole nature-divine relation.

Directly after this structure of Shelley's glimpsed from
'dome'-like (II. 27) sunset formations we have an explicit introduction to the Fairy's 'aethereal palace' itself.
Ianthe's soul journeys in the Fairy's magic car: it is a
sleep-voyage like that in Keats's *Endymion*. The palace
itself is 'likest evening's vault', a phrase showing how the
dome-feeling may blend the architectural and cosmic.
It is a 'Fairy Hall', a 'Hall of Spells', with the inevitable
dome:

> Yet likest evening's vault, that faery Hall!
> As Heaven, low resting on the wave, it spread
>> Its floors of flashing light,
>> Its vast and azure dome,
>> Its fertile golden islands
>> Floating on a silver sea. . . .   (II. 30)

Its 'pearly battlements' look Miltonically 'o'er the immense of Heaven'. But the whole description has a breathless wonder and pulsing, vital weight. The 'azure canopy' is both sky of nature and heaven, and 'golden clouds' in 'glittering billows' roll beneath; and there is music.

> 'Spirit!' the Fairy said,
> And pointed to the gorgeous dome,
>> 'This is a wondrous sight
>> And mocks all human grandeur. . . .'
>
> (II. 55)

Notice the very interesting foretaste in the thought of the last line of Yeats's *Byzantium*. From this pinnacle you look down on the 'stretched' universe and its 'countless and unending orbs' intermingled in a 'mazy motion' that repeats Coleridge's phrase for all temporal indecisions (II. 70–6). Elsewhere we are shown the Spirit standing high on an 'isolated pinnacle' above the 'flood of ages combating below', where water, as in Coleridge, specifically symbolizes the temporal world (II. 253). Shelley from the start feels himself pinnacled *in* the dome. This is important, and explains many later tangles. He is on the mountains Wordsworth normally looks up to. *Queen Mab* is interesting in its moving circularities, its orbs, spheres, 'fiery globes' (IX. 220), wheels. The ultimate positive is here given a consistent geometrical expression.

As in Tennyson's *Palace of Art*, the *Kubla Khan* paradise is, though not repudiated, yet refused as an unconditional satisfaction. 'Changeless nature '(i.e. eternity) will not have the visionary dwell self-approved in a 'celestial palace': that is, the time-world and the burdens of communal responsibility force the exhortation of 'learn to make others happy' (ii. 59–64). Shelley, like Tennyson, wills henceforth to relate his personal vision to the sufferings of mankind. The latter part of the poem does so. The typically Shelleyan antagonisms start up in line: tyrants, wars, priests, with an especial attack on Biblical mythology, somewhat like Byron's in *Cain*, only less considered. The agonies of history with their paradisal goal ahead are seen in panorama, *time* being laid out flat beneath the Fairy's dome, which becomes all but the poetic consciousness.

The technique ranges from the Miltonic inlaid phrase and the eighteenth-century abstraction such as 'musing solitude' to a Wordsworthian blank verse. The poem radiates a symbolic insight comparable with that of works of high importance before and after composed by poets in maturity. It captures something to do with the riddles of sleep and death, 'the eternal spring of life and death' (vi. 190) symbolized by *Kubla Khan*, something

> Which gleams but on the darkness of our prison,
> Whose chains and massy walls
> We feel, but cannot see.   (vi. 194)

It would pierce to some extra dimension of 'time-destroying infiniteness' and 'self-*enshrined* eternity' (viii. 206–7): and the typical Shelleyan gospel, sexual, political, and religious, works to gear this central positive to the world of his own, or any other possible, day.

Our next poem *Alastor* shows a great change: there is more darkness, depth, solemnity, with a sense of doom. The first movement is an invocation to Earth the Mother of most impressive power. No accent is forced, but mighty things revolve to the solemn pauses and cadences, the suspended and waiting paragraph movements of a blank verse modulated to harmonize with the vastest issues of nature, death, and love. The start is further weighted by the heavy architectural imagery of the 'solitary dome' of 'some mysterious and deserted fane'. Shortly after is the description of the hero's youth among awful mountainous masses: red volcano, ice pinnacles, bitumen lakes, 'secret caves' *winding* among 'springs of fire and poison'; next changing to 'starry domes' of diamond and gold, 'immeasurable' halls, crystal columns, shrines, chrysolite; and the scene of even 'ampler majesty', the 'varying roof of heaven'. We are on familiar ground. The hero wanders among ruins with a Wordsworthian and Byronic interest. He travels, significantly, East. In sleep he sees his soul's ideal: 'her glowing limbs' entrance him, but he wakes, and the vision remains lost 'in the wide pathless desert of dim sleep'. Such relation of sleep to vision may be considered a commentary on the composition of *Kubla Khan*. Sleep and death are compared as in *Queen Mab*, and mysterious vistas opened.

A frenzied quest now starts. We are introduced to a succession of watery and torrential journeys through land, sea, and caves. The poem as a whole roughly conforms to the *Kubla Khan* design: caves are in both, the quest corresponds to the river and the lifting masses variously to Coleridge's 'savage' mountain cleft, or his dome. The hero gets into a boat mysteriously driven as that in *The Ancient Mariner* (only this goes over tumultuous seas) half searching for death in the 'caverns' of ocean, the poem's progress tortured still by waves like 'domes' and 'mountains'. The boat gets into sea-shore caverns of the Caucasus where the sea is engulfed in 'winding' Coleridgian depths: all this is associated with 'sleep and death'. After elemental 'war' there is calm, next disturbed by a vast waterfall under the arms of giant trees that canopy it. There is a risk of sinking in the 'abyss', the torrent 'mingles' its roar with pleasant murmuring breezes and woodland music. Now the poet is among caves, 'aery rocks', a place found out by Death: indeed, it is Death. Tree 'pyramids' make solemn 'domes', and there is fertile paradise description. The hero meets a spirit that beckons him, and he starts off again, following a stream along the 'windings' of a 'labyrinthine' dell (cp. Coleridge's 'mazy motion'). This stream is said to 'image' the wanderings of his life, with an equally 'inaccessibly profound' source: i.e. of birth. It grows from 'childhood' to 'ghastly' age and opens out to splendid heights, only to fall into an 'immeasurable void' (cp. 'caverns measureless to man'). This he avoids, and gets on to a carefully described edge of a 'vast mountain', which even overlooks the 'bending vault of stars': it is thus a super-dome. Indeed everything is paradoxical here: the sea flows into the river and the rivers flow up mountains. But you can see what is happening: the poem aims to achieve an *ascent* from Coleridge's river to his dome. It also images that search for the meaning of life within its high inaccessible cliff-sources, as in the ruins, or in childhood; and here our birth-age river-progress *returns* finally to child images of *autumnal* brilliance. Anyway, the hero manages to die on this high chosen spot, synchronizing his end with the setting of the moon.

Shelley ends with a most noble threnody on death of weighty, sobbing, paragraph-movements, as he began. The weightiest style comes at the start and finish: in between is torrential energy. So too, lifting masses and starry domes are a framework to a torrential and labyrinthine quest, powerful at its start and finish as well as overbrooding its progress.

I point mainly to the *Kubla Khan* affinities. Though the story is in one sense tragic, the symbolism—and it is nearly all symbolism—aims to penetrate mysteries deeper than all such appearance. The torrents, labyrinths, caves, measureless abysses, dark mountain places, roofs and domes, are vividly equated with ultimates of human life and death: the use is precise, but lax and repetitive. Shelley is fond of moving in spirals and after one amazing journey gives you another just like it. The speed and mental urgency of the main story he develops to excess later. The rush of his thought is one with his rushing torrents: the phrase 'stream of thought' occurs; while the end of all 'living thoughts' in death is darkly compared to the fate of a stream's waters in the 'oozy caverns' of 'measureless' ocean (a reminiscence of Coleridge) or insubstantial cloud. Life itself is called a 'bright stream'.

In *The Revolt of Islam* Shelley relates his individual vision not only to the tragic fact as in *Alastor* but also to the wider communal and revolutionary interests suggested by much of *Queen Mab*. The story is, however, realistically insubstantial though symbolically lavish. There is a wraithly or seraph-like vagueness about the people, as people. This can be traced to the nature of the events and imagery, but also to the rhythmical technique. There is a high-pitched speed, a rush of language. The Spenserian stanza here serves effects utterly alien to Spenser's languorousness and far different also from the anvil ring or solemn toll of Byron. Such a fourth line as 'absorbed the glories of the burning skies' with its compact falling rhythm, its unit-quality, is exceptional: lines are not units, each end is at once hitched by a passionate syntax to a new beginning. Especially the crucial fourth line is hardly ever allowed to close a satisfying rhythmical quatrain as so often in Byron. Shelley seldom allows a pause at this the obvious place of rest. The emotion is keyed up and shrill, while the speed prevents one's possessing any solid suggestion. Whatever his imagistic disclosures, they pass with the flash of a camera's shutter. Look closer, with an effort, and you find, however, a significant enough series.

The natural imagery blends with the early symbolic eagle and serpent conflict and the later events to build a sense of violent, mainly ethereal and watery, conflict. Tempests in air and sea, whirlwinds, black clouds and lightning, all are frequent and realized as speedy, swirling, violent. This swift phantasmagoria corresponds to the swift lightnings of thought, and we are told so in many similes and metaphors. Thought is lightning (i. 33), there are storms of the spirit (i. 37), language is the 'light' of thought (ii. 16), but 'clouds' cause ignorance (ii. 19). Conceptions may be learned as a cloud gathers the wind that bears it, while music and poetry are again 'light' (II. 31); 'breathe the atmosphere of scorn' (II. 35) comes in naturally; feeling is a 'fountain' (II. 49), a dream-shadow is like 'mist on breezes' (III. 2), sleep produces foul dreams of 'whirlwind swiftness' (III. 22). Whirlwinds occur elsewhere as psychic equivalents. The immortality of consciousness is referred to a cloud first lighted and then invisible (IV. 31); a mind is 'piercing' like 'the morn' (VII. 30); songs are winds (VII. 33); the personality without love is smoke only sent up from ashes (VIII. 25). This impressionistic psychology is continued in the more substantial symbolisms of the many boat-journeys linking the main events. Boats are driven fast and sometimes miraculously like that in *The Ancient Mariner*, a poem whose fearsome voyage is suggested by the phrase 'fiendish bark' at III. 30. The 'ship fled fast' at VIII. 26 is typical. The speed may be explicitly related to the psychic and spiritual essences involved, as in

> And swift and swifter grew the vessel's motion,
> So that a dizzy trance fell on my brain.   (I. 48)

You can never dissociate the events in poetry from the general flow of its imagery, and in Shelley more nearly than elsewhere image is event and event highly imaginative, while all are one with his own conflicting and swift-searching consciousness. Boat journeys are thus psychic journeys and psychic conflicts hinted by watery storms and ethereal combats, with obvious opposing impressions of still depths, lighted cloud, dawn.

Analysis shows *The Revolt of Islam* to be, like *Queen Mab* and *Alastor*, continually approaching a *Kubla Khan* symbolism. The torrential boat journeys and rough seas of the tumultuous human story are continuous with higher elemental impressions and these with mountains, temples, and domes (of leaves, sky, or buildings). There is a *Kubla Khan* reminder in the bark coming from a 'chasm of the mountains' with terrific speed and energy in I. 7; and another in I. 23 of the mystic boat 'of rare device'

(Coleridge's very phrase for his dome) without any sail to catch material airs as it voyages beneath mountains over the star-reflecting deep. Religion's 'tottering dome' at II. 43 conforms to a usual manner. At IX. 35 we have, following a meditation on death, some interesting impressions. Thoughts flow as a 'stream', and 'all we are or know' is 'darkly driven towards one gulf'—a phrase that parallels Coleridge's river, 'caverns' and 'sunless sea': 'the sky's sunless dome' follows. At III. 22 death is a 'shoreless sea' (i.e. 'measureless') and 'sunless' sky.

The poem is always reaching to the vast heights of 'Heaven's mighty dome' (II. 21). The hero's youth was among both mountains and 'broken tombs' and columns left as monuments of a 'mightier' and gentler race of men: phrases recalling *Manfred*, *Cain*, and passages of Wordsworth. Their lost power is stamped 'on the fragments of yon shattered dome'. Ideas of a lost golden age may be symbolized in such ruins and both blend with those dawn idealisms of youth whose loss Wordsworth's *Immortality Ode* deplores. The 'outspread morning's radiancy' corresponds to Wordsworth's brooding 'day' of immortality. So Laon held 'lofty converse' by the 'ruined labyrinth'. With his foster-sister Cythna (who is his Psyche, the Ianthe-soul of *Queen Mab*) he wanders beyond 'aëreal mountains', among 'lawny dells' and 'boughs of incense', like the incense of Coleridge's *earthly* paradise, though next his desire to leave behind him 'some monument vital with mind' suggests the dome-like and eternal in contrast (II. 10–26). The down-fallen tyrant's palace is grandly described. He forecasts Jupiter in *Prometheus* and Saturn in Keats's *Hyperion*, with something of the latter's dignity, and his palace of death has a paradoxical grandeur. It is a tomb with a 'charnel's mist' within the 'radiant dome', yet its portals are sculptured with imagery 'beautiful as dream' (v. 22–6). There is, however, an opposing paradisal structure for the revolutionary powers, rising on a 'misty morning' from 'myriad spires of gold' which 'star' the sky:

To see, like some vast island from the Ocean,
The Altar of the Federation rear
Its pile i' the midst; a work, which the devotion
Of millions in one night created there,
Sudden, as when the moonrise makes appear
Strange clouds in the east; a marble pyramid
Distinct with steps: that mighty shape did wear
The light of genius; its still shadow hid
Far ships: to know its height, the morning mists forbid.

It rises above water, and is related both to ships and, through mists, to Shakespeare's 'cloud-capp'd towers' and to mountains generally. 'Restless multitudes' of people 'burst and shiver' round it like 'Atlantic waves' on a 'mountain-islet', but also 'dreamlike music' and 'silver-sounding tongues' of an 'aëreal hymn' play about the Altar. Female figures surround its stair and at the summit, like Mount Athos in dawn, sits 'a female Shape upon an ivory throne', corresponding to Coleridge's 'Abyssinian maid'. Its loveliness attracts the gaze as a 'burning watch-tower' the eyes of 'famished mariners' who, like those of Coleridge's poem, have voyaged through 'strange seas'. It is a finely compact miniature with all the usual symbolic meanings (v. 39–44).

A more subtle and psychological significance inheres in Cythna's sea-birth adventure. She is plunged deep: then some cataclysm at the very 'roots of the sea' reveals the sky, and the diver shoots with her to the surface, and thence to a 'cave' and 'chasm' where a *Kubla Khan* fountain 'boiled and leap'd perpetually'. The cavern resembles 'an hupaithric temple' whose 'aery dome is inaccessible'. It is a mystic place of sea-wonders including shells—of which more hereafter—and 'mystic legends' engraved by 'no mortal hand'. Cythna is fed by a sea-eagle, and has birth-pangs 'as if some living thing had made its lair even in the *fountains* of my life'; and dreams of a wondrous child. The 'prisms' in the mystic cave drop 'shadows' on the water like Coleridge's dome. The purpose of this birth-fantasy in her life's progress is vaguely determined

later. The symbolic meanings clearly concern some sub-
conscious reality in view of the emphasis on caves (cave =
soul at III. 22) and waters. The incident resembles
the under-sea experience in Keats's *Endymion*. Here we
may be content to notice the interrelation of dome, cave,
and watery experience, whether of death or life. There is
no rigid opposition, of course: still water is always a
paradise symbol. We find Coleridge's symbolism reversed: the heroine's 'mind' is one with the 'cave' and in
solitude she explores both, growing rich in the wisdom
of that 'moveless wave'—(i.e. Coleridge's dome-symbol)
whose calm reflects 'all moving things' (i.e. Coleridge's
river). I have been quoting VII. 9–31.

Just as Cythna endures a kind of death and resurrection
during her life in the narrative, so does Laon. He goes
through a crucifixion. This is by a winding cavern and
'mighty column' above ocean 'sculptured' against the sky.
He is stripped naked, raised to a dizzy height, bound with
'brazen links', and left to suffer sun-blistered torments,
a forerunner of Prometheus. He is, however, rescued by
a Hermit, 'stately and beautiful', 'reverend', and with
'giant arms' (III. 12–29). It is a movement beyond crucifixion and the Hermit is, momentarily, God. The sun-
scorched limbs he binds in 'linen moist and balmy', a
phrase with New Testament associations, while the
hermit-release after scorching agony repeats similar
symbols in *The Ancient Mariner* and, if you change sea-
death for sun-torment, the reviving of Thaisa by Cerimon
the recluse in Shakespeare. Next they go the inevitable
boat-trip, and end up by a 'grey tower', a ruin blending
nature and human art, with an 'antique sculptured roof'
and many books of ancient lore. The earthly setting
repeats that of Coleridge's hermit with similar meaning
(IV. 1–5). Notice that height-symbolism may be fused
with the agony of a tragic paradise, as in the *New Testament* and *Prometheus*—with a subsequent more explicit
'eternity' in the hermit's tower, among mountains.

In Canto VI Cythna riding on a 'black Tartarian

horse' strikes panic into the opposing forces and rescues
Laon: they speed off together, the wondrous horse's hoofs
grinding the rocks to 'fire and dust', his strong sides
turning the torrents to spray. They reach a mountain
whose crest is 'crowned with a marble ruin', a hill which
'overhung the ocean': our usual pattern. 'A shattered
portal' faces the 'eastern stars', it is a home of things
'immortal', with the usual 'hanging dome of leaves',
sweet flowers, and music. Thus are men 'piloted' through
'caverns strange and fair of far and pathless passion' while
the 'stream of life' (a repeated image) bears our 'bark' on.
The lovers' passion is ecstatically described: their thoughts
are as 'light beyond the atmosphere'. A 'wandering
Meteor' now hangs high above 'in the green dome',
blessing them, as eternity is consummated on earth:

> . . . What is the strong control
> Which leads the heart that dizzy steep to climb,
> Where far over the world those vapours roll,
> Which blend two restless frames in one reposing soul?
> *It is the shadow which doth float unseen,*
> But not unfelt, o'er blind mortality. . . .

Which serves as the neatest of commentaries on *Kubla
Khan*, picturing in sexual terms the blending of opposites
in a new dimension, creating harmonious unity from
troubled duality, with phrases, especially 'shadow' and
'float', that make the relation clear (VI. 19–37). The green-
magic setting points to *Prometheus*.

We have had various domes or other vertical paradises:
those of Laon's youthful fervour, Cythna's solitary cave
with its blissful dreams, the pyramid of revolution, the
pinnacle of a martyr's crucifixion, hermit peace, and love
triumphing. All are knit together at the close where
Laon and Cythna die together both for their revolutionary
gospel and for love of each other, and wake to an immortality accompanied by a mysterious child. This last
cresting ascent is preluded by long and violent description (Cantos X and XI) of those horrors of famine and
disease that lead to the sacrifice. Analogies to *The Ancient*

Mariner are striking. A 'burning sun' rolls on 'day after day' over a 'death-polluted land' of 'thirsting air' and 'rotting vapour'. Nature is paralysed, beasts die 'in helpless agony' gazing on each other's faces. Wells are choked with 'rotting corpses'. Laon and Cythna, blamed for these trials, are to die 'linked tight with burning brass' on a pyre among hissing snakes. In the 'dim labyrinths' of the people's tortured minds we are told that hope 'near imagined chasms' struggles with despair (x. 13–46). Maniacs like 'spectres' run from a 'death-fire' and lurid 'blue' flames strike an uncanny, Coleridgian, feverish light (xi. 12). A child, whom we met earlier *comforting the tyrant*, pleads for Laon's life (xii. 6). Laon offers himself for death, comparing a young nation to an eagle—a recurring symbol in Shelley—whose 'golden plume' floats moveless on the storm, and tells of genius rearing monuments beneath the 'dome' of a 'new Heaven' (xi. 23–4).

Cythna arrives (xii) on the black charger. They lie together on the pyre; the 'veil' dividing life from death is all but lifted; and next death proves to be music and song and love, by the 'waved and golden sand' of a 'clear pool'. A boat like 'a curved shell' arrives guided by the Child with 'silver' wings and they journey together, the Child, who now turns out to be, also, *Cythna's dream-child* and is called a *'plumed seraph'*, telling how after their death the pyre-smoke 'hung in many a hollow dome and spire'. There the 'flood of time' still rolled after the lovers had glided down 'death's mysterious stream': the river fitting both time and death from the temporal aspect. But now we begin to focus the eternal, and are told of that 'better genius' of the world (=Coleridge's monarch) 'whose realm is spread' round 'one mighty Fane', beside Elysian islands. He it is who has commanded the Child to guide them there. The usual pattern unfurls yet again. The boat flies a mazy course between a *Kubla Khan* 'chasm' of 'cedarn' (Coleridge's word) mountains, through a 'long and labyrinthine maze' of 'winding' stream. 'Mighty mountains' with prehistoric Cyclopean piles lifting in 'turrets' frown above. Through the dome-suggestion of star-roofed caves they voyage, virtue surviving 'mortal change'. They seem to rise, water is ethereal, there is spray, sunbows, and a 'silver mist', which becomes next gold. The boat is suspended on some breathless heavenly lake, with snow-bright mountains and radiant isles and afar, like a 'sphere', the 'Temple of the Spirit'. With that the poem ends. Again, labyrinthine water leads up to a spheral and sacred architecture.

This obsession is deep-enwoven: so, very aptly, the whole poem is introduced by the poet's journey with the lady he finds by the sea in a fast boat towards ice-mountains (Shelley's fondness for ice parallels Coleridge's) and ethereal heights leading to a Fane, made by no mortal hand, 'likest Heaven' (in the natural sense) at the turn of sunset into moonlight, when the sky and marmoreal floods are paved with fire. This Fane symbolizes the poem to follow, or poetry in general. Here is its description:

> Like what may be conceived of this vast dome,
>   When from the depths which thought can seldom pierce
> Genius beholds it rise, his native home,
>   Girt by the deserts of the Universe;
> Yet, nor in painting's light, nor mightier verse,
> Or sculpture's marble language, can invest
>   That shape to mortal sense—such glooms immerse
> That incommunicable sight, and rest
> Upon the labouring brain and overburdened breast. (1. 50)

'Incommunicable sight' recalls *Kubla Khan*. There are 'lawny islands' beneath the Fane's 'aërial heap'; sculptures resemble 'life and thought', the roof from within is compared to clouds, has 'orbs' and stars, moons and meteors, all worked by 'subtlest' and 'divine' power, a 'hollow hemisphere'. Beneath, in the world of time, are 'labyrinthine aisles', where walls show stories of 'passionate *change*, divinely taught': we might compare Keats's *Grecian Urn*. Great men of the past form a senate reminding us of Pope's *Temple of Fame*, their white hair like mountain snow. It is a 'dome of woven light';

o

indeed, all but a 'sunny pleasure-dome with caves of ice'. The poet sees now two mysterious lights gliding in 'circles' like 'meteors' on a river's shore, revolving round each other and dilating and commingling into a unity, geometrical harmony being dynamically employed. Next the form of Laon appears distinct to tell his story of passionate sacrifice and spiritual victory. He and Cythna are now birds of calm after the 'world's raging sea', like the eagle of VII. 27 whose peace with the 'nautilus' balances our earlier eagle-and-serpent contest (I. 8–20). Air and water are both suggested in the name Cythna with its undertone of 'cygnus'; just as Laon faintly suggests Leo, or lion.

I do not pretend all this makes easy reading, but Shelley must be studied with an eye to these symbolisms. In *The Revolt of Islam* he tries to relate his personal paradise-intuition to many experiences: natal, psychological, revolutionary, sacrificial, passionate, with a blend of all at the close. His reliance on similar *Kubla Khan* mechanisms marks a weakness comparable to Milton's on music and human artefacts, but the poem certainly *aims* to expand further, and to use these in interpretation of wide human statement. Story and symbolism alternate. An exact coalescence of the fanciful with the dramatic or narrative is rare: perhaps only found in the crucifixion-episode and those moments where Cythna appears on her black charger. For the most part realism suffers, but it suffers, at least, in a precise cause. Shelley is attempting to enmesh the river-and-dome mechanism with those social problems to which he dedicated himself in *Queen Mab*. Moreover, there is in *Kubla Khan* a relation undeveloped within the mechanism itself. The dome rises above the life-stream: the two are juxtaposed, not continuous. But mortality is pressed with desire to know if and how the time-river plunging to the death-caverns leads back, or up, to the eternity-dome. This problem Shelley's imagery always attacks, and hence his paradoxical journeys with rivers seeming to flow *uphill* from sea to heights in *Alastor* and *The Revolt of Islam*: which may be related to many strange statements (as in Wordsworth's *Ode* and often in Shelley) where a penetration into the past, whether of man or race, is used as an exploration of the higher dimension; with which also we might compare all *inaccessibly high* river-sources and Coleridge's image of divine reality as a sun to which our backs are turned.

II

Queen Mab opposes sculptural-visions to harsh human wrong, and in *Alastor* dream-longing creates a tragic and romantic adventure amid symbols of vast nature and moonlit splendour. In *The Revolt of Islam* Shelley is attempting to gear a certain positive intuition to the harsh world of his experience. What is that intuition? And what are, to him, good and evil?

Shelley seems to have realized his own personality with an almost premature finality reflecting the wholeness of cosmic life. Consequently, his poetry, though aware of horrors, entirely lacks fear: he deliberately seeks out mid-night ghosts (*Alastor*, 23–9; *Intellectual Beauty*, 49–52) to force ultimate answers; and how different is this from Coleridge's quivering susceptibilities! There is, corre-spondingly, slight sense of subjective sin. Shelley likes snakes and attributes to others his own basic purity:

> I hate thy want of truth and love—
> How should I then hate thee?
>
> (*Lines to a Critic*)

He neglects, however, those manifold colourings, mostly evil, that lie between the purity of God and the purity of the inmost self. He rarely creates *persons* from a wide acceptance of good *and* evil as does Shakespeare: his first tyrant-studies in *The Revolt of Islam* and *Prometheus* are sawdust figures. However, though that mass of varied material Shakespeare lifts towards *The Tempest* has a weight Shelley's work lacks, yet, to a judgement believing in a final and inclusive harmony, the judgement of Pope's

Essay on Man, he rejects only unrealities. His monistic faith, moreover, presents one aspect of Shakespeare's own progress, and that is why Shelley so closely resembles Ariel; more profoundly, indeed, than a superficial equation might guess. He is a poet who from the start breathes that rarefied element to which all poetry, semi-consciously, aspires. His violent imagery of tempest and rushing torrent shows him trying to hitch man's destiny to an all but inhuman speed. As with St. Paul, the 'slight trouble of the passing hour' shall give way to a new dimension of human existence. Living inside the push of creation, its naked fire in his veins, he is properly at home only with that end—whether in time or eternity—to which existence is travailing. He *is* the future, the eternal, the cosmic and spiritual whole. That is why his poetry is less cathartic than prophetic.

Shelley's main characteristics of (i) trust in his own, subjective, consciousness, (ii) holistic enthusiasm, expansion, and ascent, and (iii) prophetic energy, are neatly expressed in three of his most famed lyrics: his *Cloud*, *Skylark*, and *West Wind*.

His clouds are, of course, ubiquitous. I have already noticed how explicitly symbolic of the subjective consciousness are Shelley's watery, vapoury, and ethereal impressions. His use of them corresponds precisely to Shakespeare's comparison of cloud-formations to the individual consciousness approaching dissolution in *Antony and Cleopatra*. Shelley's *Mont Blanc* starts with

> The everlasting universe of things
> Flows through the mind . . .

and continues with a close equation of 'thought' with 'waters'; and in *Fragments Connected with Epipsychidion* we find human existence equated with clouds in point of death and resurrection and the varying colour-reflections of all psychic life. That equation, precisely, is implicit in his poem *The Cloud*. The central symbol is of eternal though changing substance; scintillating, evanescent, dissolving but indestructible. The cloud is not even a psychic essence known as an object, but rather the very 'I' of personality: that is why the poem runs throughout in the first person. 'I change, but I cannot die' refers to both the cloud and the central 'I am' in humanity. There is thus a naïve purity and childlike merriment suffusing its happiness. It laughs 'silently' at its own apparent end, and indeed the whole lyric has a lilting, laughing melody. Both its childlike quality and varied enjoyment of its own experience among stars and moon and earth make it more precisely symbolize Shelley's own *poetic* consciousness, his finest vision being elsewhere expressed through just such symbols of laughter and child-simplicity. What is the 'I' of us all? This: 'the daughter of earth and water' on the one side, and the 'nursling of the sky' on the other. The cloud's transmutations are felt as symbolic of (i) birth and (ii) resurrection: to Shelley, as to St. Paul, these mysteries involving each other. The doctrine beautifully renders pantheism and the inwardness of human experience identical.

To a Skylark symbolizes a universal expansion. *The Cloud* was a moon-and-dawn poem: this directly faces sunlight. To argue that the bird does not really resemble the things it is compared to misses the point. It is not very like a 'high-born maiden' or a 'glow-worm' and 'rose embowered', phrases sounding respectively more akin to the worlds of Tennyson and Keats. But to understand the rush of imagery it releases we must get into Shelley's mind. The skylark is all but himself. As a light is lost in light, as a poet's meaning may be blurred by its own radiances, so, we are told, is this bird's music melted: its music being thus made to resemble Shelley's own, its ethereal destiny felt to be his. Indeed, Shelley's own method of progressing through what might be called repetition of song with variation of height, as in the *repeated* symbolisms of *Alastor* and *The Revolt of Islam*, imitates the skylark's peculiar technique. The bird thus becomes to him a universal symbol of that 'unbodied joy', that cosmic life of which he is himself the voice; and must be associated not only with light, sun, stars, but with things quite unlike itself. Shelley therefore uses un-Shelleyan imagery to express his intuition of *sky-lark-ness* within all detailed manifestations. He aims not at all to give a vivid picture of the bird (Wordsworth's poem does that far better), but uses it as a window through which to examine the universal substance: in it he focuses the cosmic. Both these poems lift us above earth: we are *amid* the elevations Coleridge and Wordsworth regard.

The *Ode to the West Wind* objectifies Shelley's third characteristic: prophetic energy. The wind is a symbol of resurrection like the cloud and of fine motion like the skylark, expressing, however, rushing energy as the skylark soaring joy. The poem has a more exact pattern than is usually supposed. The first stanza treats of earth; the second of air; the third of water. The fourth stanza combines the three elements in one, light or fire not being emphatic in this, comparatively, purgatorial and troubled poem of conflict. Fire therefore only enters in the 'sparks' of the last stanza which are the future justification of the cold hearth and half-dying ashes of the present; the 'spring' to that 'winter' the poet is forced to endure. This stanza equates the wind with the poet's own prophetic consciousness: all three poems make a similar equation. Though each stanza expresses the central force, or vision, hardest realities are included. The opening here is crammed with deathly impressions: ghosts, pestilence, corpses, and graves, the wind dominating all such in its course. Stanza II has a magnificent image of riotous elemental confusion, the 'tangled boughs of heaven and ocean' suggesting psychic conflicts of passion and spirit till the vast stage becomes a single gigantic actor in person of 'some fierce Maenad' whose locks are the full sky in storm. The wind is throughout destructive as well as creative, tearing at forests, blackening the sky, and, in the third stanza, stirring up under-sea 'palaces and towers', the paradises slumbering in unconsciousness, for its purpose. Yet those are of lesser dignity than that other eternity of tragic agony when the whole concave of storm-lashed night is seen as 'the *dome* of a vast sepulchre'. The wind is forcing man from easy paradise to a more majestic, if awful, destiny: whereby this, perhaps the greatest of Shelley's shorter poems, far outdistances *The Cloud* and *Skylark*, with a prophetic and moral energy more impressive than happier revelations. In its wild speed and deep undertones, its balance of serenities and rising, gathering power, its massive swaying movement and fury of impact alike, the poem is a masterpiece of orchestration. That my close relation here of the natural forces exposed to human personality is no intrusion, the poem itself witnesses: 'Be thou me, impetuous one!'

Of these three poems two make vertical, though naturalistic, structures, and the third deals in swirling energy within a vastly apprehended 'dome'. They may also be characterized as poems of (i) magic, moonlight, and dawn; (ii) expansion and sunlight; and (iii) tragic intuition. This same sequence—I am not suggesting a sequence of composition—I shall retrace later in terms of some longer poems. But next I note shortly some similar light and dark variations in certain passages of dome-symbolism.

Domes may be variously brilliant and sombre, but in nearly all there is direct eternity-suggestion. In his *Euganean Hills* Shelley sees Venice first as a 'peopled labyrinth of walls' among waters, and passes directly to sunrise and bright imagery wherein

> Column, tower, and dome, and spire
> Shine like obelisks of fire,

pointing from ocean's 'altar', as the 'flames of sacrifice' used to rise from 'marble shrines' to pierce 'the dome of gold' in the temple of Apollo's oracle. The pattern is normal: human life, water, and labyrinths blending into the sacred with temples and domes, the whole shot through, as in Shelley is usual, with naturalistic and cosmic force. There is a *Hymn of Apollo*, where the god speaks of Heaven's 'blue dome'; and the *Ode to Heaven* praises and Heaven's natural glory of an 'eternal' and 'ever-canopying dome' over-arching all temporal acts, past and future, and corresponding to the sky-dome which broods over Wordsworth's child as at once its master and true immortality. Each is called a 'presence'. Next, however, the poet questions the ultimate validity of any *naturalistic* faith; and ends in doubt. The ode compactly expresses three normal Shelleyan modes: (i) naturalistic, (ii) trans-cendental, and (iii) agnostic.

The *Ode to Liberty* sets 'Time's fleeting river' against 'kingliest masonry'. 'Citadels' of freedom rise over the 'tempestuous' waters of tyranny in 'tower-crowned' splendour. Next anarchy's 'idle foam' is contrasted with a 'strange melody', while we are told how

> Art, which cannot die,
> With divine wand traced on our earthly home
> Fit imagery to pave Heaven's everlasting dome.

From Coleridge onward, domes are always likely to repre-sent the poetic consciousness. Later, during a passage of Shelley's fiercest vociferations against 'kings' and 'priests', he longs for wisdom to kindle lamps 'within the dome' of a dim world. There is thus no consistently radiant use of the figure. In *Mont Blanc* the mountain expresses not only the 'infinite' but much of cruelty and rocky inconscience, yet somehow, as in Wordsworth, a 'power' is felt in its 'tranquillity':

> . . . there many a precipice,
> Frost and the Sun in scorn of mortal power
> Have piled: dome, pyramid, and pinnacle,
> A city of death, distinct with many a tower
> And wall impregnable of beaming ice.

'Scorn' recalls *Queen Mab* and points on to Yeats's Byzantine dome. There are 'vast caves' and Coleridgian torrents 'in tumult welling' from 'secret chasms'. A 'still and solemn power' concludes earlier grimnesses:

> The secret Strength of things
> Which governs thought, and to the infinite dome
> Of Heaven is as a law, inhabits thee.

The poem scarcely adds anything to Wordsworth, but the similarity itself shows the extent of Shelley's tonings. Domes are often dark: as in that 'dome of a vast sepulchre' in the *West Wind* or the terrific image in *A Vision of the Sea* where a screaming blast rends the cloud-columns sustaining the tempest's 'dome'; and in *The Tower of Famine* the tower rises over 'sacred domes' and 'brazen-gated temples' and the abodes of wealth, dwarfing them, itself at once symbol and accuser. Often, of course, the dome-structure may, as in these last examples, seem to be generated by time's turmoil or agony rather than any eternity. There is, however, no lack of precision. Shelley is always inflating his temporal struggles to cosmic proportions, playing on heights where time and eternity mingle. That is why in *Adonais* the dome is actually contrasted with the eternal:

> Life like a dome of many-colour'd glass
> Stains the bright radiance of Eternity.

Life is the concave, and eternity the convex, approach, and *Adonais* ends with tempestuous boat-ascent to the eternal star. Eternity is the objective view of subjective experience: hence the importance of poetry.

My comments in this section are designed to prepare for more complex analyses. I am not observing Shelley's order of composition. The *Ode to the West Wind* preceded both *Cloud* and *Skylark*; and all followed the *Prometheus*. One must lay no heavy emphasis on Shelley's development during his last blazingly creative years, wherein he controls and uses for his purpose various levels of insight with a Dantesque and Shakespearian ease.

III

In *The Christian Renaissance* I discussed the theological skeleton of *Prometheus Unbound*, equating Prometheus

with Christ; Jupiter with Satan—or, in so far as Satan is
not allowed personal reality, the satanic attributes of God
the Father; Demogorgon with the human imagination or
Holy Spirit during the era of conflict; and Asia as that
spirit in perfect accomplishment superseding provisional
mechanisms of philosophy and poetry. I observed that
Demogorgon goes into the 'abyss' with Jupiter, but
omitted to notice his return in Act IV; which Act is,
however, somewhat in the nature of a final curtain-call for
all the dramatic persons except Jupiter; while his re-
appearance seems the more reasonable in that the subject
of his words relates back to the past (which is our present)
of human existence. My remarks now are to touch more
specifically the poetic substance, its outer flesh, so to
speak, and body: whereby we shall discover that the
sufferings of Prometheus are the prelude to a more complex drama not usually observed.

In *The Revolt of Islam* we noticed a continual stream-
and-dome symbolism and a reiterated attempt to relate
this to a violent narrative action. In *Prometheus* Shelley
masters a more satisfying fusion of movement with stillness, of action with artistic design, and consequently no
extreme symbolisms, geometric or natural, take precedence over dramatic realism. The vast Caucasian and
mountainous setting—and the stage directions need full
attention—are themselves both its dome of precious
agony and place of liberation. *Prometheus* has a mass and
weight, a majestic and slow glacier-like movement, quite
different from the earlier poem: it is truly dramatic rather
than narrative. Shelley himself once deplored in his work
the 'absence of that tranquillity which is the attribute and
accompaniment of power'. Here he attains repose, as in:

> The curse
> Once breathed on thee I would recall. Ye Mountains,
> Whose many-voiced Echoes, through the mist
> Of cataracts, flung the thunder of that spell!
> Ye icy Springs, stagnant with wrinkling frost,
> Which vibrated to hear me, and then crept

Shuddering through India! Thou serenest Air,
Through which the sun walks burning without beams!
And ye swift Whirlwinds, who on poisèd wings
Hung mute and moveless o'er yon hushed abyss,
As thunder, louder than your own, made rock
The orbèd world!   (i. i. 58)

There is slowness or stillness in 'stagnant', 'crept', 'poisèd', 'moveless'; and feeling of mass in 'mountains', 'India', 'orbèd world'; of vastness which is not emptiness but rather a substantial and living cosmos. Heavy stresses are aptly placed in 'cataracts', 'thunder', 'vibrated', 'shuddering', 'rock'. Carefully placed pauses apply a break to the flow, piling the content into an accumulation and reservoir of emotional meaning. It is a massive world crammed with slow movement and deep music. The chafing unrest of Shelley's other style here matures into a stillness, a process made clearer by a speech where speed is plastically presented, and the verse moves slow:

The rocks are cloven, and through the purple night
I see cars drawn by rainbow-wingèd steeds
Which trample the dim winds: in each there stands
A wild-eyed charioteer urging their flight.
Some look behind, as fiends pursued them there,
And yet I see no shapes but the keen stars:
Others, with burning eyes, lean forth and drink
With eager lips the wind of their own speed,
As if the thing they loved fled on before,
And now, even now, they clasped it. Their bright locks
Stream like a comet's flashing hair: they all
Sweep onward.   (ii. iv. 129)

Motion is frozen into a poetic stillness, time's fleeting moment is locked in formal stability, like the figures on Keats's urn. A fusion of Coleridge's torrent and dome is implicit throughout the dramatic stability of *Prometheus*.

A massive eternity is felt to master yet not exclude temporal events. Any Shelleyan extravagances become part of a whole not of that quality; and any shrill notes part of an orchestration rich and deeply varied. Details of human history are minor groupings round the base of the vast central and archetypal drama uplifted into a higher dimension. The horrors of future history foreseen by Prometheus during the Furies' visit and the songs of human heroism sent by the Earth for his comfort both refer to the usual Shelleyan likes and dislikes: but the greater drama overarches with Prometheus, Asia, Panthea, and the Earth speaking a weighty blank-verse of unhurrying pace whose very accents echo an eternal assurance. The time-sequence of history seems to move in a different dimension from the action of Prometheus' defiance and liberation which takes place, as it were, out of time altogether. So, though the dominating atmosphere gives, from the very start, a sense of natural majesty and cosmic life, yet within this atmosphere the sternest facing of evils is possible. We have Prometheus' fore-knowledge of the Crucifixion, phrased with masterly reserve, sympathy, and poetic tact:

> Remit the anguish of that lighted stare;
> Close those wan lips; let that thorn-wounded brow
> Stream not with blood; it mingles with thy tears!
> Fix, fix those tortured orbs in peace and death,
> So thy sick throes shake not that crucifix,
> So those pale fingers play not with their gore. . . .
>
> (i. i. 597)

There is no lack of either realism or reverence. There is, moreover, a deeply realistic wisdom and subtle power of diagnosis in such lines as those following of the Furies' description of unending human evil, of humanity's rooted psychic paradoxes. Shelley is perfectly well aware of all such: he is averse only from making them a basis of creation. Now both this historic suffering, with all that suggested by the comforting spirits too, is compressed into a few pages. The Furies disclose what seems a distant future; but the comforting spirits immediately after arrive with reports from human history. Time is all but rendered subordinate to simultaneity. The historic process

is suggested within the circling whole of the main superhuman action—Prometheus is clearly called a 'god' although he must also be often considered as mankind—
and that greater whole is a different process, the outer and
doming formation of the inner movement-into-stillness
we have observed in the verse. Shortly, too, the main
action strides beyónd and outside contemporary history,
which was, with Prometheus' suffering, at best a prologue,
to dramatize the central statement, the liberation of
Prometheus and awakening of Earth; from which again
flow back blessings on the human race in time. Precise
and rigid distinctions are not to be sought: I merely aim
to show the kind of freedom the poet's mythopoeic faculty
exploits, and the kind of relation the poetic architecture
here may be supposed to bear to the architectural symbolisms interspersing the action of *The Revolt of Islam*. Those
symbols have become a total technique, within which
reminders of normal actions in time take subsidiary,
though essential, place.

This pervading stillness into which the Shellyan speed
now *matures* blends into that sense of a breathless dawn-
expectancy so heavily charging the poetic action. It is
a 'tingling silentness', to quote a phrase from *Alastor*;
and indeed the weighty yet throbbing verse at the start
and close of *Alastor*, together with its massive feeling for
the Earth, makes it a true forerunner of the mighty
Earth-song *Prometheus*. Here the dawn of a new physical
creation is in the air from the start: Prometheus' first
invocation, where the ethereal blends with the massive
under mountainous symbols of glaciers and ice, of moon
and sun, is so charged. But a more explicit dawn flushes
the later action. Asia, alone in her vale, awaits Panthea's
arrival from Prometheus:

> This is the season, this the day, the hour;
> At sunrise thou shouldst come, sweet sister mine,
> Too long desired, too long delaying, come!
> How like death-worms the wingless moments crawl!
> The point of one white star is quivering still

> Deep in the orange light of widening morn
> Beyond the purple mountains: through a chasm
> Of wind-divided mist the darker lake
> Reflects it: now it wanes: it gleams again
> As the waves fade, and as the burning threads
> Of woven cloud unravel in pale air:
> 'Tis lost! and through yon peaks of cloud-like snow
> The roseate sunlight quivers: hear I not
> The Aeolian music of her sea-green plumes
> Winnowing the crimson dawn?   (II. i. 13)

Still expectancy is poetically realized by alternations of waning and gleaming hope, with the unanalysable process of dawning light on clouds delicately stitched in words, stillness melted into change. 'Unravel' is a homely metaphor suiting Shelley's habitual feeling for the *interwoven* quality of all natural, and especially ethereal, phenomena. 'Quivers' blends motion and stillness, carrying on the similar qualities of 'shuddering' and 'vibrated' in Prometheus' first speech. Striking colours occur: white, orange, purple, roseate, sea-green, crimson. The central moment of Asia's transfiguration is accompanied by a dawn lyric:

> Child of Light! thy limbs are burning
>   Through the vest which seems to hide them;
> As the radiant lines of morning
>   Through the clouds ere they divide them;
> And this atmosphere divinest
> Shrouds thee wheresoe'er thou shinest.   (II. v. 54)

Such golden streams rise on our first heavy glacier and ice imagery, the vast conception recalling Coleridge's 'sunny pleasure-dome with caves of ice'. But here the ice is replaced by a warming, spring-like, joy. Dawn is the key-colour, key-note. The narrative climax concerns the rebirth of a natural, human, or divine reality known in some earlier dawn of creation, as golden-age intimations rise mist-wreathed from the dream-waked consciousness. Such thoughts illuminate a strange stanza (II. v. 98–110) describing an upward progress from Age and Manhood

through Youth to Infancy and thence through Death and
Birth into a 'diviner day': it is also a journey from icy
caves through rough to smooth seas and on to an earthly
paradise. We may recall Wordsworth's great ode,
Coleridge's divinity located *behind* the consciousness, and
Shelley's own uphill torrents. 'Birth', 'death', 'dawn',
'youth', 'age', must in such a poem as *Prometheus* be felt
not as time-links, but qualities: when a new sort of poetic
grouping at once takes form.

A glowing dawn suffuses our drama as from pale agony
the impregnable glory steps free, closely recapturing the
Pauline vision. Panthea tells her dream:

> his pale wound-worn limbs
> Fell from Prometheus, and the azure night
> Grew radiant with the glory of that form
> Which lives unchanged within, and his voice fell
> Like music which makes giddy the dim brain,
> Faint with intoxication of keen joy. . . . (II. i. 62)

The physical form burns with seraphic beauty:

> . . . the overpowering light
> Of that immortal shape was shadowed o'er
> By love; which, from his soft and flowing limbs,
> And passion-parted lips, and keen, faint eyes,
> Steamed forth like vaporous fire; an atmosphere
> Which wrapped me in its all-dissolving power
> As the warm aether of the morning sun
> Wraps ere it drinks some cloud of wandering dew.
> I saw not, heard not, moved not, only felt
> His presence flow and mingle through my blood
> Till it became his life, and his grew mine,
> And I was thus absorbed, until it passed,
> And like the vapours when the sun sinks down,
> Gathering again in drops upon the pines,
> And tremulous as they, in the deep night
> My being was condensed. (II. i. 71)

Shelley's precise scientific and atmospheric interests are
one with his spiritual intuitions. 'Rays of thought' occurs
immediately after, and words like 'steamed', 'wrapped',
'dissolving', 'absorbed' (Dr. Moffatt's word for a Pauline

intuition: man 'absorbed by love'), 'condensed' demand precise attention. That the subject's consciousness should be a 'cloud' is quite Shelleyan. There is, as so often, a breathless, still expectancy, as in 'tremulous', 'moved not'. Love is a supernatural, overpowering presence who *overshadows* a more naturalistic union, felt as a dawn-like absorption of cloud by sun, passing into condensation at sunset.

This dream leads on to Asia's transfiguration, with music. Who is she? She embodies love and beauty, and is called 'daughter of Ocean' (ii. iv. 168), though also (at iii. iii. 108, 151) herself calling Earth 'mother' (cp. 'daughter of earth and water' in *The Cloud*). Her name is relevant. India is magnetic to Shelley. The hero of *Alastor* travels East and has his central vision in Cashmir, meeting in sleep a dream-maiden who clearly acts Asia to his Prometheus, the analogy being further pointed by the tragic climax on Caucasus. There is the eminently successful lyric *The Indian Serenade*. Moreover, *Fragments of an Unfinished Drama*, which aims to press the *Prometheus* vision yet further, is wholly Indian. Some 'far Eden of the purple East' is the magic land outlined in *Epipsychidion*, a phrase to be associated directly with 'looking towards the golden Eastern air' in the same poem. The East is always dawn-suggestive. In Shakespeare we have the strong Indian element in the fairyland of *A Midsummer Night's Dream* with Oberon's fine dawn-passage, as well as the East and West balance of *Antony and Cleopatra* and such phrases as 'O Eastern Star!' applied to Cleopatra at a pivotal moment in Shakespeare's supreme positive vision. There is, of course, a whole vein of Eastern interest in both the poetry and prose of the eighteenth century, and romantic dome-paradises of the *Kubla Khan* sort in Wordsworth and Coleridge. Byron is saturated in oriental sympathies: there is the Indian maid of Keats's *Endymion* to balance the Abyssinian maid in Coleridge; and so on. We find a continual embracing of oriental glamour throughout the Western imagination, as though it sensed there some magical wells fertilizing man's Western progress. The union of Prometheus and Asia has therefore widest references, such a phrase as Asia's 'and the Celt knew the Indian' (ii. iv. 94) underlining the general emphasis. Asia grows from this mystic Indian dawn-setting. Here is a fine stage direction (ii. i):

> Morning. A lovely vale in the Indian Caucasus. Asia alone.

Asia's part in the general liberation is central She, with Panthea, goes on a dark journey to Demogorgon. It is a psychic descent into the chasm before renewal, with analogies in legend and ritual; a daring submission to the 'snake-like doom' (ii. iv. 97) as a way to wisdom, corresponding to Colcridge's caverns and snakes. The conversation with Demogorgon I have elsewhere dealt with, indicating its honest facing of an inability to solve ultimate problems in philosophical and theological terms. The incident only temporarily holds up the rising dawn, which next rolls in another wave of roseate cloud, dissolving to gold at Asia's transfiguration. Panthea tells her how she is changing, there is music and a voice hymns the lyric of adoration. She is shown as regaining a state previously known but lost. She is becoming love incarnate—or discarnate: it makes no matter, since such antinomies are quite transcended, a process helped by subtle imagistic confusions of materiality and immateriality in terms of light and music.

The general liberation involves not only the reunion of Prometheus and Asia but, even more emphatic, the awakening of Earth. There is a release and a rebirth. Nature becomes divine. Shelley has for long expressed a man-nature fusion through his peculiarly ethereal imagery. Thought is continually as rays of light, swift streams, birds; in *Hellas* a matter of 'quick elements', which are paradoxically creating an eternal present, past and future being 'idle shadows' of their speed. Shelley's impressionism aims to capture and define the elusive mystery of

P

consciousness itself. It follows those tendencies of Shakespearian 'swift thought' and bird-imagery I have analysed in *The Shakespearian Tempest*. In *Prometheus* birds winging the wind, and fish in the wave, are (i. i. 660, 684) compared to thoughts. The subject-object fusion is in such phrases peculiarly self-conscious. Now Shelley's problem—it is everyone's—is to submit his leaping and piercing thought to the demands of actuality; that is, here, of Earth; and *Prometheus* celebrates an extension of his man-nature fusion, so that all nature, earth as well as light, air, and water, becomes mind-impregnated. The two Fauns at the end of ii. ii discuss a mystical music in terms of nature, with a magical yet earthy impressionism of green and golden fire, woodland, watery 'pavilions' and 'lucent domes.' So the earth itself is shown awaking. Shelley's imagination is being geared to the weightier element, and all the evils of existence are immediately involved. Ages past the Earth suffered a fall: earthquake, inundation, toads in 'voluptuous chambers', plague, famine, poisonous weeds, all accompanied the fall, as in Milton (i. i. 164–79). Now this is to change.

What can such prophecies mean, here and elsewhere? Can the lion ever lie down with the lamb in a universe patently patterned on an interweaving of destruction with creation? Yet something very definite is indicated. Prometheus tells the Spirit of the Hour to take a 'curved shell', a 'mystic shell', and to breathe into it, 'loosening its mighty music' throughout the 'orbèd world' (iii. iii. 65–81). This 'ocean' shell was Asia's marriage-gift from Proteus. Its music is the love-music, foam-born, to be now felt flooding the dry arteries of earth: the lighter elements are no longer to be sole symbols of ecstasy. Compare the action of water in Keats's 'Bright Star' sonnet; and Wordsworth's shell-symbol, how with its mystic sea-music, itself ocean-born, it blends the aerial and the solid, time and space, its patterns perhaps suggesting a rainbow light, its curve the geometric harmony. All elements concrete and abstract blend in it, including art:

> See the pale azure fading into silver
> Lining it with a soft yet glowing light:
> Looks it not like lulled music sleeping there?
>
> (III. iii. 71)

It symbolizes the oceanic music within the inanimate and solid. So Earth's awaking is our central event:

> *The Earth:*   I hear, I feel;
> Thy lips are on me, and their touch runs down
> Even to the adamantine central gloom
> Along these marble nerves; 'tis life, 'tis joy,
> And through my withered, old, and icy frame
> The warmth of an immortal youth shoots down
> Circling.   (III. iii. 84)

Notice 'circling' and the emphatic solids ('adamantine', 'marble') related to age and death. The contact of Prometheus' lips releases her life. Henceforth men and beasts are to draw only blessings from her mothering power, with death a loving 'embrace' and return home. Ages since she first 'panted forth' her spirit in 'anguish' at man's suffering, dying at his pain (III. iii. 125). Her transformations thus depend on man's consciousness. The lion perhaps will never lie down with the lamb, but slaughter may be known as a kind of love, disintegrating bodies felt as a sweetness, graves become a gentle love-intercourse with twining roots and earth. To any mind knowing all physical creation as a throbbing, golden, *personal* lover, much might be explained. So here the rock-like and dead substance springs to an all but human life. Therefore a new person enters our drama: the lost life, or soul, of the Earth rises as a most attractive child.

The Child's appearance is exquisitely described, a felt presence (as in Panthea's dream) preluding its entrance: in no poem is 'atmosphere' itself so vital, so pulsing. There is (III. iii. 131–47) a 'breath', a 'violet's exhalation', something fills the surrounding rocks and woods with 'serener light and crimson air, intense yet soft'; some new tingling essence feeds the growth of 'serpent vine' and dark ivy, the 'golden globes' of fruit suspended in their

'green heaven'. How weighty, thick, opaque, the intangible mesh of imagery. Now 'it'

> . . . circles round,
> Like the soft waving wings of noonday dreams,
> Inspiring calm and happy thoughts, like mine,
> Now thou art thus restored.

So the mysterious presence shapes itself into a *circling*,
like those revolving orbs of *The Revolt of Islam*; in which
we may recall also the dominating part played by a child.
Next the circling forms into the Child, who is the 'Spirit
of the Earth'. It leads the way to the cave of peace.

Caves are mentioned throughout Shelley with psychological and universal connotations. Asia's descent to
Demogorgon involved 'caverns hollow' (ii. i. 178) and
there a stage-direction included a cave. Prometheus on
his liberation tells Asia of a cave (iii. iii. 10–63) where he
and she will dwell for ever watching human affairs with
a purified simplicity similar to that outlined in Lear's
speech to Cordelia. It is to be a paradise of human art,
the new eternity-wisdom being akin to poetry. The cave
is to be felt, in part at least, subjectively, as a state of being.
Prometheus is, however, never precisely a man, and not
quite a god: we may call him Man. Yet he is also to
watch men from the cave. The Spirit of the Hour (i.e. *of
Time*) is to return there, its 'car' to be stilled, and coursers
to rest 'pasturing flowers of vegetable fire' in a wonderful
temple with sculptured 'Phidian forms', whose 'dome' is
'fretted with graven flowers', and where carved 'wingèd
steeds' mock the flight from which they now find repose,
the Keatsian eternity of art supervening on action (iii. iv.
108–21). The cave is associated with a temple: nature
with religion. The Earth independently refers to a cave
directly after Prometheus' speech, but with no apparent
recognition of it. It was here she 'panted forth' her spirit
in ages past, and this cave she now offers to Prometheus
and Asia. It, too, is related to temples: first to one devoted to the evils of religion in man's fallen state (decep-

tive oracles, war, &c.); and next to some wondrous centre of Prometheus-worship, mainly Greek, with fine description of its 'most living imagery' and 'Praxitelean shapes' (III. iii. 124–75). It is here that the lamp of human hope has been kept burning through the ages of trial. Clearly, the cave-temples referred to by the Earth and Prometheus are the same; they stand for that forest 'fane' built in 'some untrodden region of the mind' of Keats's *Psyche*; and the dual aspects of (i) nature, and (ii) religion and art reflect the dual partners, Earth and Man, in *Kubla Khan* and Wordsworth: for all this may be said to expand those. It is right that the Child—properly the creation of this fusion—should lead us to the cave, which next appears dramatically actualized in scene-direction.

The poetry now takes on a new, breathless adoration, a sacramental, yet utterly unforced, paradisal fervour, an awe which is both a peace and a tingling joy, all centred on the Child-Spirit. The favourite colour here, green, is exquisitely used in collaboration with light: this is indeed a poem of 'vegetable fire'. The stage-direction reads: 'A Forest. In the Background a Cave':

Ione: Sister, it is not earthly: how it glides
         Under the leaves! how on its head there burns
         A light, like a green star, whose emerald beams
         Are twined with its fair hair! how, as it moves,
         The splendour drops in flakes upon the grass!
         Knowest thou it?

Panthea: It is the delicate spirit
         That guides the earth through heaven. From afar
         The populous constellations call that light
         The loveliest of the planets; and sometimes
         It floats along the spray of the salt sea,
         Or makes its chariot of a foggy cloud,
         Or walks through fields or cities while men sleep,
         Or o'er the mountain tops, or down the rivers,
         Or through the green waste wilderness, as now,
         Wondering at all it sees.   (III. iv. 1)

This is the spirit of wonder in man so close akin to worship and yet so often confined to childhood. The solid exposition of the magically unearthly, yet earth-born, is noteworthy: 'emerald beams' that 'twine' with 'hair', 'splendour' turning to 'flakes'. Panthea's speech uses a magical impressionism to something more than a fairy-like purpose: the fanciful is thick-knitted into an amazing actuality, the abstract becomes uncannily concrete. The human realization, too, presents a strangely convincing child. It objectifies the purified consciousness, and its 'wonder' is the sense of child-wonder, the paradise-sense causing nostalgia in Goethe, Wordsworth, and many others. Panthea goes on to say how it once loved Asia, drank light from her eyes, talked childishly to her, told her all it had seen, 'for it saw much but idly reasoned what it saw', and called her, though no one knew its true origin, 'mother'. At this instant (III. iv. 24) the Child runs to Asia, again calling, 'Mother, dearest mother', asking for the old times again, the old play and happiness, and says it has grown 'wiser' now: childlike, maybe, rather than childish. The whole passage, especially the relation of motherhood to a sparkling, almost erotic, joy is to be compared with the sterner maternal conceptions of Wordsworth; as well as with Cythna's under-sea experience, Asia's reunion with the Child-Spirit repeating that of Cythna with her 'seraph' child, and Prometheus corresponding to the similarly mountain-crucified Laon. Observe that the Child calls Asia 'mother', a term also used by Asia in addressing the Earth. The 'spirit' of the earth therefore appears as grandchild to the Earth itself: for the Earth, or nature, needs *the link of human consciousness*, especially the symbol of human beauty and sexual love, to realize its own soul or life. The symbolic meaning is beautifully precise.

The Child describes its wanderings, saying how it used to dislike loathly animals and hard-featured men with faces merely masks of pride, insincerity, ignorance (all mental sins, repeating the Gospel stresses); but how, as the new music burst forth, each mask dropped away as a foul disguise. Moreover,

> . . . when the dawn
> Came, would'st thou think that toads, and snakes, and efts,
> Could e'er be beautiful? Yet so they were,
> And that with little change of shape or hue.
> All things had put their evil nature off.   (III. iv. 73)

Which again suggests, as in Coleridge's *Ancient Mariner*, the new state to be not so much a change of objective fact as a new dynamic relation where fact ceases to be wholly objective: that is, a state of artistic insight, the in-seeing of love; or again, a speeding level with some swifter reality so that 'fact' is no longer a past participle, a ghostly memory, but something impregnated with still immediacy. The Spirit of the Hour speaks a parallel description containing lines of finest psychological precision which should be read carefully by anyone doubting Shelley's importance as a great humanist. The root evil is diagnosed as an insincerity, a double-faced tortuous mental process 'which makes the heart deny the *yes* it breathes' (III. iv. 150); a thought comparable to Pope's 'His can't be wrong whose life is in the right' (*Essay on Man*, III. 306), and paralleled by New Testament wisdom. Evil is a denial of essential life; while the mind, instead of pursuing its function of *reflecting*, has become hostile and critical. Now, however, men are found

> Speaking the wisdom once they could not think,
> Looking emotions once they feared to feel,
> And changed to all which once they dared not be,
> Yet being now, made earth like heaven.
>   (III. iv. 157)

Fear, pride, jealousy, envy, are gone. 'Ill shame' has vanished from love. Yet, though free from guilt and pain, men are not exempt from chance, death, and change: which are, however, henceforth their 'slaves'. The eye having altered alters all. A change of *being* is announced, which at once involves the transcendant and eternal and goes far beyond any facile ethic.

In the final act, which sums up the whole, these thoughts

are continued in the Earth's paean on man's new ascendancy:

> Man, one harmonious soul of many a soul,
> Whose nature is its own divine control,
> Where all things flow to all, as rivers to the sea;
> Familiar acts are beautiful through love;
> Labour and pain and grief, in life's green grove
> Sport like tame beasts, none knew how gentle they could be.
>
> (IV. iv. 400)

Evils, that is, cease to be evil: but troubles persist. Henceforth all mean passions, bad delights, and selfish cares are not exactly destroyed, but found aspects of 'a spirit ill to guide, but mighty to obey', reminding us of Pope's trust in basic human passions. Language in the higher state therefore becomes poetry, 'a perpetual Orphic song', since poetic technique, the natural medium of supermen, exists by control and exposition of 'a throng of thoughts and forms' which were else, as in our own social intercourse, 'senseless and shapeless' (IV. iv. 415–17): a balance of abstract 'forms' with sensible 'shapes' in the theoretic tradition of Theseus' well-known passage. Deepest issues are certainly inexplicable in normal speech. We might remember Asia's awkward question to Earth: apart from all rhapsodies about the thrills of its new life and man's new-found oneness with nature, does the individual cease at death or doesn't he? She can only answer: 'It would avail not to reply', and,

> Death is the veil which those who live call life;
> They sleep, and it is lifted.   (III. iii. 113)

That is, what we call death is a veil obscuring a reality which those who have attained illumination know to be the true life; so that when they appear to sleep in death the veil is lifted once and for all. Shakespeare, Shelley, and Keats are together in their emphasis on sleep as an approach to understanding of death: remember its importance from the start in *Queen Mab*. However, the Earth's answer remains somewhat arbitrarily unsatisfactory. The terms of the discussion are inadequate: some more dramatic, symbolic, statement will be needed.

So far, we might point in *Prometheus* to (i) profound myth and (ii) profound thought. But there is a passage in Act IV, again devoted to the Child-Spirit, where a perfect *fusion* of the mythopoeic and philosophical faculties is both the subject of the passage and in strong technical evidence while we read. The metaphysical symbolism matches in quality Coleridge's highly condensed *Kubla Khan* and Yeats's two *Byzantium* poems. To call it a statement of 'ultimate reality' reduces it to triteness, but it is certainly no less. What happens is this. Though the myth has been hitherto interpretable best in terms of changed conscious-ness, yet that is an approach only, and partly wrongs the objective scheme: Prometheus is, dramatically, a Titan, not a man; the Child a child, not a mental faculty. Yet to possess the significances we have to perform a provi-sional translation into other terms: which terms, since they do not exhaust the symbolic meaning, must remain partial. The symbolic whole is elusive or unbelievable. The very nature of mythical statement provides a rising and baffling problem, to us and maybe to the poet him-self. So he tries yet again to interweave closest thinking with the Child, his primary figure: for that it certainly is, the focal point of the later action, the magnetic centre which draws to it all other primary significances in person and symbol.

Panthea and Ione have visions of the Earth and Moon spirits ('Mother of the Months' suggesting, like the Hour-spirit earlier, time, while the Earth = space). Coleridge's 'caves of ice' are in the new consciousness:

> Clear, silver, icy, keen, awakening tones,
> Which pierce the sense, and live within the soul,
> As the sharp stars pierce winter's crystal air. . . .
> (IV. iv. 190)

Ione describes the moon-chariot appearing through the forest where two openings mark two 'runnels' of a single rivulet. The 'chariot' or 'boat' is guided, as elsewhere, by a 'wingèd' seraph-child. After Ione's description Panthea describes the earth-vision:

Panthea: And from the other opening in the wood
Rushes, with loud and whirlwind harmony,
A sphere, which is as many thousand spheres,
Solid as crystal, yet through all its mass
Flow, as through empty space, music and light:
Ten thousand orbs involving and involved,
Purple and azure, white, and green, and golden,
Sphere within sphere; and every space between
Peopled with unimaginable shapes,
Such as ghosts dream dwell in the lampless deep,
Yet each inter-transpicuous, and they whirl
Over each other with a thousand motions,
Upon a thousand sightless axles spinning,
And with the force of self-destroying swiftness,
Intensely, slowly, solemnly roll on,
Kindling with mingled sounds, and many tones,
Intelligible words and music wild.
With mighty whirl the multitudinous orb
Grinds the bright brook into an azure mist
Of elemental subtlety, like light;
And the wild odour of the forest flowers,
The music of the living grass and air,
The emerald light of leaf-entangled beams,
Round its intense yet self-conflicting speed,
Seem kneaded into one aërial mass,
Which drowns the sense. Within the orb itself,
Pillowed upon its alabaster arms,
Like to a child o'erwearied with sweet toil,
On its own folded wings, and wavy hair,
The Spirit of the Earth is laid asleep,
And you can see its little lips are moving,
Amid the changing light of their own smiles,
Like one who talks of what he loves in dream.
Ione: 'Tis only mocking the orb's harmony.

(IV. iv. 236)

The suggestion is continually concrete, sometimes mechanic or homely: 'solid as crystal', 'mass', 'axles', 'grinds', 'emerald', 'kneaded', 'alabaster'. The impact is similar to Shelley's early statuesque and geometric style in *Queen Mab*, though, of course, much else of intense accompanying activity is now included. 'Music and light' flow as water, the lighter continually expressed in terms of the heavier element. An infinite multiplicity is felt in the one unity, carried across by the reiterated 'thousand's, the circularity of the 'sphere' symbol with all its unity-impact assisting, as in Dante. A paradoxical statement is convincingly attained since the 'swiftness' being circular is 'self-destroying' and therefore slow: 'intensely, slowly, solemnly roll on': in which we should mark the reserve force and sense of inevitable ordained movement. The speed is, again, 'intense' and 'self-conflicting'. A motion-into-stillness such as that always suggested by *Kubla Khan* river-and-dome symbolisms in general, and the blank verse of *Prometheus* in particular, is here closely involved in circularity. The first part of the speech is metaphysical and geometrical, with symbolisms of philosophic harmony, the innumerable spheres (cp. all 'domes'), such as created the Ptolemaic and the Dantesque systems. But this geometric harmony is next shown as churning into natural phenomena of the kind exploited so vividly by the Renaissance imagination, 'grinding' the brook into mist and light. Next the odours of flowers and 'music' of 'living' grass and air (sharp expression of the living harmony within nature such as that so often symbolized by the music-breathing shell), with light heavily 'emerald' from physical 'entanglement' with leaves (phrases that intentionally transpose the material and immaterial), are felt radiating from that central philosophic core of harmonious revolution which steadily 'kneads' them into 'aërial mass'. The comprehensive spiritual *is* the higher mass and solid: and that drowns the sense; transcends, as often elsewhere in Shelley, though never so impressively as here, all sense-distinctions, so that the inanimate becomes a voice and light has weight.

What is this strange machinery doing? What is this

vastly yet subtly conceived factory of axles and spheres supposed to be at? Why is nature being 'ground' or 'whirled' into 'mist' and 'aërial mass'? Throughout this essay I have been at pains to show that such ethereal imagery, whether of speed, vapour, or light, is in Shelley especially emblematic of human consciousness. So what we are watching is this: the earthy and heavily physical being forced to generate the conscious, which in turn includes and transcends that same solidity into a new 'mass'. The process repeats that already symbolized whereby the Earth needs mankind in order to know its own life, so that its 'spirit' becomes its own grandchild, Asia (an erotic symbol) being the needed link. So here the active and central agent is again the Child, the Earth-Spirit, yet son of man. Shelley is to this extent a humanist: the child is the final fact. Its first appearance materialized from a mystical, abstractly conceived, circling. So now it rests, lovingly described, *inside* the philosophic sphere, central to that geometrical and cosmic urge which generates of nature the transcendent.

The sleeping figure with its just moving lips recalls Keats's idea of poetry as 'might half-slumbering on its own right arm'; or the sleeping Adonis in *Endymion*. It is smiling, and Ione comments:

'Tis only mocking the orb's harmony.

Why? We glimpse the purified consciousness, the clairvoyance of Jesus and Blake, mocking (cp. the *alternation* of symbol and action elsewhere) all such geometric eternities. The conclusion to Dante's *Paradiso* shows similarly concentric circles enclosing a human form, but how exactly they relate, how a sense of inner, or outer, cosmic harmony may be fitted to man's tragic experience, though (as in high tragedy) revealed in a flash of intuition, eludes his expression. Now Shelley at this point advances, resolving the antinomy in terms of a gentle humour: an essence not properly so used in the ancient world, Hebraic or Hellenic, and outside the scheme and direction of

Dante, yet one which, since its subtle use in Chaucer and Shakespeare, is perhaps now necessary to a comprehensive poetic statement. Not only here but continually elsewhere (e.g. in Pope and Byron) humour performs an otherwise impossible fusion. So ends our passage of 'intelligible words and music wild', or rather one wherein these two strains in Shelley, the rush of excited thought and the repose of myth and symbol, enjoy perfect union.

Next the Child (Wordsworth's 'mighty prophet') becomes a terrific symbol of Keats's 'might':

Panthea: And from a star upon its forehead, shoot,
　　　　Like swords of azure fire, or golden spears
　　　　With tyrant-quelling myrtle overtwined,
　　　　Embleming heaven and earth united now,
　　　　Vast beams like spokes of some invisible wheel
　　　　Which whirl as the orb whirls, swifter than thought,
　　　　Filling the abyss with sun-like lightenings,
　　　　And perpendicular now, and now transverse,
　　　　Pierce the dark soil, and as they pierce and pass,
　　　　Make bare the secrets of the earth's deep heart. . . .

　　　　　　　　　　　　(IV. iv. 270)

These hammers of flame and fierce gyrations—like those of certain passages in *Queen Mab*—are used to show Keats's 'supreme of power' now piercing, revealing, redeeming, and *annihilating* all past agonies of Man and Earth. The whole passage is magnificent, though too long to quote, and characterized by remorseless images of the rocky, jagged, and grim in history or prehistory, with a ruthless, gnashing ferocity of phrase. And only in its place beside and in direct relation to such a passage must we judge, if 'judging' be our aim, the triumph song that succeeds.

In the *Fragments of an Unfinished Drama* Shelley aims to re-express the central message of *Prometheus*. The plan involves an Indian setting and the intentional whole was to have approximated closely to the pattern of Shakespeare's *Tempest*. Here I can only point to one deeply important passage where through a magic star-visitor Shelley precisely blends throbbing life with the inanimate, which becomes, again, a child before our eyes. The Lady dreams how a star fell from heaven and rested 'mid the plants of India'. Then:

> There the meteor lay,
> Panting forth light among the leaves and flowers,
> As if it lived, and was outworn with speed;
> Or that it loved, and passion made the pulse
> Of its bright life throb like an anxious heart,
> Till it diffused itself, and all the chamber
> And walls seemed melted into emerald fire
> That burned not; in the midst of which appeared
> A spirit like a child, and laughed aloud
> A thrilling peal of such sweet merriment
> As made the blood tingle in my warm feet. . . .

Next, murmuring 'low, unintelligible melodies', it places seeds in the mould of a vase, and a mystic hand next pours over them liquid light, fertilizing the magic growth. This child's appearance recalls the orbs forming into persons in *The Revolt of Islam* and the Child-Spirit's similar arrival in *Prometheus*.

The importance of moon-and-stars and sleep in Shelley I have not sufficiently emphasized, but from *Queen Mab* and *Alastor*, where the hero's quest concerns a sleep-vision, onwards, both are continual. I shall now notice *The Witch of Atlas*.

The poem is very compact. Its phrases, like Panthea's, compress the intangible into concrete forms:

> She took her spindle
> And twined three threads of fleecy mist, and three
> Long lines of light. . . .   (13)

Again, there are 'intertangled lines of light' (25). The poem's lady 'kneaded fire and snow together' (35) for her purpose. There is, too, a wonder and splendour burning through greenness as in *Prometheus*, and the word 'emerald' occurs often. 'Emerald' crags 'glowed in her beauty's glance' and deep water is a 'green splendour'

(28). The poem is remarkable for carefully housed and concretely projected fire-variations:

> Their spirits shook within them, as a flame
> Stirred by the air under a cavern gaunt. (11)

The *still* flame is seen to flicker. In a marvellous cave there are

> Carved lamps and chalices, and vials which shone
> In their own golden beams—each like a flower,
> Out of whose depth a fire-fly shakes his light
> Under a cypress in a starless night. (20)

'Shakes his light': light burns from metal solids, which are also flowers, itself felt as living. Elsewhere the Witch 'shakes' light out of funeral lamps (70). We might recall the similar splendour falling 'like flakes' in Prometheus. Such 'green and glowing light' (39) is one with the 'living spirit' (34) within all manifestations whether of nature, man, or, as with our last phrase, a magic boat; and the fire-solidification marks a sense of spiritual *substance*, that fiery seraph-body which is the 'naked beauty of the soul' (66). Here is a crowning gem:

> Men scarcely know how beautiful fire is—
> Each flame of it is as a precious stone. . . . (27)

These, I think, reach the poem's core, a close realization of the magical and unearthly which is yet earth-twined and concretely imagined. The close interdependence of the vital and solid approaches Keats's larger, less compacted, symbolisms, while also resembling the sharp phrase-hardening of Yeats's later style. The linear rhythms also point to Yeats. The lines have a similar ring or rap, a terse, finished, manner of statement, almost abrupt. My quotations have provided clear instances. Here is another:

> Beneath, the billows having vainly striven
> Indignant and impetuous, roared to feel
> The swift and steady motion of the keel. (46)

The imagery of fierce sea *controlled* resembles Yeats's 'dolphin-torn' and 'gong-tormented' sea. A consonantal technique and homely imagery may give tautness as in

> The steepest ladder of the crudded rack . . . (55)

and

> She ran upon the platforms of the wind.   (55)

But, reserved though it be, no poetic idiom houses a more vital and unearthly magic. The phrases are 'atoms of inextinguishable thought', or vision. Each stanza makes a compact, terse, usually completed, statement, and in no poem does Shelley so clearly obey Keats's advice to 'load every rift with ore'. Finally, the poetic rhythms often approach, but no more, a keen, almost Byronic, humour; a pith and pregnancy of wit just left undeveloped, thereby contributing to, without despoiling, the gossamer charm.

The Witch is a remarkable lady, whose title is quite unjustly derogatory. She is a dream-projection and, partly, an incarnation of poetry itself. Shelley's own poetic experience is clearly built into her, and we watch, even more clearly than in *Prometheus*, the myth-making faculty at work; that queer business of using one's imaginative experience to create something surprising to oneself. Self-objectification may prove uncanny and revelatory. Mental confession alone cannot study the human mind: the myth-making faculty can. Shelley here very subtly objectifies and personifies his own poetry to serve as an exploitation of magic.

From now on I shall not give references: my analysis moves in a sequence corresponding to the poem's own order.

You can see why the Witch is shown as knitting with light, since to her, and Shelley, light is substantial. Moreover, considering the sun as the ultimate behind all positive vision and the moon as nevertheless an *easier* romance-medium, we see why sun and moon references are in turn used to introduce her. Her mother is 'one of the Atlantides'—almost, I think, Mother Earth; her father, the Sun, whose kiss dissolves her (the mother) to a golden joy from which she becomes in turn vapour, cloud, meteor, star. We may remember Panthea's pre-

cisely similar love-account. The 'Mother of the Months',
the Moon, has bent her bow 'ten times' and as often commanded the seas since first in Atlas' cave the 'dewy
splendour' (cp. Cythna's birth-fantasy) took shape. The
cave is, in fact, a womb, while the 'cavern' and 'secret
fountain' at the start have as direct physiological meanings
as the ten months' duration. Similar nature-human suggestion occurs in *Kubla Khan* and *The Triumph of Life*.
The child is next an 'embodied power' who warms the
cave. Star-imagery has been inwoven into her mother's
experience preceding, or during, the birth; and now the
heroine's eyes are as openings into 'unfathomable night'
through a temple's, probably domed, roof. She *is* the
dark prenatal magic of night, of sleep. While the fountain
she lives by is now 'sacred' and a normal enough birth-
symbol, the cave-womb association becomes explicit: the
'enwombed rocks' have brought her forth.

After this exceedingly complex and not quite clear
attempt to explicate birth-mystery, the poem's lady
becomes a personification of magic. She negates death-
instincts, as does the conclusion to *Prometheus*, and
animals are by her regenerated. The approach, in homage,
of animals, nature-deities, rustics, and kings may suggest
(i) the lower orders of creation integrated into a human
birth, and (ii) the adoration of a divine birth in the New
Testament. When she clothes herself in mist, being too
beautiful in nakedness, there is dual suggestion of the soul
clothed in a body, a usual Shelleyan figure, and human
dress: she resembles Asia. There follow gossamer stanzas
concerning her magic properties, including power to
make death a rich dream-joy. Often we had best equate
her with the *poetic consciousness*, if only to assist our
approach: Shelley is writing, you see, of a supernatural
state, or person. Her cave has carvings of ancient lore,
like that in *Prometheus*, concerning the proper path from
man's fallen state back to a golden age matching in harmony the 'sacred stars'. The sense of natural sanctity here
is comparable with that of Keats. Whether the cave still

Q

symbolizes the womb is doubtful: rather the Witch now personifies the birth-quality, in both its child-purity and magic unconsciousness. The cave's carvings are, however, things of ancient art and learning: the sub-conscious and super-conscious meet. The Witch symbolizes a potentiality wherein all dangerous forces of the elements, time, and man's will are mastered: again, a reminder of *Prometheus*. Spirits do her bidding, penetrating, like Ariel, 'the earth', 'matted roots', and the 'gnarl'd heart of stubborn oaks': her power interpenetrates the insentient. Yet she is herself independent of mortal nature. Her cave-roof is (to suggest a magic guided by sexual *instinct*) paradoxically *lighted* by her fountain: on it she reads her scrolls of ancient wisdom. She also, being poetry itself, embroiders a 'pictured poesy'. The impressionism is Keatsian, the more so for the presence of 'sandal wood, rare gums, and cinnamon'.

She has a boat, which Apollo 'bought'—strange term in such a poem—from Venus for whom it was first intended as a 'chariot', though proving too weak. It was made from a love-plant, and perhaps also symbolizes poetry: Wordsworth uses the symbol similarly in introducing *Peter Bell*. True, the Witch is already such a symbol, but Shelley is nothing if not lavish, and we have yet a third following. The Witch creates out of 'fire and snow' mingled with 'love' a new being resembling Goethe's Homunculus, the mixture recalling the sunny-ice of Coleridge's dome, symbol of the purified, yet inclusive, poetic consciousness. This seraph-form is *sexless*, its bosom swelling 'lightly' with 'full youth', yet incorporates *the best of both sexes*, strength and gentleness, and is excessively beautiful with an artistic 'purity'. It is thus super-sexual rather than a-sexual, as is the creative consciousness, and, perhaps, the evolutionary or transcendental goal of mankind. Coleridge's Apollo-form in *The Destiny of Nations* is a direct analogy; and the Witch herself is later called 'sexless'. Anyway, he sits in the boat's prow, a guiding force, like the Child-navigator in

The Revolt of Islam who takes hero and heroine to Heaven, the seraph-consciousness there ruling and guiding the sexual partnership. Here he lies as an 'image' with 'folded wings and unawakened eyes', 'busy dreams' playing on his countenance, with 'rapid smiles' and 'warm tears' aroused *'from that full heart and brain'*. Though closely resembling the sleep-smiling Child in *Prometheus*, he is more mature: a child super-man, as it were. He is close to Shakespeare's Ariel, spirit of poetry; yet perhaps more inclusive.

We now have various poetic expeditions. The boat of poetry voyages through Shelleyan scenery, sometimes reminiscent of *Kubla Khan* and *Alastor*. It flies on the wind or lingers by 'pools' of 'content'. Next it descends cataracts that either 'shiver' into 'golden air' (i.e. paradisal vision) or 'sepulchre' themselves in 'unfathomable' 'chasms' (i.e. more tragic vision), but remains always guarded and up-borne by 'circling sunbows' (i.e. divine, dome-like assistance) that 'light it far upon its lampless way'. The symbolisms are normal. There are, also, labyrinths. To ascend from 'the labyrinths of some many-winding vale' upward to 'the inmost mountain', to attack that most difficult poetic job of moving *from river to dome* which elsewhere makes Shelley's streams flow up-hill, the Hermaphrodite's seraph-purity is especially needed. He is therefore now *awaked*, representing poetry fully *conscious*, and, in glorious imagery mixing light and snow (Coleridge's sunny-ice again), is seen spreading his wings to speed 'like a star up the torrent of the night', while the pinnace cleaves 'the fierce streams towards their upper springs'. Or they (witch, seraph, and boat) may voyage under a waning moon (another Coleridgian reminder), where the Lady cannot rest content with 'visions', the relation of voyages to poetic experience being explicit. Now she makes herself a dome-paradise amid and above storm, a 'windless haven' among stars, constructed of clouds' 'windy turrets' *beneath* which stars twinkle, set among other clouds like inaccessible mountain crags.

Here, where the 'outer lake' under 'the lash of the winds'
scourge' 'foamed like a wounded thing'—the imagery is
tempestuously ferocious—and the cormorant momentarily
lit by lightning seems a wind-wandering and wrecked
'fragment of inky thunder-smoke', her haven remains a
'gem', an 'engraven' copy of Heaven: against sea and
ethereal storm stands firm the minute precision of art's
eternity. You can see how constantly our dome-structure
remains basic in contrast or comparison with watery and
ethereal turmoil.

She may play pranks before the late moon, 'as a sick
matron', starts her journey. An almost cynical turn of
phrase deliberately tones down the glamour, as in Byron
and the later Yeats. From their 'hollow turrets' of white,
gold, and vermilion clouds she calls her spirits, who
arrive in 'mighty legions', each troop, somewhat like
Milton's Satanic host, 'emblazoning its merits' on
'meteor flags'; and these make 'proud pavilions' out of
the atmospheric textures upon the 'calm mere', as many
pleasure-domes over water. Such is their Queen's 'imperial tent'

> as may be seen
> A dome of thin and open ivory inlaid
> With crimson silk—cressets from the serene
> Hung there, and on the water for her tread
> A tapestry of fleece-like mist was strewn,
> Dyed in the beams of the ascending moon.

The ethereal is often here given a textile expression, a
newly concentrated extension of Shelley's continual use of
'woven' in atmospheric description. So the Witch sits on
a 'throne' overlaid 'with starlight', listening to tales from
earth, growing moon-pale, weeping and laughing by
turns. She rules waters and reptiles, riding a dolphin
like Arion, 'singing' through the 'shoreless air', 'following
the serpent lightning's winding track'—a deliberate
imagistic photography rendering almost still the in-
expressibly swift—or running on the wind. How like
Ariel she is! Yet these are all images of violent action,

against which are set those of circular harmony, when she
moves to soft upper regions 'which whirl the earth in its
diurnal round', and joins in the angelic chorus. On such
days earth knows intimations of a mystic happiness.

The poem now changes to a more Keatsian tone. We
have had moonlight, starlight, subdued fire, marvellous
storms and mystic dome-pavilions ethereally wrought.
Next we explore a legendary Egypt and the wonders of
sleep.

This movement is fittingly introduced by a voyage on
the winding Nile as he 'threads' Egypt and Aethiopia,
leading to notice of 'cities and proud temples' and many
'a vapour-belted pyramid' on its banks: the heights as
usual lifting above the winding river. There follows a
striking image of blossom-strewn lakes and 'naked boys
bridling tame water-snakes' or 'charioteering ghastly
alligators' (cp. the dolphin-riding spirits in Yeats's *Byzantium*); and next boy and beast sleep together after the
'pomp' of their 'Osirian feast' within the 'brazen doors of
the great labyrinth'. Again, see how boy-forms, seraph-
forms, like the tyrant-comforting child in *The Revolt of
Islam*, are safe with fierce antagonists. Remember the
reptiles in *The Ancient Mariner*. This impossible union,
like Isaiah's of lion and lamb, child and asp (cp. child
and basilisk in *The Revolt of Islam*, v. 49–50), preludes
descriptions of sleep's labyrinthine mystery.

The Witch goes

> Through fane and palace-court, and labyrinth mined
>   With many a dark and subterranean street
> Under the Nile, through chambers high and deep
> She passed, observing mortals in their sleep.

These fanes, subterranean passages and chambers, th
Nile itself, are more psychological than geographical.
The Witch, like the Child in *Prometheus* and Shakespeare's Queen Mab, moves through the world of dream;
seeing now two lovers linked pictorially in a beautifully
plastic and Byronic image, their locks creeping 'like ivy

from one stem'; and now 'old-age with snow-bright hair
and folded palm'—the line limning the riches of age,
sanctity, and marmoreal peace in one swift stroke. Un-
restful dreams are passed over by this 'holy song': she
herself is, like Coleridge's dome, by them undisturbed,
though mankind are as 'weak mariners', only too troubled
as they make an 'unpiloted and starless' course over a
'wild surface to an unknown goal'—to Coleridge's
'caverns measureless to man'. The Witch is now rather
below, than above, that winding course, in 'calm depths'
among 'bright bowers of immortal forms', beneath the
'restless' tide of existence. Depth is always liable to
replace height in these eternity-symbolisms. She sees *into*
all sleepers, exploring the true 'naked beauty' of an outwardly disfigured form. To those most beautiful she
gives in 'deep sleep' a magic drink; makes them men of
genius, so that they live thenceforth 'as if some control
mightier than life were in them'; and to these death's
eternity is a pleasure-house:

> as a green and over-arching bower
> Lit by the gems of many a starry flower.

This happy death is curiously described in lines powerfully illustrating the closely realistic and disciplined
approach to a theme more usually given a fanciful expression. The Witch undoes the embalmers' work, shakes
light from the funeral lamps. She took

> The coffin, its last cradle, from its niche,
> And threw it in contempt into a ditch.

We have a pulsing immortality in terms of sleep and
magic vegetation:

> And there the body lay, age after age,
>   Mute, breathing, beating, warm, and undecaying,
> Like one asleep in a green hermitage,
>   With gentle smiles about its eyelids playing,
> And living in its dreams beyond the rage
>   Of death or life; while they were still arraying
> In liveries ever new, the rapid, blind
> And fleeting generations of mankind.

This suggests Shakespeare's Hermione-statue, the sleep-smiling child in *Prometheus* and Keats's pulsing architectures. But the Witch thwarts the purposes of those who are evil, making them comically reverse their behaviour in dream, and two stanzas of pithy satire deal with Shelley's old antagonists, priests and kings. Yet how poetically fresh that aversion seems when accorded so precise and detailed, so truly creative and original, an expression. Now soldiers in sleep beat their swords to ploughshares. Young lovers, not yet joined, dream of their union, but 'ten months' shows the union, through the Witch's magic, to be real, as though this dream were very much more than a fancy-language after all. She also, through sleep, unites friends, like those in *Christabel*, long-parted. Sleep in this poem is at once the source, nurse, and redeemer of waking life, which is felt as a shallow unreality in that comparison. The Egyptian tonings are kept up through these stanzas, since the mystic lore of ancient Egypt may be supposed to have possessed a more authoritative insight into sleep and dream than Western science can approach. The use precisely resembles Yeats's use of Byzantine civilization. In Shelley magic and moonlight, or dawn-awakening, are, of course, continually given Eastern associations. In *The Witch of Atlas* we tread the borders of a consciousness wherein sleep, not waking, is the truer life: which points towards Keats. And what then of death?

The Witch marks an attempt to create a composite figure of supernature from all Shelley's intuitions of sleep and dream, poetic creation and especially poetic symbolism, his own psychic conflicts and eternity insight, and, at the start, that even more final mystery than death, the darkly magic quality of birth. There is a steady progress from the mainly feminine 'seraph'-child in *The Revolt of Islam*, through the pivotal and half-metaphysical Child in *Prometheus*, to the super-sexual Hermaphrodite and alligator-boys in *The Witch of Atlas*. Shelley attempts to penetrate both the womb and purpose of creation through

fine use of his mythopoeic art; to force that art to reveal
the ultimate mystery.

Its more magical propensities forbid *The Witch of Atlas*
to develop further that more metaphysical vigour found
in the greatest passage of *Prometheus*. Its realism is therefore limited; some would say its fancifulness unlimited.
Magic is easier to realize in terms of moonlight and sleep
than through sun and a virile humanism. The contrast is
that between a moonlit fairyland and the summoning
horns of Theseus, the wise humanist, as dawn breaks in
A Midsummer Night's Dream. Shelley made one supreme
attempt after *Prometheus* to waken his dream-world as the
Hermaphrodite is *wakened* for hardest ascents; to render
magic actual, show it burningly incarnate.

Epipsychidion develops the rosy dawn-joy of *Prometheus*
as *The Witch* its mystic wonders. Naturally, a sexual
theme is necessary; wherein the union of partners, as
once in *The Revolt of Islam*, corresponds directly to that
transcending of antinomies found within Coleridge's
dome. The poem's manner is ecstatic and superlative:

> Thou Moon beyond the clouds! Thou living form
> Among the dead! Thou Star above the storm!

What would normally be climax-impressions in poetry
are here a level style. Love is felt as at once a supreme
positive and conquering power. Emily—the name is
scarcely suitable—incarnates earlier romance-dreams such
as that of *Alastor*. She perfects 'youth's vision'; a divine
'presence' trembles through her limbs; she is compared
to all nature's wonders and is, indeed, that original and
inclusive Beauty 'which penetrates and clasps and fills the
world', her 'mortal shape' being symbolically expressive
of 'some bright Eternity'. That 'eternity' suggests a
superconsciousness, and such transcendence is, as so often,
given vertical form in terms of an experience 'too deep for
the brief fathom-line of thought or sense'. Paradox plays
its part:

> The glory of her being, issuing thence,
> Stains the dead, blank, cold air with a *warm shade*

> Of *unentangled intermixture*, made
> By Love, of light and motion: one intense
> Diffusion, one serene Omnipresence
> Whose *flowing outlines* mingle in their flowing . . .

Which is a precise and detailed formulation of an experience that negates our usual mental distinctions, using, indeed, the normal ingredients, but mixing them differently. Something is *made* from all the senses, sight, 'fragrance', warmth and cold, music, some fluidity of which these are aspects but which to receive as one whole is quite supernormal. Love here is that totality, immediately reflecting and drawing on the inexhaustible totality of life:

> True Love in this differs from gold or clay,
> That to divide is not to take away.

Herein 'each part exceeds the whole'. The poet eventually feels love 'penetrating me with living light'. Love's fire is *active*, a thing of 'magnetic might', or 'lightning'. It is the supreme power able to burst the charnels of all-conquering death.

The mystical and metaphysical experience leads to an extreme—even for Shelley—boat-and-dome ascent. He invites his love to 'a far Eden of the purple East', a Paradise of 'Elysian' and 'golden' air. Like that in *The Revolt of Islam* it is 'an isle 'twixt Heaven, Air, Earth, and Sea': which makes at once nonsense and an all-inclusive sense, the isle being really as much around and interpenetrating, as within, the natural universe. The island is itself erotically felt as the Earth in *Prometheus*, human love and semi-divine nature enjoying a vital reciprocity. The heavenly ascent clothes itself next in dome-formation. The 'chief *marvel* of the wilderness' is an ancient 'tower' built in some golden age by an Ocean-King for 'delight'. Like Kubla Khan's it is called a 'pleasure-house', yet also 'sacred' to (i) his sister, and (ii) his spouse: a thought to which I shall return. It, like Coleridge's 'miracle of rare device', is vast and wondrous, called 'Titanic', made in 'the heart of Earth', growing out of the mountains:

from the living stone
Lifting itself in caverns light and high . . .

This recalls Coleridge's 'sunny pleasure-dome with caves of ice'. Its ancient and learned carvings are now erased, giving place to ivy and wild-vine, and through its roof-tracery patches of moonlight or 'star atoms' or 'fragments' of day are seen

Working mosaic on their Parian floors.

It is called, perhaps inadequately, a symbol of 'reality'. The architectural blends into the more natural and cosmic dome-formation of the sky. This pleasure-house the poet has filled with 'books and music' and all

Those instruments with which high spirits call
The future from its cradle . . .

which associates the mystic elevation, as does Coleridge, with the artistic consciousness: for all this, indeed the whole poem, is a purely psychic adventure, or structure. Cosmic dome-imagery recurs:

Let us become the overhanging day,
The living soul of this Elysian isle,
Conscious, inseparable, one.

This is the brooding 'day' of Wordsworth's *Immortality Ode*. The realized soul *is* the cosmic. The poet's desire is extreme: not to enjoy, or be lost in, the higher dimension, but to *be* that dimension; that is to be, not a lover, but *that love itself composed of two lovers*; and yet to remain fully conscious. He asks the normally impossible. Hence his ecstatic whirl of words to describe a union slaying duality, at once an expansion and absorption, as when two meteors expand their 'spheres' into one. Shelley uses 'winged words', that is poetry, to reach the unreachable, as a way to know self-loss, to live annihilation,

ever still
Burning, yet ever inconsumable.

The phrase drives in the poem's already obvious affinities to Shakespeare's *The Phoenix and the Turtle*. Whatever our private judgements on the torrential phraseology, we must face this ambitious attempt

> to pierce
> Into the height of Love's rare Universe.

That is, to possess within daylight consciousness—the poem is intellectual, not dreamy—the inflooding of a transcendental comprehension; to control and enjoy pure, unimpeded, ecstasy.

This is certainly no conventional love-poem. Let us examine it more closely. Emily is felt as an incarnation of all earlier love-dreams:

> There was a Being whom my spirit oft
> Met on its visioned wanderings, far aloft,
> In the clear golden prime of my youth's dawn . . .

The 'Being' corresponds to the vision in *Alastor*, and was like that known among 'enchanted mountains' and 'the caves of sleep'. She is, however, brighter, a fiery visitant within the 'dreary cone' of our temporal existence, and leaves a blank which, we are told, neither prayer nor verse can satisfy. An attempt at secondary realization has resulted only in 'electric poison' and 'killing air': some form, one may suppose, of lust. Shelley has 'rashly sought' his idol's shadow in 'many mortal forms' until at last, as a hunted deer',

> I turned upon my thoughts, and stood at bay.

He faces, instead of being driven by, his inward longing: the thought resembles that in Thompson's *Hound of Heaven*. Now he sees one resembling the 'glorious shape' of his vision somewhat as the 'cold chaste moon' resembles the sun. The original shape, we must note, remains a 'sun'. 'Cold' and 'chaste' are important, so is the 'icy flame' that 'warms but not illumines'. A certain super-humanity is denoted corresponding to Coleridge's sunny-ice, almost to Keats's Moneta. Next 'all is bright' between 'the Heaven and Earth' of his 'calm mind', the dualism of actual and ideal resolved. He sleeps 'within a chaste cold bed', endures a period of passionless passivity, neither alive nor dead, wherein Death and Life are no longer at war but *similar*. He is again agonized by longing—the present experience repeating the earlier one in the typical Shelleyan manner—and endures misery, 'a death of ice', smiled on by the 'white Moon': that is, an agonized chastity and severance. At this point Emily appears in a setting recalling Beatrice's appearance in Dante's earthly paradise. She is the lost 'being', called 'Incarnation of the Sun', and associated with blazing dawn and power. Sleep-wonders become awake and actual.

We must, however, see this experience as continuous with the earlier visions. What, precisely, was that 'being' with Shelley from youth? It must be related to (i) his own thoughts, (ii) visions of childhood or youth, and (iii) aloneness: there is a certain mystic inwardness about it similar to that celebrated in *The Phoenix and the Turtle*. Hence strange phrases, again recalling Shakespeare, concerning the *identity* of lover with loved, such as 'would we two had been twins of the same mother' and 'I am part of thee': the one suggests Laon and Cythna and Byron's Manfred–Astarte relationship, and the other Cathy's 'I *am* Heathcliff' in *Wuthering Heights*. Such works dramatize a love beyond the normal approach of opposites through sexual passion, a love blending sexual excitement with the purity of an ingrained similarity, almost identity. Hence a sisterly relation may occur, as in Melville's *Pierre*, where Isabel, a sister-figure, draws the hero from normal love. Heathcliff and Cathy were brought up together. So Shelley addresses his ideal as both 'spouse' and 'sister', a combination repeated in our pleasure-house built by an Ocean-King as 'sacred to his sister and his spouse'. His ideal is, definitely, 'my heart's sister'. The object is, you see, similar to, or even *within*, the subject. Hence

When a voice said:—'O thou of hearts the weakest,
The phantom is beside thee whom thou seekest'.
Then I—'Where?'—the world's echo answered 'Where?'

'The Kingdom of Heaven is within you.' His idol is both 'this soul out of my soul' and a 'veiled Divinity'. There-fore, as the ecstasy of union is approached, the poet re-iterates this supernormality. The poem's experience is almost *auto*-erotic:

> Twin Spheres of light who rule this passive Earth,
> This world of love, this *me*.

The italics are Shelley's. The world—earth, sea, &c.—next described is, as so often, himself; or he is it. Again, with emphasis on purity:

> To whatsoe'er of dull mortality
> Is mine, remain a vestal sister still;
> To the intense, the deep, the imperishable,
> Not mine but me, henceforth be thou united
> Even as a bride, delighting and delighted . . .

The proposed union is a realization of his own identity and is 'pure' without ceasing to be physically exciting:

> the wells
> Which boil under our *being's inmost* cells,
> The fountains of our *deepest life* shall be
> Confused in passion's golden purity.

'Purity' involves some conception of the impure, and it would seem that not only lust (256–62) but, in their degree, all mortal unions (267–8) have failed, degrading the image torturing the soul from youth. Yet some final physical consummation is also indicated.

There is, moreover, a blissful agony. The concluding ecstasy is at once a fiery dissolution and perfect self-realization, and earlier phrases prepare for it. His longing forces a tragic existence, making of this world 'a garden ravished' and driving such as he to strive prophetically for some 'later birth'; and he afterwards passes through an icy death. But, as so often in Shelley, agony and death are also positive adventures, toned fierily. So he is lured to deep wisdom by his vision, which makes the 'cold common hell' of mortal existence 'a doom as glorious as a fiery martyrdom', and leads him dizzily, as a moth to a flame, towards 'a radiant death, a fiery sepulchre'. There is a straight-line development from child-memory to super-personal realization—the mysterious 'Being' was met *often* 'in the clear golden prime of my youth's dawn'—with the sexual violently included, but sin (except for the 'electric poison') side-stepped: Shelley is living in his poetry a development Christian theology asserts to be impossible—hence the many golden-age and Eden impressions, the word 'golden' being emphatic—yet his phrases are directly reminiscent of Christian mysticism. He is, as it were, incorporating child-magic and child-innocence into a sexually mature yet transcendental relationship. We can say either that *Epipsychidion* expresses a unique experience of the poet; or, which is more valuable, aims to reveal a new dimension of normal existence, new shafts of transcendental power slanting upward from human actuality as we know it. The final union symbolically realizes an utterly time-vanquishing eternity. Indeed, I know no passage so vividly smashing, exploding, the temporal, as a bird breaks its shell. Which comparison raises the question: what *is* this new birth?—this transcendental creation?

We need not here rest content with 'Eden' and golden-age impressions; nor with Coleridgian reminders of honey-dew (twice) and domes; nor even with nature-vitalized, though this may help, as in the erotically felt paradisal nature:

> Till the isle's beauty, like a naked bride
> Glowing at once with love and loveliness,
> Blushes and trembles at its own excess:
> Yet, like a buried lamp, a Soul no less
> Burns in the heart of this delicious isle,
> An atom of the Eternal . . .

Both the 'pleasure-house' and island are really as important as the lady, and here one becomes the lady. All equally symbolize the super-personal state. The island is the Earth of *Prometheus*, with Emily corresponding to Asia. Now such revelations in Shelley often clothe themselves paradoxically in such images of nakedness, and the naked form revealed may take various shapes. In *Fragments connected with Epipsychidion* we read:

> And what is that most brief and bright delight
> Which rushes through the touch and through the sight,
> And stands before the spirit's inmost throne,
> A naked Seraph? None hath ever known.
> Its birth is darkness, and its growth desire;
> Untamable and fleet and fierce as fire,
> Not to be touched but to be felt alone
> It fills the world with darkness and is gone.

How closely this resembles that moment in *The Revolt of Islam* where two restless forms in love union are felt to be creating some super-personal presence in eternity. Our sixth line here clearly recalls Shelley's *self-dramatizing* phrases, 'a pard-like spirit beautiful and swift' in *Adonais*, and 'one too like thee, tameless and swift and proud' in the *West Wind*. Love-sight (and we need not necessarily suppose a complete union) is creative, not in time but in eternity, of a 'naked seraph', corresponding to childbirth in the temporal order. The main poem early addresses its object as 'Seraph of Heaven' as well as 'angel'. Sex is really indeterminate. Shelley himself knows his poem holds a 'riddle' (Emily merely acting as a release-mechanism) and compares the general experience to that behind (i) Dante's *Vita Nuova* (see his prefatory note), and (ii) —in the *Fragments*—Shakespeare's Sonnets with reference to love and 'friendship' and caustically humorous remarks on the 'dull intelligence' of most readers, a warning implicit also in the introductory lines on the poem's difficult 'reasoning' and 'hard matter'. Difficult, indeed. For we already have manifold suggestions of (i) a woman as (*a*) spouse and (*b*) sister; (ii) an angel; (iii) a seraph; (iv) *innocent* child-dreams; (v) *innocent* passion; (vi) revitalized nature; and (vii) a pleasure-house: all are the one 'veiled divinity', and yet all Shelley's own *anti-self* (233), as appears from 'identity' passages and lines recently quoted. In the *Fragments* there is more reference to 'serene infancy', 'immortality', the 'awakening spirit', 'sister-spirits'—the poet feeling himself as *feminine*—and those who 'mix in death'. Our only solution is through some imagined creation embodying both sexes to balance the fully controlled and *possessed* union of lovers the poem craves. The *Fragments* once throw out such a hint:

> And others swear you're a Hermaphrodite;
> Like that sweet marble monster of both sexes,
> Which looks so sweet and gentle that it vexes
> The very soul that the soul is gone
> Which lifted from her limbs the veil of stone . . .

In two of Shelley's works, *The Revolt of Islam* and *Prometheus*, a seraphic child plays a central, guiding, part, as in Isaiah; and in one, *The Witch of Atlas*, it becomes, specifically, a hermaphrodite, that is, a bisexual creation, which is there directly regarded as personifying precisely this ambitious sort of sunlight poetic assertion we are here analysing. In *Epipsychidion* Shelley treads the brink of a new state of being; or rather springs 'sandalled with plumes of fire' (as when the awakened Hermaphrodite spreads his wings in *The Witch*) towards a full sexual and bisexual integration—remember Wordsworth's idea of the creative personality reaching paradise—in direct line with child-purity. All this is suggested by the title, 'Epipsychidion'. The Eros-experience gives birth to, indeed itself *is*, a young hermaphroditic seraph-form outspeeding thought. We therefore have here a most valuable development of New Testament doctrine ('become as a little child', 'their angels do always behold my Father which is in Heaven') yet incorporating further all that sexual virility necessary to-day for any revitalizing of the once fiery faith:

> If I were one whom the loud world held wise,
> I should disdain to quote authorities
> In commendation of this kind of love :—
> Why there is first the God in Heaven above,
> Who wrote a book called Nature, 'tis to be
> Reviewed, I hear, in the next Quarterly;

And Socrates, the Jesus Christ of Greece,
And Jesus Christ Himself, did never cease
To urge all living things to love each other,
And to forgive their mutual faults, and smother
The Devil of disunion in their souls. (*Fragments*)

Shelley is injecting the fullest positive and human dynamic, now lost, into an age-old doctrine: which seems not at all *limited* to physical intercourse, nor to the temporal order itself, but is mainly concerned with some super-physical and eternal dimension.

IV

There are, however, tragic problems not strictly faced in either *The Witch* or *Epipsychidion*. In *Prometheus* the problem of the cause of evil is deliberately, almost unnecessarily raised, and *intellectual* defeat admitted; similarly there is an admitted intellectual inability to solve the problem of death. In *The Witch of Atlas* the Witch once mourns, rather ineffectually, over the transience of mortal nature (23–5), and later is said to pass by instances of evilly-disturbed sleep with the dangerous poetic reservation that such are 'not to be mirrored in a holy song' (62). There are limits to her magic. She exists in a dimension outside both 'error' and 'truth', which are called, at the start of her poem, twins born from the incestuous union of Time and his daughter Change; that is, she exists outside (i) the intellectual consciousness, and (ii) time. *Epipsychidion* breaks into golden existence without sacrificing reason, yet its subject is personal, and a thousand evils, especially social evils, remain. Yet must not all temporal horrors be incorporated into any substantial eternity? I pass to examine works where Shelley exerts his eternity-powers to soak up, if it may be transmute, such all but insoluble problems. That is, we pass from the magical to the tragical.

In *The Cenci* he identifies himself with as bad a dramatic person as our literature affords. There is a moral antithesis of an utterly evil against a greatly good person.

R

Both are remarkable studies, Beatrice possessing a dignity and power comparable with that of Lady Macbeth, and, at the trial, Vittoria Corrombona or Milton's lady in *Comus*, while also showing affinities with Shakespeare's Isabella and Byron's Angiolina. Opposite her stands Count Cenci, a monstrosity so vast that his murder by Beatrice becomes a good, thereby lending an ethically noble person the essential power generally inseparable in literature from evil: a queer and fascinating dramatic transposition. Yet the play, as a whole, lacks texture. It has slight atmospheric weight. The use of storm in one unimportant scene is a weak Shakespearian imitation to be most emphatically contrasted with Byron's thoroughly organic symbolism in *Marino Faliero* and *Sardanapalus*, or Coleridge's in *Remorse* and *Zapolya*. But, though offering a dramatic antithesis rather than a dramatic conflict, and failing to radiate significances from every angle, as does *Macbeth*, *The Cenci* does not lack either human inwardness or cosmic universality: indeed, as with so much of Shelley's work, it offers both while neglecting intermediate particulars.

Cenci himself dominates as an all but cosmic evil. He is a tyrant-father. Remembering Jupiter, we can call him a minor god:

> Thou, great God
> Whose image upon earth a father is . . .
>
> (II. i. 16)

His children are up against a universal force. He compares himself to 'the world's Father' (IV. i. 106) expecting God to fulfil his paternal curse; and, again, sees himself as Heaven's scourge, like Tamburlaine (IV. i. 63), as a fiend 'appointed to chastise' (IV. i. 161). He sees his own evil as positive, with God on his side: which differentiates him from even his nearest dramatic relatives, the villainous pair in *The Duchess of Malfi* and Shakespeare's Richard III. Shelley gets inside his villain's criminality, and displays, most acutely, its sadistic origin; for Count Cenci gives

way to a 'fearful pleasure', a 'giddy sickness' of 'horrid
joy' (IV. i. 164–7), surrendering to a wicked bliss, to
what Nietzsche, in a similar diagnosis, once called 'the
bliss of the knife'. Such an insight may prove a way to
understanding and sympathy in its suggestion that no
criminal desires evil, as such, but is searching pathetically
for his own paradise. Strangely therefore, by imagining
the worst possible monster, you find evil again positive
and therefore purified: Shelley's monistic cast of mind is
valuably in evidence. We may further suggest that the
sadistic instinct in man makes direct contact with the
positive in cosmic evil. The relation is cemented by a
thoroughly Hardyesque use of irony in IV. iv that suggests
a mocking providence. An interesting speech of Orsino's
—he is a queer, Bosola-like, person—discusses the risks
of a self-anatomy that reveals 'dangerous secrets' and, by
revealing evil thoughts, makes way for crime (II. ii.
110–12). I cannot here pursue this analysis, but we see
how deep the diagnosis, which may be related to kindred
explorations in *The Borderers* and *Remorse*, goes. By this fear-
less adventure Shelley enriches his work, and our next
important poem shows a new sympathy with evil, with
a tyrant-figure rather than a martyr central: Shelley is
trying to *understand* his tyrants. The Child (=poetry)
comforts the tyrant in *The Revolt of Islam* (v. 21) The
inclusive and cathartic poetic imagination is beautifully
witnessed, since by identifying himself with evil Shelley
grows in love and power. Count Cenci directly points
his creator to *Hellas* and *The Triumph of Life*.

In *Hellas* the Shelleyan faith is forced agonizedly to
face the harshest evil of contemporary European actuality.
This involves an acceptance of Christian positives closely
analogous to Shakespeare's expanded use of orthodox
mythology in *Henry VIII* after the more personal spiritual
adventures from *Hamlet* to *The Tempest*. The close relation of Shelley's *Prometheus* to Christianity becomes explicit,
Prometheus and Jupiter now reappearing as Christ and
Satan in the prologue. A later lyric asserts the equation.

Christ is a 'power from the unknown God' and a 'Promethean conqueror', treading a 'triumphal path' of 'thorns', 'death', and shame':

> The moon of Mahomet
> Arose, and it shall set;
> While blazoned as on Heaven's immortal noon
> The Cross leads generations on.   (211–24)

Shelley's more pantheistic intuition drives towards fulfilment in Christian symbols. The play, or dramatic poem, is realistic in theme, though universalized in treatment. It treats of the Graeco-Turkish war; while, opposite the forces of tyranny, and, in especial, Turkey, whose tyrant, Mahmoud, is our central, though scarcely a dominating, figure, suffering heroism is presented with a typical fervour. Against 'the citadels of sanguine kings' are pitted the 'armies of the eternal' with attendant self-sacrifice that remains 'sepulchred in monumental thought' (412–20). Whatever its outward fate, the good remains eternalized in some other, more spiritual, dimension. In 'monumental' we may feel our dome-image subtly recurring; 'thought' we can call 'spiritual experience'.

Indeed, the poem continually returns to such eternity-glimpses:

> But Greece and her foundations are
> Built below the tide of war,
> Based on the crystalline sea
> Of thought and its eternity . . .   (696)

Where the thought-eternity equation is clear. 'Built' and 'crystalline' echo former dome-imagery, though here the eternal structure sinks below rather than lifts above the temporal waters ('tide of war') and is indeed contrasted with the more superficial 'temples and towers' (692) of tyrannic glory. The use of depth corresponds to the dark realism of the poem, but the vertical dimension is still emphatic. A similar conception is elaborated later in a magnificent passage (762–85), wherein the whole material universe is felt as unreal in contrast with 'the Fathomless',

who is said (with a New Testament echo) to care for
'meaner things' than Mahmoud the Tyrant can 'dream'.
The great 'whole' of nature, its past and futurity alike,

> Is but a vision; all that it inherits
> Are motes of a sick eye, bubbles and dreams;
> Thought is its cradle and its grave, nor less
> The future and the past are idle shadows
> Of thought's eternal flight—they have no being:
> Nought is but that which feels itself to be.

The Shakespearian reminiscence shows how little such
correspondence argues plagiarism, since no one will question the Shelleyan authenticity of this passage. Notice that
time is a two-dimensional shadow-language compared
with the eternal reality; how this reality is now felt to be
itself *moving*; and how 'feels' in the last line serves to
extend the content of 'thought'. The speech is uttered by
Ahasuerus the Jewish prophet who is gradually demoraliz-
ing, or rather regenerating, Mahmoud the Tyrant. He
continues

> Thought
> Alone, and its quick elements, Will, Passion
> Reason, Imagination, cannot die;
> They are, what that which they regard appears . . .
>   (795)

The phraseology is again closely Shakespearian, Shakespeare's use of 'swift thought' having similar implications.
   Shelley's intuition grows more inward. Yet he does not
assert some bodiless abstraction to be real and all objective
shapes unreal, but rather that the true object seen or felt
by us is in some mysterious way *more us than itself*; as when
Romeo calls Juliet his own 'soul'. Words clearly tangle
us in paradox. Shelley, however, hits at a vast truth and
is only phrasing, as it were, the inverse of the Wordsworthian statement: inorganic nature = the deeps of
personality. We had always best think in terms of fusion
with equality of status accorded either side. The doctrine
is specifically poetic and poetry the only witness of its
truth, for in poetry alone objective imagery *is* inward

thought or feeling, and I have continually noticed how Shelley's especially ethereal imagery derives from his almost too clear-sighted perception of this, and a consequent outflow of impressionism corresponding to what Shakespeare in *Henry V* terms 'the quick working-house and forge of thought'. In *Hellas* he explicitly expounds a doctrine implicit in *The Revolt of Islam*.

Ahasuerus' words grow wilder. 'Thought', he says, is outside 'time' and 'place' (801–2), but, if Mahmoud wishes for prophecy, he is warned that the future will only resemble the past (805), and is shown a vision of hideous war-destruction with implications both historic and prophetic. The intuition is precisely that of *Kubla Khan* where the dome rises above temporal tumult wherein *ancestral* voices are *prophesying* war. *Hellas* concentrates on the worst horrors of warfare. Shelley is attacking the problem of evil on a new, and deeper, level; the ethic of *temporal* progress is denied; and wars must persist, since 'what was born in blood must die' (811). The logic is imaginative: war, being a concentration of death-horrors, is merely a surface aspect of what is anyway a universal law. The argument is developed:

> Inheritor of glory,
> Conceived in darkness, born in blood, and nourished
> With tears and toil, thou seest the mortal throes
> Of that whose birth was but the same. The past
> Now stands before thee like an incarnation
> Of the To-come.   (849)

Birth is felt as turbulent after the *Macbeth* and *Kubla Khan* manner. All temporal existence lies under a curse, and all temporal power, as the spirit of Mahomet the Second next asserts, ends in death and ghostly empire. So Mahmoud, learning wisdom, cries 'woe' on *both* 'the wronged' and 'the avenger'; 'the destroyer' and 'the destroyed'; those who 'suffer' and those who 'inflict' (893–902). That is, in place of a one-way didacticism, even of the most general good-versus-evil kind, the *whole drama* of temporal existence is clouded, and our list of opposites logically

culminates in those 'who are born' and 'those who die'.
Mahmoud realizes that his own miserable present must
have seemed a golden and paradisal future to past ages,
and that hope remains perpetually cheated (923–8). Evil
indeed now usurps, as in our earlier towers and temples,
the privilege of height, each semi-chorus in turn seeing
'victorious wrong' riding on the 'pyramid of night', on
the tempest's 'black pyramid', while one group even cries
to be lifted there, as though in frenzied fascination
(940–7, 952–66). Those upper reaches are thunderous,
and lightning their only light, the use of 'pyramid' mark-
ing a fear that the eternity-dimension itself is under the
dominion of evil. In such passages the choric commentary sounds a note familiar in Hardy's *Dynasts*
(Shelley's close spiritual kinship to Hardy has not been
properly observed). But next we return to a more positive
hope prophesying ultimate victory for good (as, indeed,
does Hardy too) and move to what seems the only possible
solution, replacing earlier indecisions of heavenly depth
and stormy elevations by our more habitual image of
serene architectural height above troubled waters:

> And now, O Victory, blush! and Empire, tremble
>> When ye desert the free—
>> If Greece must be
> A wreck, yet shall its fragments reassemble,
> And build themselves again impregnably
>> In a diviner clime,
> To Amphionic music on some Cape sublime,
> Which frowns above the idle foam of Time.
>
> (1000)

Notice the building to, or by, music, as in *Kubla Khan*;
and time, as so often, felt through water-symbolism. So
the temporal drama gives way to a rejuvenation such as
Prometheus asserted, wherein joy, light, music and fragrance

> Burst, like morning on dream, or like Heaven on death,
>> Through the walls of our prison.   (1050–8)

Now *bright* eternity succeeds temporal pain. The message

is both psychological and apocalyptic, and Shelley's attempt to blend creative purpose within the temporal order with a strong feeling for the impossibility of an established success except in the eternity-dimension—if there—always holds a fine Christian balance.

We end with one of the most powerful song-lyrics in our language:

> The world's great age begins anew
> The golden years return . . .

Time and eternity are blended through a statement of *eternal* recurrence similar to that celebrated in Nietzsche's *Zarathustra*. Imagine Coleridge's mazy river coiling round and lifting itself to form a spiral and thereby generating, in the mathematical sense, our dome-formation: that would be one way of getting the river into the dome. The lyric ends on a tragic note, but this argues no retraction. Rather it the more firmly outlines inevitable, yet ascending, recurrence against human frailty. Certain elements close-knit in this final song are displayed in separation earlier, in a passage where purely temporal, rather than eternal, recurrence in the objective universe is contrasted with the immortality of subjective experience:

> Worlds on worlds are rolling ever
> > From creation to decay,
> Like the bubbles of a river
> > Sparkling, bursting, borne away.
> But they are still immortal
> Who, through birth's orient portal
> And death's dark chasm hurrying to and fro,
> > Clothe their unceasing flight
> > In the brief dust and light
> Gathered around their chariot as they go.   (197)

Notice this 'chariot': I refer to it later. Birth is here radiant, as in Wordsworth's *Immortality Ode*, rather than turbulent, as in *Kubla Khan*, but the chasm of death recalls Coleridge. Human immortality stands outside the creative process, yet has, as we are next told, its own progress through successive incarnations advancing according to merit. The scheme is probably too temporal in impact to be quite satisfying. The variations are, of course, inexhaustible, and I only aim to show how *Hellas* involves them in an attempt to make sense of its grim action. Shelley's own note concerning the 'Gordian knot of the origin of evil' is at once modest and interesting. He follows Pope in regarding human 'desire itself' as 'the strongest and the only presumption that eternity is the inheritance of every thinking being'. Again, there is emphasis on (i) thought, and (ii) eternity.

We find an even sterner questioning in the unfinished *Triumph of Life*. Its plan, rhyme-scheme, incidents, and phraseology are modelled on Dante and the whole transmits a similar austerity. Shelley's fondness for *terza rima* matches his tendency to proceed through repetition and expansion, as in a widening spiral. I attempt a short paraphrase of this difficult poem.

The poet sees humanity at its usual deluded and chaotic purposes, its highly 'serious folly'. A Moneta-like 'shape' appears in a chariot. Though a figure of death and *blind* destruction, it yet possesses dignity:

> So ill was the car guided—but it passed
> With solemn speed majestically on.

Shelley's old antitheses are breaking down. Neither the tyrant in *The Revolt of Islam* nor Jupiter in *Prometheus* were 'majestic'. *The Cenci* and *Hellas* mark a developing acceptance, and here our central figure, symbolizing 'life', is exceedingly complex. My last quotation from *Hellas* had a 'car', and we may remember the car in *Queen Mab*. The symbol is important in Dante, Milton, Shelley, and Keats, suggesting a transcendence-in-motion to be both compared and contrasted with domes. We may, provisionally, call it 'dynamic eternity'. Here it is first associated with human suffering, except for those who willingly renounce temporal hopes. Round it whirls the 'wild dance' of human existence, described by phrases such as 'savage music', 'agonising pleasure', and 'whirlwinds'; while sexual unions are brief lightnings, themselves fiercely destructive, before death. Positives of harmony, circularity, and union are evilly toned, just as in Dante's whole scheme circularity applies, though not with equal emphasis, to Hell, Purgatory, and Paradise. Shelley is denouncing the limitations of a purely humanistic existence, and simultaneously injecting an awareness of cosmic, Hardyesque, evil into his harmonious symbolisms. A one-time sufferer, now in Dantesque wise a distorted root, asserts that the 'shape' in the car is 'life'. The speaker turns out to be Rousseau, chosen to typify the naturalistic or humanistic philosopher.

The poem starts a new, yet repetitive, movement, after the somewhat baffling manner of *The Revolt of Islam*. Rousseau is now thoroughly chastened. Had his spirit, he says, been 'with purer nutriment supplied' he would be in better case. Yet his fault, it would appear, lay not in too self-reliant a humanism, but rather in too little self-knowledge: *as though deepest self-knowledge involves both evil and the transcendental*. So he explains how men now 'chained to the car' were truly wise and noble men, lacking one thing only, to 'know themselves', *intellectual* powers having failed to 'repress the mystery within'. Life, their own profoundly rooted life, gets the better of their trivial learning, and this life is a transcendent, not a naturalistic, reality. Hence its projection into car-imagery. It is, too, not necessarily pleasant, and knowing oneself may involve the horrors of *The Cenci*. The poem is fascinatingly paradoxical: 'good' and the 'means of good' are actually felt as incompatible. But no paradox is more strange than that central to the poem, how all 'life' conquers greatest men in the 'battle' they wage with her: wherein we see clearly that by 'life' Shelley now all but means 'death'. In contrast, the purely temporal existence is imagined as an ever-changing play of pictures on a false glass, a two-dimensional shadow-play. Supreme figures of the ancient and modern world, including

Christian thinkers who have unwittingly blotted out the sun (i.e. God) they worship, are shown in subjection to the car. Rousseau indeed claims to have been a creator, but only of 'a world in agony': a confession applying to many a great thinker of the post-Renaissance world.

The poem now starts a third movement. Rousseau indulges in a metaphysical autobiography. His birth was a blissful sleep by a 'mountain', 'cavern', and 'gentle rivulet'. As in *Kubla Khan* and *The Witch of Atlas* nature-imagery may suggest a more human configuration, and the presence of maternal suggestion here might be supported by a closely sequent image, though in a different relation, of a child and its mother's breast. What Heaven or Hell lay before he 'woke to weep' (remember *King Lear*) the speaker does not know. Next, the dawn-joy is remembered, as in Wordsworth's *Immortality Ode*, during the boy's growth. The primal 'light from the orient cavern' turns to a 'shape all light', who is exquisitely described as an absolute-personification closely resembling that in *Epipsychidion*, and corresponding, very precisely, to Wordsworth's 'vision splendid'. The youth questions her (cp. perhaps Wordsworth's 'obstinate questionings', though these really refer to a later stage) as to the meaning of this 'perpetual dream' of existence. But now she melts—the Wordsworthian process ('fade into the light of common day') closely repeated—as a dawn-star at dawn into a new and all-dissolving light; that is, into the light of mature reason; yet still, like the star in the poem *To a Skylark*, remaining subtly felt, remembered, within the greater light. The 'new vision', as it is termed, corresponds to the matured intellectual consciousness, which in Wordsworth is called a 'prison'; and yet this consciousness is clearly also of eternity-stuff (as in the 'thought' of *Hellas*) and to be directly related to all domes (the dawn-joy being rather enjoyment of an *earthly* paradise); to such circular symbols as we found in *Prometheus*; and to cars. It may be therefore both fearsome and transcendent. Here it is in full action and panoply:

But the new Vision, and the cold bright car,
With solemn speed and stunning music, crossed

The forest, and as if from some dread war
Triumphantly returning, the loud million
Fiercely extolled the fortune of her star.

A moving arch of victory, the vermilion
And green and azure plumes of Iris had
Built high over her wind-wingèd pavilion,

And underneath aethereal glory clad
The wilderness, and far before her flew
The tempest of the splendour, which forbade

Shadow to fall from leaf and stone . . .

The 'cold bright car' corresponds to Coleridge's 'sunny' dome with 'caves of ice'. But the impressionism may also touch Wordsworth's 'prison-house' as when we hear of the 'cold light' of reason 'whose airs too soon deform' (i.e. disfigure) the human countenance. Both aspects, kindly and fearsome, are to be included. Miltonic dignity and the Wordsworthian awe of superhuman presences and worship of an all-terrible god reside in 'stunning', a word which occurs also in a similar passage of Coleridge's *Remorse*; while the chariot's triumphant victory-progress recalls Milton's Messiah. Coleridge's dome rose above war-tumult, and also above nature and trees: so, too, this car passes *over* the forest. The car is a 'moving arch' (cp. Tennyson's *Ulysses*), yet one with sky, colourful as a rainbow and so vertically omnipresent, like Wordsworth's brooding 'day' of immortality, that it casts no horizontal 'shadows'. The two aspects of nature and human fabrication so often coalescing in sky-dome passages recur; and both are housed within the phrase 'wind-winged pavilion'. Here eternity itself moves, the car-symbol expressing eternity-in-action. Shelley works at a profound synthesis of time and eternity, good and evil, not unlike that of Keats's Moneta, and his transpositions are all poetically coherent and purposeful.

THE NAKED SERAPH: AN ESSAY ON SHELLEY 255

The new perception of evil as entwined within the
absolute opens vistas of horror, corresponding to the
prison-world of Wordsworth's *Ode* and the horrors of
Tennyson's *Palace of Art*. With a passing tribute to
Dante, Shelley engages in description of these: shadows,
phantoms, vampire-bats, chattering apes, vultures, charnels cluster the' page. Ghostly evil forms becloud the
universe. A reference to 'lawyers, statesmen, priest and
theorist' is interesting in its Pauline sense of legalized and
academic rigidity working in double-harness with root
evils, even death. We are facing the dangers of the intellectual consciousness, in orthodox phrase 'the fall', which
creates both death-knowledge (as at line 59 in our present
poem) and those rigid professional charlatanisms Pope,
after the manner of Christ himself, attacked. Each, of
course, is at once cause and effect of the other, with an
oscillatory action. We meet next a Keatsian horror at the
passing of youthful grace and care's disfiguring lines.
From the crowd (i.e. mankind) steam up, as it were,
shadows, cloudy essences of evil suffering, which are
wrought, as 'the sun shapes the clouds', into those evil-
formed spirits already described by the *'car's creative ray'*.
The phrase is extremely important. Notice that the
creativity described is not temporal but vertical. We watch
a process similar to that circular grinding and milling I
have so emphasized in *Prometheus*, and both passages
depict the generation in eternity of essences extracted, as
it were, from the temporal order. Here the mysterious
process is itself darkly toned, though the originating
power remains a vast sun. We watch a compelling, inevitable, purpose forcing man from paradisal birth and
an earthly paradise into spiritual agonies for its own ends.
Such an intuition is tragic, yet not hopeless: indeed, it
conditions the only hopes worth entertaining. Shelley
now asks, 'Then what is life?' What *is* this mysterious
eternity, these cruel yet majestic cars, spheres, domes?
This mind-stunning and inhospitable music? The poem
is, unfortunately, like *Kubla Khan* itself (according to

Coleridge) and Keats's first *Hyperion*, not completed, and we accordingly have to wait for the answer.

We must not assume that the works just noticed mark a retraction of earlier statements or even a totally new insight. The highly charged and more or less naturalistic positives of *The Revolt of Islam* and *Prometheus* are all placed beyond tragic experience: the victories were never facile and always involved transcendental categories. *Adonais*, *Epipsychidion*, *The Cloud*, and *To a Skylark* follow *The Cenci* and are contemporaries of *Hellas*. Shelley finally is working to relate the agonies of existence to the one invulnerable positive, the 'nature's naked loveliness' of *Adonais* and the blazing humanism of *Epipsychidion*. Perhaps of all his work *The Sensitive Plant* most securely expresses his general problem and its answer. Nature, in the plant nurtured by a lady, is stricken by the 'chariot' of winter, but the poet refuses to allow death to overcome a positive joy. In *The Triumph of Life* he works to probe the meaning of that chariot. His favourite symbol of an eagle and serpent battling in mid-air repeats the opposition of albatross and reptile in *The Ancient Mariner*, but from the start Shelley, as in the early action of *The Revolt of Islam*, gives the serpent full *sympathy*. His spiritualized fervours may be over-emphasized, deflecting our minds from his essential realism and urgent message; so may his optimism. There is no facile revolutionary expectation. His keenly satiric poems, *Swellfoot the Tyrant* and *The Mask of Anarchy*, deserve attention. Moreover, disagreement with his moral or political ideas must be allowed only a minor emphasis: far more important is the specifically resolving action of his poetry. The antinomial terms in all such subsidiary studies must remain abstractions, and awareness of this was perhaps at the back of Shelley's fluid use of abstract categories from the start. We can always put our own conflicts in their place, and get on with the real business of poetry, concerned more precisely with symbolism. Then we shall feel

Shelley as a figure of both agony and revelation. His later eternity-intuitions are troubled, but beside such mechanisms, which the Child in *Prometheus* was seen as *mocking*, we must remember his keenest spear-points of *human* vision. An archetypal moment in his work is that of the binding in brass links of his hero Laon on a mountain pinnacle where naked physical suffering in shivering icy crucifixion or sun-blistering agony is a step, as in *Prometheus* and *Epipsychidion*, to that other nakedness, so repeatedly emphasized, of magic rebirth and victorious eros-impregnated life in nature or in man, which is at once resurrection and espousal and seraphic purity; and these may assist to penetrate those darker mysteries of the eternal purpose in *The Cenci*, *Hellas* and *The Triumph of Life*.

Additional Note, 1958.

The Fragments connected with *Epipsychidion* are also discussed in my book on Shakespeare's Sonnets, *The Mutual Flame* (1955). *Julian and Maddalo* is discussed in my *Lord Byron: Christian Virtues* (1952) and *Lord Byron's Marriage* (1957).

THE PRIEST-LIKE TASK: AN ESSAY ON KEATS

I

KEATS resembles Shelley in emphasis on both the moon and sleep. He, too, uses the chariot-symbol powerfully. He has his caves, mazes, and architectural splendours. But he also has many excellences peculiarly his own. His work is, to use Bradley's excellent phrase, 'dense'. It is at once weighty, rounded, and naturalistic. The architectural and naturalistic elements of *Kubla Khan* are from the start found in *organic cohesion*. He is never shrill, and always capacious. The verse moves slow, with vowel sounds in 'full-throated ease' turning out images that revolve, as the urn in his *Ode on Indolence*, with stately sequence. Each image is enjoyed to the full, tasted, before it is let pass, fading with, to use his own figure, a sunset glory. Spontaneity prevents any charge of the ornate. We are in danger of missing the wood for the trees: but both wood and trees are there. Indeed, Keats is definitely earthy and arboreal in imagistic choice rather than ethereal. No traditional light-imagery of a general un-realized sort, itself almost, by use, become of the order of an abstract concept, provides any too facile poetic synthesis of mind and object. The moon is felt as an object, almost a person:

> Thou dost bless every where, with silver lip
> Kissing dead things to life.   (*Endymion*, III. 56)

See what a lot is there condensed: the mysterious levelling alteration irrespective of objects that moonlight performs; its strange ability to create a sacred and romantic glamour, rendering the inanimate mysteriously significant and vital; the use of 'kissing' to saturate the statement with specifi-cally romantic and erotic feeling; personification in 'lip';

and concrete, sculptural weight in 'silver'. Keats loves the sculptural and also chariots, like Milton and the earliest and latest Shelley. *Sleep and Poetry* has a fine chariot. In *Endymion* Cynthia's car is addressed, axle and all (ii. 190), and Venus comes in a 'silver car'

> Whose silent wheels, fresh wet from clouds of morn,
> Spun off a drizzling dew. (ii. 519)

The mechanical and naturalistic live together in a single intuition. In *Sleep and Poetry* 'pleasure's (poetic) temple' is Coleridgian, but Keats's poetry makes slight distinction between the dome and river of *Kubla Khan*. Hence, precisely, its easy sweep, the feeling transmitted of some unusual accomplishment. It has the assurance of his own swan: 'Oft have you seen a swan superbly frowning . . .' (from a poetic letter to Charles Cowden Clarke). He here writes of a

> sonnet swelling loudly
> Up to its climax and then dying proudly.

Each image is thrown up rounded and whole as a physical creation, with subjective interpretations lending depth. The Miltonic solidities are present, with a similar smoothness and rondure, but they are all newly *alive*. There is a god-like creative delight and a superb artistic repose; with also a god-like recognition of and pleasure in the sombre as well as the fiery, the sad as well as the happy, which, in the organic nature-reflecting quality of his world, is felt purely as a necessary balance.

This creative method can be partly defined in terms of his wide range of sensory perception. Visual imagery is not over-emphasized, with a corresponding flatness of result, but rather you tend to touch, to smell, to taste, to feel the living warmth of one object after another. And yet none of these sense-impressions are direct: they are rather our own critical abstraction from a more complex whole. Keats writes with a feeling for an object which makes us aware of its weight or smoothness or warmth without any too direct assertion on his part: there is

s

always more than the one simple appeal. He is continually losing himself in one whole of experience after
another. With this reservation we can point to a valuable
distinction. He does not offer much that is unpleasing to
the tactile sense: the jagged or rough plays small part.
Hence our strange awareness of the sculptural throughout
a poetry largely concerned with nature, and of the smooth
in statement however painful the emotions employed.
His use of smell is most varied and subtle, contrasting with
Shelley's less-realized 'odours'. The sensory suggestion
is mostly pleasant. Closely allied is his almost excessive,
and indeed at the first not always so subtle, use of taste.
His references to eating or drinking contribute, as in
Shakespeare's *Antony and Cleopatra*, to the strangely
physical impact of his poetry as a whole. His *Lines on the
Mermaid Tavern* are typical:

> Have ye tippled drink more fine
> Than mine host's Canary wine?
> Or are fruits of Paradise
> Sweeter than those dainty pies
> Of venison?

Which, in its reference of some diviner substance to something very substantially material, illustrates the physical
nature of Keats's apprehension generally. As for drink,
Bacchic voluptuousness with a drowning of consciousness
first in sensation, and next in forgetfulness, may be felt
as almost the perfection of experience. 'Honey' and 'bees'
are often mentioned, together suggesting a complex of
sweet taste and droning slumberous music. Clearly,
Keats's poetry is brimful of sensuous richness in tactile
and sculptural yet exquisitely living attraction; in rich
stones, and smooth surfaces; in earthy fecund nature;
in warmth and perfume and taste; until the mind is all
but drowned, fumed, intoxicated by a pleasure just stop-
ping short of a cloying sweetness. There is nothing deca-
dent in it, however. 'O, he had swoon'd, drunken from
pleasure's nipple' (*Endymion*, II. 868) suggests a typical
blend of intoxication with health-giving nourishment.

Shelley often touches a similar experience: in his *West Wind* the 'sense faints' in 'picturing' lovely under-sea foliage; his *Indian Serenade* repeats the idea of fainting; 'I faint, I fail' is a natural climax elsewhere; and in the great passage of *Prometheus* the senses are intoxicated and overruled at once. But what Shelley experiences Keats instinctively *lives*. Dizziness is a frequent impression. This expanding of sensory delight to the limit of consciousness is all but the central fact of his work, early or late.

Which leads to his even more amazing emphasis on sleep. Shelley was a sleep-worshipper: Keats a positive fanatic. Hardly a page is without a reference given some luxuriant realization. Its very darkness is here attractive, and indeed such words as 'dusky' and 'ebon' are characteristic of Keats's liking for darkness as a positive luxury. What Mr. Middleton Murry has called his 'Indolent' letter and his later *Ode on Indolence* are both culminations of a prepossession evident in his earliest work. One of his first poems is aptly *Sleep and Poetry*. Elaborate quotation is unnecessary: you have only to open the book. But a few words on the part played by sleep in *Endymion* are necessary.

The poem is, as it were, one long swoon, or at the least the occasion for a number of separate ones. In Book I there occurs this fine invocation:

> O magic sleep! O comfortable bird,
> That broodest o'er the troubled sea of the mind
> Till it is hush'd and smooth! O unconfin'd
> Restraint! imprisoned liberty! great key
> To golden palaces, strange minstrelsy,
> Fountains grotesque, new trees, bespangled caves,
> Echoing grottos, full of tumbling waves
> And moonlight; aye, to all the mazy world
> Of silvery enchantment!—who, upfurl'd
> Beneath thy drowsy wing a triple hour,
> But renovates and lives? Thus in the bower,
> Endymion was calm'd to life again.   (i. 453)

Notice that sleep is (i) an introduction to paradise symbols of the *Kubla Khan* sort, and (ii) at once a magic release and an outpouring of health for daylight living. Elsewhere a passage recalling Shakespeare's Queen Mab speech can delicately characterize the insubstantiality of both fairy palaces and 'the Morphean fount' itself, but it remains a rich description (I. 739–56). And here is the sleeping Adonis:

> Sideway his face repos'd
> On one white arm, and tenderly unclos'd,
> By tenderest pressure, a faint damask mouth
> To slumbering pout . . .   (II. 403)

Which may remind us of Shelley's child-spirit. Throughout we are endued 'with power to dream deliciously' (II. 708). In Book IV there is a long description of Sleep 'slow journeying with head on pillow' (IV. 361–89), associated with origins in the 'old womb of night' and 'caves forlorn', yet with his own *moving*, adventuring, dignity and deep mysteries:

> His litter of smooth semilucent mist,
> Diversely ting'd with rose and amethyst,
> Puzzled those eyes that for the centre sought.

Two winged 'raven horses' (compare Cythna's black steed in Shelley) are 'in slumber dead', Endymion and his lady sleeping on their pinions in mid-air (IV. 398–404), while love-adventures form duskily:

> Yet he turn'd once more to look
> At the sweet sleeper—all his soul was shook—
> She press'd his hand in slumber.   (IV. 452)

The whole poem is, as it were, 'pillow'd in lovely idleness' (IV. 467). 'Pillow' is a favourite word. The Cave of Quietude, with all the psychic and spiritual connotations Mr. Murry gives it in his essay 'The Meaning of *Endymion*', is nevertheless a place of especially profound sleep: for sleep to Keats is not at all a simple thing but rather the entry to final mysteries. This cave is given heavy and tragic tonings, with all the troubles of mortality emphatic enough, but, though all men know the agony, yet

THE PRIEST-LIKE TASK: AN ESSAY ON KEATS 263

... few have ever felt how calm and well
Sleep may be had in that deep den of all.

Whatever its meanings, a sleep all but a death, induced
by a drink of *melting ice*, is their crown:

> Happy gloom!
> Dark Paradise! where pale becomes the bloom
> Of health by due; where silence dreariest
> Is most articulate; where hopes infest;
> Where those eyes are the brightest far that keep
> Their lids shut longest in a dreamless sleep.
> O happy spirit-home! O wondrous soul!
> Pregnant with such a den to save the whole
> In thine own depth.   (IV. 537–45)

The complexities of the poem, its main conflict indeed,
that of the Indian girl balanced with Dian, concern the
relation of waking life to a divine dream:

> I have clung
> To nothing, lov'd a nothing, nothing seen
> Or felt but a great dream!   (IV. 636)

Yet the dream turns out to be reality.

The poem dramatizes less the antagonism than the equation of the Indian girl with Dian, of reality with dream; a
movement implicit in Endymion's sleep-journey with his
mortal lady, and the choice of an Indian, with all the associations of (i) duskiness, and (ii) romantic magic, to symbolize
the actuality of love. In both Shelley and Shakespeare
'Indian' suggestion has extreme mystic force, as I have
noted in writing of Asia in *Prometheus*. The nearest of
kin in literature to *Endymion* is probably *A Midsummer
Night's Dream*, where we have India in close association
with fairyland and fairies, which fairies are symbols of
dream, of sleep. There too the moon is a ruling symbol.
Changeable love-loyalties occur in both works. That
breathless sense of the mystery of dead night and coming
dawn which Shakespeare so skilfully projects is of
Keatsian quality. And, should we doubt the profundity
of sleep and dream impressions in Keats, we might attend

to many passages not alone in Shelley but in Shakespeare too: the troubled sleep-speeches of Henry IV and Henry V; the part played by sleeplessness and nightmare in *Macbeth*; the three passages noticed in my *Wheel of Fire* all concerning sleep that I use there to distinguish the mental territories of *Macbeth*, *Lear*, and *Antony and Cleopatra*, especially Cleopatra's dream, with its recapitulation of Romeo's; and the extreme importance of sleep in the higher visions of *Pericles*, *The Winter's Tale*, *Cymbeline*, *The Tempest*, and *Henry VIII*. With these in mind we may more naturally breathe the atmosphere of Endymion's adventures in the glittering corridors of Earth and lucent caves of Ocean, and his flight on dusky-feathered steeds through air; above all, his finding of an unguessed and resolving unity, not unlike the recognition conclusions in Shakespeare's final plays, at the close, so that he ends his labyrinthine quest, his bright and dusky voyages alike, in a mysterious 'deathful glee' (IV. 945). Just before the resolution he is about to become a hermit, with 'mossy cave', the final synthesis alone saving him from the hermit and mossy stump solution of *The Ancient Mariner*. Dream and sleep are laid on heavily to the last: see the passage commencing 'As feels a dreamer . . .' (IV. 889–900) with its intuition of people meeting each other in a sleep-world possessing its own independent laws of existence.

Poetry itself is, in *Sleep and Poetry*, called 'might half slumbering on its own right arm', and this is, paradoxically, the 'supreme of power'. The intuition is analogous to that of Wordsworth's *Tintern Abbey*. Keats's reference to a mood of 'effeminacy' in his Indolent letter is important, while in a passage from *Richard II* which I have often discussed Shakespeare treats of a creative consciousness in terms of the mind becoming the 'female' to the soul. The power of creation may be said to come from a union of sleep and waking: Coleridge's *Kubla Khan* was fished from the depths of a sleep-consciousness. Shelley's child in *Prometheus* is first seen as half-sleeping and next shown as a symbol of power, and a similar conception is likewise implicit in

> Four maned lions hale
> The sluggish wheels; solemn their toothed maws,
> Their surly eyes brow-hidden, heavy paws
> Uplifted drowsily . . .   (*Endymion*, II. 643)

The peculiar virtues of Keats's poetry are conditioned by its slumberous quality.

These are what might be termed subjective character-istics, and I pass to notice further Keats's more objective realizations, though in no writer is this distinction more untenable to a final judgement. Here is an example of Keats's heavy, rounded perception:

> The vine of glossy sprout; the ivy mesh,
> Shading its Ethiop berries; and woodbine,
> Of velvet leaves and bugle-blooms divine;
> Convolvulus in streaked vases flush.
> > (*Endymion*, II. 412)

Which illustrates the following qualities: smooth or soft surfaces—'glossy', 'velvet', 'streaked'; sculptural round-ness—'sprout', 'bugle-blooms', 'convolvulus', 'vases'; denseness—'mesh'; duskiness—'Ethiop'. Rich vowel-sounds are, as always, in evidence. This is all so typical that when in *Sleep and Poetry* we find

> A laughing schoolboy, without grief or care,
> Riding the springy branches of an elm,

we are startled by the Wordsworthian perception; but when on the next page we find 'a dusky space made by some mighty oaks' we are again at home. The 'capacious wheel' of the chariot in this poem is what we expect of verse-movement, image-weight, and psychological content. Keats's nature is very un-Shelleyan, also un-Words-worthian. Yet, though heavy and sculptural, there is no lack of pulsing warmth, the geometrical and architectural being perfectly interfused with the naturalistic and vital. Keats actually surpasses his predecessors in acute perception of natural significance, of some almost human vitality in vegetable and earthy life, in the heavenly bodies; in, we may say, the very texture of the earthy universe and its elements.

The charioteer in *Sleep and Poetry* 'talks to the trees and mountains'. In *Endymion* 'sleeping kine' by moonlight 'dream of fields divine' (III. 57); and a 'ditty', at II. 829–35, was told by a 'cavern wind' to a 'forest old', who in turn tells it 'in a dream' to a 'sleeping lake' where a poet finds it. In such passages poetry, sleep and dream, and a certain human, if sleepy, consciousness in nature are all entwined. Indeed, Keats's interest in sleep is one with his perception of a kind of consciousness within manifestations usually felt to be half-conscious only or quite inanimate. The problem and mystery are identical. Like his moon, his own poetry passes across the world of nature or human sleep, miraculously 'kissing dead things to life'. This is precisely why his mythological figures are so deeply realized. No one in English literature, no Elizabethan even, has found the symbolic grammar of Greek mythology so exactly focused to his own purposes. He does not borrow: he sees what was seen by the race-mind that peopled woods with satyrs and rivers with nymphs, and knew the sun and moon as divine charioteers. So his Dian, Apollo, Neptune are real. In *Endymion* a river talks, as in *Comus* and *Lycidas*. But no English poet has so light a touch, so unswerving a tact in mythological treatment: for Keats never loses sense of the natural object, however precisely it be personified. Here is an illustrative description of Neptune's under-sea palace of 'proud domes', 'rich opal domes', and 'jasper pillars' (*Endymion*, III. 833–49):

> Far as the mariner on highest mast
> Can see all round upon the calmed vast,
> So wide was Neptune's hall: and as the blue
> Doth vault the waters, so the waters drew
> Their doming curtains, high, magnificent,
> Aw'd from the throne aloof;—and when storm-rent

> Disclos'd the thunder-gloomings in Jove's air;
> But sooth'd as now, flash'd sudden everywhere,
> Noiseless, sub-marine cloudlets, glittering
> Death to a human eye: for there did spring
> From natural west, and east, and south, and north,
> A light as of four sunsets, blazing forth
> A gold-green zenith 'bove the Sea-God's head.
> Of lucid dépth the floor, and far outspread
> A breezeless lake, on which the slim canoe
> Of feather'd Indian darts about, as through
> The delicatest air: air verily,
> But for the portraiture of clouds and sky:
> This palace floor breath-air,—but for the amaze
> Of deep-seen wonders motionless,—and blaze
> Of the dome pomp, reflected in extremes,
> Globing a golden sphere.   (*Endymion*, iii. 865)

One is less inclined to select the inevitable 'doming curtains', 'dome pomp', and 'golden sphere' of the description for special regard than to observe how all such—in *Sleep and Poetry* too and elsewhere—are so perfectly embedded in the organic whole that there is no symbolic 'mechanism', but rather a soft mesh of inter-tissued, yet heavy-rich, soil-like, poetic substance. Identity replaces contrast. Keats is always seeing the *eternal dimension* of the *lower elements themselves*. The sea-palace, in becoming a palace, does not at all cease to be the sea. Ocean plays the part of clouds, water as an embracing element replaces air: and yet finally (1005) the palace 'whirls', inducing giddiness. Not only is the place one of heavy watery substance. Neptune himself is likewise projected:

> And the great Sea-King bow'd his dripping head.
>   (iii. 890)

Oceanus rides on an 'oozy throne' (iii. 993): the liquidity of all solids is maintained. Venus is the 'ooze-born goddess' (iii. 893). The use of 'dripping' and 'oozy' is vivid. There is no facile elemental anthropomorphism, nor any overstress of the human. The personification is, as it were—quite apart from the water-suggestion—technically fluid. The nearest analogy in English poetry is probably Spenser's Morpheus in Book I of *The Faery Queen*, though less finely realized than Keats's steed-borne figure in *Endymion*. Keats's modernization of myth is original and authentic: Diana really is the moon; Sleep, *though voyaging*, really *is* asleep, and so forth. The poetic technique lives in phrase after phrase with a serene assurance the synthesis Wordsworth expounded and Shelley dramatized.

Many gods are finely honoured, sometimes with hymns. The address to Dian in Book IV well exemplifies again the natural realism of Keats's mythology; and that offered to Neptune, Venus, and Cupid in the palace of Neptune just noticed is rich, not only in naturalisms such as 'shell-borne king sublime' (III. 965) but in a peculiar trick (that lilting phrase is an example) used also for Bacchus in Book IV and Pan in Book I, involving rhymed half-line interspersions, often conclusions to swaying movements of other variously chosen rhyme-schemes, that seem to make the verse circle back and dance, sway, with a light ritualistic abandon before the deity concerned. Especially is this true of the exquisite hymn to Pan, himself a deification of Keats's own loved poetic earthiness. It has, by the way, a most interesting introduction:

> Thus ending, on the shrine he heap'd a spire
> Of teeming sweets, enkindling sacred fire;
> Anon he stain'd the thick and spongy sod
> With wine, in honour of the shepherd-god.
> Now while the earth was drinking it . . .
>
> (I. 223)

See how the living earth is one with the ritual. The speech is heavy with characteristic touches. So is the long ritual hymn that follows. Pan is to Keats 'dread opener of the mysterious doors leading to universal knowledge' (I. 288), and, in somewhat Wordsworthian phrase, 'the unimaginable lodge for solitary thinkings' (I. 293). The earthy god is one with palatial eternities making a miniature *Kubla Khan*:

> O thou, whose mighty palace roof doth hang
> From jagged trunks, and overshadoweth
> Eternal whispers, glooms, the birth, life, death
> Of unseen flowers . . .   (I. 232)

The especially pagan and ritualistic approach of the hymn is central to Keats's naturalism. The unification of man and nature fleetingly embodied by others Keats quietly, unobtrusively, celebrates. He is officiating, with the unhurried and assured pomp of a professional priest. Before this hymn we have a flower-strewn 'marble altar', 'sacred sward,' and the 'old piety' of the company present. Throughout *Endymion* piety and ritual are emphasized and terms of the sort scattered everywhere in other poems: 'incense', 'sacrifice', 'temple', 'fane', 'altar', &c. In the Dedication Sonnet to Leigh Hunt the poet complains that

> No wreathed incense do we see upborne
> Into the east, to meet the smiling day . . .

No nymphs approach: the man-nature opacity has clanged down as an iron gate. Wordsworth wrote a similar sonnet, but normally eschewed such symbolisms, which are, however, Keats's direct method of approach, recognition, and communion.

This synthesis of the pagan-ritualistic with a modern nature-perception is one with a general synthesis of human art and religion with the objective and elemental universe; that is, of Coleridge's dome with his rocks, trees, and rivers in *Kubla Khan*. We have seen how perfectly these are intermeshed in Keats's description of Neptune's domed and watery palace. It happens elsewhere. In Book II of *Endymion* the hero adventures 'into the sparry hollows of the world' (II. 204) to view the 'silent mysteries' of the earth (II. 214). He comes on

> A dusky empire and its diadems;
> One faint eternal eventide of gems.   (II. 224)

It is at once cavern and palace where 'some monstrous roof curves hugely', with 'winding passages', leading to 'silver

grots'—'silver' is a reiterated metal in Keats—'sapphire
columns' and a 'flood of crystal': the metallic and architectural mixing with the natural, both earthy and liquid.
There are a 'hundred waterfalls' and a mystic and astound-
ing 'orbed diamond': the usual nature-dome balance.
This orb is like a 'sun' rising over 'chaos'. It is, like
Coleridge's dome, a thing striking 'amazement':

> past the wit
> Of any spirit to tell, but one of those
> Who, when this planet's sphering time doth close,
> Will be its high remembrancers.   (II. 249)

Who are, we are told, great poets of Greece and England:
the orb *is* poetry, as in Coleridge. The adventurer passes
through a 'marble gallery' and 'mimic temple', 'complete
and true in sacred custom', to where appears 'through a
long pillar'd vista' a 'fair shrine' and, poised on 'tiptoe',
a 'quiver'd Dian'. You can see how, without any rigid
oppositions at all, the close mesh of impressions presents
(i) nature, (ii) the architectural and geometric or circular,
and (iii) the specifically ritualistic and religious; the last
being the fusing medium of the other two. Coleridge's
cavern and dome are being *identified*. There is later (II.
593–640) an even finer nature-architecture synthesis:

> So, with unusual gladness, on he hies
> Through caves, and palaces of mottled ore,
> Gold dome, and crystal wall, and turquois floor,
> Black polish'd porticos of awful shade . . .

Notice the word 'black'. It is a place of 'wild magnificence', a phrase blending the two elements of 'caves' and
'dome'. 'Spiral' is likewise set beside 'ruggedest loop-
holes'. There is a 'void', and 'enormous chasms', with the
'foam and roar' of subterranean waters on 'granite'; and
a thousand 'silvery' fountains whose 'sprouting columns'
—phrase now uniting the watery, vegetable, mineral, and
architectural—rise 'a poplar's height' and enclose his
'diamond path' with '*fretwork*' that yet 'streams' and is
'*alive*'. All elements are intermingled and interchanged

with each other and with human artifice. It gets even
more involved:

> every minute's space,
> The streams with changed magic interlace:
> Sometimes like delicatest lattices,
> Cover'd with crystal vines; then weeping trees,
> Moving about as in a gentle wind,
> Which, in a wink, to watery gauze refin'd,
> Pour'd into shapes of curtain'd canopies,
> Spangled, and rich with liquid broideries
> Of flowers, peacocks, swans, and naiads fair.
> Swifter than lightning went those wonders rare;
> And then the water, into stubborn streams
> Collecting, mimick'd the wrought oaken beams,
> Pillars, and frieze, and high fantastic roof,
> Of those dusk places in times far aloof
> Cathedrals call'd.

Liquidity forms into solids of human artistry from line to
line: 'lattices', 'watery gauze', 'canopies', 'broideries';
then becomes heavier—'wrought oaken beams', 'pillars',
'frieze', and 'fantastic roof'; ending with religious suggestion in 'cathedral'. We meet, obviously, only what we
expect when five lines farther on we find the scene canopied by 'a vaulted dome like Heaven's', gem-bespangled,
where, through the usual movement, the domed and architectural becomes again the heavenly and cosmic.

Of course, the subtle interchange of elements, similar
to that in the great passage of Shelley's *Prometheus*, is the
objective view of Keats's inclusive use of all senses already
observed. Notice, too, his fondness for both the heavy
and the dark ('dusk places' in our last passage) which
recalls his interest in sleep. As sleep tops his sensuous
indulgences with a swooning pleasure, so his intermixture
of elements—though never, as with Shelley, in abstraction from vividly *realized* particulars—together with his
human-natural mythology and ritualistic piety in general
build a sense of sacred significance in the natural, often
the specifically inanimate, world. Yet there is not
Goethe's tingling and seething activity in Keats's nature,

nor Shelley's torrential and energic movement. Rather we have a feeling of repose, of slumberous life, of that power any artist knows to exist paradoxically not so much in what he does as what he leaves undone. So the sub-jective and objective approaches coalesce: Keats's feeling for nature is precisely one with his feeling for sleep. They are best unified under the moon-symbol as when the moon is felt 'kissing dead things' to a withdrawn, mysterious, life; or by the frequent references to vast woods where a numinous, silent, yet weighty presence is felt in an archi-tectural and vital stillness more powerful than motion. We shall find later that the nature-sleep equation leads on to the even more important relation of love to death.

Keats's peculiar playground where sleep meets waking life and the inanimate takes its own deep unheard breaths sets the scene also for many kindred images where motion and stillness seem to meet. In *Sleep and Poetry* 'steeds' are seen to 'paw up against the light' balancing on their hind legs. The title-line 'I stood tiptoe upon a little hill' with its poised movement is an example. So are Diana on tiptoe and 'tiptoe Night' listening to the nightingale in *Endymion* (ii. 261, i. 831). A famous sonnet showing Cortez and his followers struck dumb in mid-adventure by the inrush of spacious sight, and looking at each other 'silent upon a peak in Darien', is another, where the very stillness has dramatic or narrative force. Motion may be dissolved in an expansive silence:

> E'en like the passage of an angel's tear
> That falls through the still ether silently.
> (From *To one who has been long in city pent*.)

A wide area, buoyed up and momentarily still, gives us the poised vividness of an attractive line from *The Eve of St. Agnes*:

> And the long carpets rose along the gusty floor.

This poem has elsewhere an exquisite image of movement and repose together in 'carved angels' with 'hair blown back, and wings put cross-wise on their breasts'. In *Lamia*

THE PRIEST-LIKE TASK: AN ESSAY ON KEATS 273

an interior is elaborately described in terms of glades, blending the architectural and natural from the human and artistic side. In all these Keats steers between the static engraved images (usually of still objects) in Milton and the violent motion of Shelley, where, even if motion be subdued to a *poetic stillness* as in *Prometheus*, the motion described is often itself vigorous. In Keats this is not so: short, steady, weighty, or maybe just past or expectant, movement is given sculptural form; or, conversely, some weighty and expansive solid is sensed as pulsating and alive. In *Sleep and Poetry* the 'broad swelling smoothness' of ocean is felt balancing 'patient weeds' that dwell in an 'undulating home': the image recalls a similar impression ('the swan's down feather') in *Antony and Cleopatra*. Spatial and temporal conceptions are thus continually blended. We face vital eternity, the mystery subduing motion and stillness into one harmony; or stillness and silence that says more than words, as in those favourite eternity-reminders, great oaken senator-like trees.

What may be called the sensuous greediness of Keats's imagination remarkably coexists with such profundities and subtleties, while all converge on the crucial problem of human love. The sensory perception is throughout so acute and thirsting that love becomes almost synonymous with swooning, if not death. The experience expressed by Shakespeare's Troilus of fear lest actual love-contact be a death has Keatsian parallels. In *Endymion* love is the 'chief intensity' beyond the 'oneness' of what appears to be a mystic communion. Greatest men have 'let occasion die' in order to 'sleep in love's elysium'. The passage grows ecstatic and almost Shelleyan in parts, and ends with a striking thought: how can we be sure that the mysterious union of human lovers does not accomplish a purpose beyond our understanding? does not, indeed, keep all nature at its work? (*Endymion*, I. 795–842.) The pain of love is well characterized: 'Half-happy by comparison of bliss is miserable' (II. 371). *Endymion* has moments (in its earthy, i.e. more *materialistic*, adventure) of physical enjoyment that recall Marlowe: as in the description of Adonis at II. 387–427, or Arethusa at II. 936–48. There is, however, a youthful exuberance with a natural fecundity and absence of undue human emphasis, sensuous perception, that draws Keats far nearer the perception of human loveliness being only part of a wider Shakespearian health in *Venus and Adonis* than the just perceptible decadence of Marlowe. In Book IV the Indian Maid defends love as intrinsic to nature's more earthy and creative enjoyment. There are most frankly physical phrases, 'delicious' being a dangerously weak, but significantly Keatsian, choice in this relation. Indeed, love is a matter of biting:

> His plump white arms, and shoulders, enough white
> For Venus' pearly bite.   (*Endymion*, IV. 213)

Endymion's devotion to Dian is once accused of presumption against physical love, therefore against all elements, against the tie binding mankind: against flowers, rivers, and the tombs of the great. The poem concludes by equating Dian and the Indian girl: that is, spiritual and fleshly love. Basically, love is to Keats a frankly physical enjoyment, but so is almost everything else, basically. And with him each and all develop as we watch, or read, into various profound disclosures. The word 'spiritual' would wrong, however, his work, the continual unity of what are often tugging opposites being evident at every stage of our analysis.

Melancholy is with him from the beginning both sincerely felt and luxuriantly enjoyed. The Indian girl's 'Sorrow' song (*Endymion*, IV. 146) marks an early development. A delicate humour is felt within the lilting, yet also sad, rhymes. In a person you would name it 'attractive': it is at once a sadness of eye and merriment of voice, a conscious youthfulness that makes no effort to be anything but itself. This characteristic of the early Keats, one with his especially *intimate* physical touches— Milton's line 'pillows his *chin* upon the orient wave' (of the sun) in his *Nativity Ode* is exactly Keatsian—blossoms richly here. The thought, too, is profound. Why, the girl asks, does Sorrow take the 'natural hue of health' from the 'vermeil lips' of happy youth? Is it to supply some need of the natural world? To tip the daisy with redness, give light to the glow-worm, music to the nightingale? Which recalls Keats's idea of human love as feeding the outer universe, and both passages illustrate his innate sense of a creative partnership between man and his setting with no necessary superiority attributed to either side, as in Wordsworth, where the human mind enjoys, I feel, a certain precedence. Sorrow here is 'constant' and 'kind', and Keats's later tragic understandings implicit. But the move on to the exquisite description of Bacchus is equally characteristic. There is no sharp distinction: sorrow is luxuriant, revelry and love a swoon consummated in unconsciousness. Bacchus, in a sequence of amazingly realized images, challenges all the mystic and religious glamours of the East, only to give place to the girl's remembrance of the other intoxicant of melancholy as the lyric circles back:

> Come then, Sorrow!
> Sweetest Sorrow!
> Like an own babe I nurse thee on my breast:
> I thought to leave thee
> And deceive thee,
> But now of all the world I love thee best.
> (*Endymion*, IV. 279)

The lamentations of Constance in *King John* and Cleopatra's death-scene present a similar association of tragic sorrow and maternal possession.

The Indian girl has lost her 'maiden prime' in grieving. Keats's pagan sensuousness does not forget that there is something subtly wrong with human love: that it is subject to a tragic necessity, and that ugliness—as in *Comus*—may be at the core of its luscious bloom. The Circe incident of *Endymion* (III. 314–688) during the *water*-adventure (earth and water in II and III prelude the

T

higher realm of sleep in iv) exploits degradation and misery. The associations are, on the one side voluptuous love; on the other, cruelty and animals in bestial suffering. Snakes occur, with the image 'like the eye of gordian snake', and the beasts departing in air 'like one huge Python'. There is no emphasis on any sin-struck conscience, but an objective sense of potential hell within physical love is clearly symbolized, pointing on to *La Belle Dame Sans Merci* and *Lamia*.

II

Lamia is a queer poem. The heroine is half-serpent, half-woman. She claims she was once a woman; is now transformed to one; is loved; but finally shrivelled back to her serpent form by the eye of philosophy. We are forced to dislike and fear the Sophist's 'keen' and *'cruel'* eye: 'philosophy will clip an angel's wing'. The Sophist is, within limits, right: yet the issue remains indecisive. Lamia seems to have been originally a woman, and extreme descriptive care is given the beauty of her serpent form, Keats expending on it his very richest elaborations of colour. Though *Lamia* is in part a bitter enough statement of mental power dissolving beauty, the whole abounds in a rich poetic joy. The conception touches that acceptance of the serpent symbolized in *The Ancient Mariner*, as later the girl's nervousness and fear of recognition recall Geraldine's behaviour in *Christabel*. It is, indeed, striking how much of other poets' work is implicit in Coleridge's three best-known poems. The loveliness ruined by the Sophist may also be related to *Kubla Khan*. Lamia, with the help of nameless powers, constructs a palatial home for herself wherein to celebrate her nuptial with Lycius. Here Keats expands magnificently:

> About the halls, and to and from the doors,
> There was a noise of wings, till in short space
> The glowing banquet-room shone with wide-arched grace.
> A haunting music, sole perhaps and lone
> Supportress of the faery-roof, made moan

Throughout, as fearful the whole charm might fade.
Fresh carved cedar, mimicking a glade
Of palm and plantain, met from either side,
High in the midst, in honour of the bride:
Two palms and then two plantains, and so on,
From either side their stems branch'd one to one
All down the aisled place; and beneath all
There ran a stream of lamps straight on from wall to wall.
So canopied, lay an untasted feast
Teeming with odours.

'Wide-arched grace', 'faery-roof', 'aisled place', 'canopied' all build a dome-like cathedral structure, which blends with the splaying palms and heavy cedar. Sacred groves (as in the *Ode to Psyche*) and cathedral aisles have an obvious architectural relation: Shelley's domes are often forest canopies. Here there is an especially beautiful blend of the natural and the decorative. The whole is a 'faery' structure and built to music, like Coleridge's dome to be built 'in air' to the Abyssinian maid's 'symphony and song'. We have light, a liquid flow of it, weightily streaming down the hall to balance Coleridge's 'sunny' palace. Notice the continually preserved sense of weight: the banquet-room itself 'glows', light burning out from solids. But the description goes further, to 'enrich' the 'fretted splendour' and 'marbled plain' with 'jasper panels', while now 'creeping imagery' of smaller trees 'bursts' forth. It buds while we watch, flowering in stone. No English writer has so exquisitely set himself to such destruction through a poetic technique of the stone-life antinomy. His interiors are fertile growths, his ethereals solid, his solids fluid, his light weighty, yet with each object remaining its particularized self. It is a room of 'wealthy lustre' filled with 'pervading brilliance and perfume'. Ritualistic tonings elevate its breathless magic:

Before each lucid pannel fuming stood
A censer fed with myrrh and spiced wood,
Each by a sacred tripod held aloft,
Whose slender feet wide-swerv'd upon the soft
Well-woofed carpets.

The smoke rises to the 'high roof' with a 'light voyage'. The circular plays its part in the 'sphered tables' themselves 'insphered' by seats, and the 'heavy gold' of goblets. Keats is not, however, lost in any factitious light-enjoyment, but remembers how the wine comes from the 'gloomy tun', a phrase sensing the cool cellar depths and their musty fragrances. Never was description so loaded with sense-splendours, of perfume (again in 'fragrant oils'), taste, surfaces, blazing warmth. There is also music:

> Soft went the music the soft air along,
> While fluent Greek a vowel'd undersong
> Kept up among the guests . . .

How well the phrases suit his own poetry. There follows a striking description of revelry: 'when the wine has done its rosy deed', and 'soon was god Bacchus at meridian height': lines which delightfully capture a unity (such as that Milton's *Comus* half opposes and half admits) between the inspirations of drink and natural or cosmic excellence. The whole description reminds one most of the early poetic atmosphere of *Timon of Athens*. Here it is a solidly blazing, softly burning, pleasure-dome directly related to a dream of sexual love. That 'dome' which Coleridge looks up to and Shelley often seems to float above, Keats is always deep *inside*. There are many swoons, pillows, &c., and an interesting remark occurs earlier:

> It was no dream; or say a dream it was,
> Real are the dreams of gods.

But not those of men: not that of Lycius anyway. Under the Sophist's eye the 'stately music' ceases, the 'myrtle' sickens, and the 'icy' coldness of her hand now replaces nuptial warmth. She is shrivelled back to a serpent. But, in losing Lamia, Lycius loses not only love but life itself: which all but restores her lost honours.

This serpent coldness may lead us on to the other coldness of *The Eve of St. Agnes*. Here it is:

> St. Agnes' Eve—Ah, bitter chill it was!
> The owl, for all his feathers, was a-cold;
> The hare limp'd trembling through the frozen grass . . .

A quivering sensuousness of perception is one with an inward, Shakespearian, sympathy. Such a mind only can properly feel and project itself into another's pain: and such physical sympathy is probably at the root of all sympathy. If enjoyment at its purest be mental or spiritual, sympathy at its purest is more likely to concern a physical than any other suffering. The very statues are, characteristically, imagined as feeling:

> his weak spirit fails
> To think how they may ache in icy hoods and mails.

Cold blends with impressions of dim religion and old age in the Beadsman at prayer mourning for men's sins. There is Angela, an 'old beldame weak in body and in soul', a 'poor, weak, palsy-stricken, churchyard thing'. Cold, age, death: and to Keats, as to Webster, this associates normally with medieval religion. From this icy setting burns the central love-story. Porphyro sees Madeline go to bed. Warmth is finely exploited. The coloured glass, described in a famous passage of richest tinctures, throws 'warm gules' on her breast. Her jewels are 'warmed' from contact with her body. Then,

> Soon, trembling in her soft and chilly nest,
> In sort of wakeful swoon, perplex'd she lay,
> Until the poppied warmth of sleep oppress'd
> Her soothed limbs, and soul fatigued away.

The store of sensations is inexhaustible: here warmth blends naturally with sleep. This poem is even richer in sleep than *Lamia*. As in *Endymion*, a dream comes true, since Madeline has prepared herself to receive the wondrous midnight visitations of St. Agnes' Eve. She first thinks Porphyro part of her dream: he actually is said to 'melt' into it, and a union of sleeping and waking life is cleverly dramatized. Outside there is sharp 'sleet' and 'iced gusts': these contrast with love's warmth and sleep and the usual Keatsian display of foods, extravagantly rich. 'Silver', always a favourite impression, is outstanding: 'a silver taper's light', 'silver twilight', 'silver shrine'. This silver-impressionism recalls Pope's in *The Rape of the Lock*: the two poets show similar tendencies—both love ritual-tonings, while Pope's *Temple of Fame* rivals Keats in architectural vitality. The story is framed with the icy pallor of its start and close:

> And they are gone: aye, ages long ago
> These lovers fled away into the storm.
> That night the Baron dreamt of many a woe,
> And all his warrior-guests, with shade and form
> Of witch, and demon, and large coffin-worm,
> Were long be-nightmar'd. Angela the old
> Died palsy-twitch'd, with meagre face deform;
> The Beadsman, after thousand aves told,
> For aye unsought for slept among his ashes cold.

The dim religious interior assists this framing of warm and youthful love by eternity. The poem speaks with a quiet-voiced verse and especially soft, yet rich, tones and shadowed sculptures in half-light. Wider issues concerning the *Romeo and Juliet* opposition of family feud and personal love are slightly etched.

This coldness is an intuition of death, love's final enemy. *Isabella* is more explicit. There is more of a human story than in *Lamia* and *The Eve of St. Agnes*: it is, practically, the story of *The Duchess of Malfi*, with a kindred exploitation of luxuriant semi-physical horror. Love is contrasted with family villainy and death. The heroine's tragic progress is aptly accompanied by a seasonal summer–autumn–winter sequence, love at the first having led her from 'wintry cold' to 'summer clime' and 'ripe warmth'. Her brothers' villainy is directly alined with capitalistic tyranny and gives us Keats's only passage of social and economic satire. The poem is, however, focused mainly on death. The return of the buried Lorenzo (as usual it is a sort of dream, a 'vision' in 'drowsy gloom') is given all the physical detail of the similar ghost in Collins's poem on Highland superstitions; his once 'glossy hair' is marred, 'cold doom' has struck his lips, his ears are 'loamed'. But there is a sensuous acceptance of horror that distinguishes this from the more spiritualized and nervy apprehensions of Collins and Coleridge, and recalls Webster. Here is a crucial passage:

> Who hath not loiter'd in a green church-yard,
> And let his spirit, like a demon-mole,
> Work through the clayey soil and gravel hard,
> To see skull, coffin'd bones, and funeral stole;
> Pitying each form that hungry Death hath marr'd,
> And filling it once more with human soul?

As in Webster, a vast negative universal may be said to use poetically a purely human and social evil (in Isabella's brothers) to project itself. There is a curious unselfconsciousness in Keats's development of his queer story. Isabella's keeping and caressing of Lorenzo's head mixes love and horror in an almost too questionable fashion:

> Pale Isabella kiss'd it, and low moan'd.
> 'Twas love; cold,—dead indeed, but not dethroned.

Romeo's speech before Juliet's supposed dead body and Hamlet's Yorick meditations both trace a somewhat similar territory, but with a difference. Juliet is only supposed dead, and Hamlet puts aside the skull with a gesture of disgust. Yet Keats is celebrating in his way a kindred sense of love's royalty to that in Shakespeare's work as a whole. Isabella treasures the skull in the soil of Basil plants, and Basil means 'king': horror and love become one. The dead thing now breeds life in the plant, is part still of that life that bred itself. The solution is intrinsic and physical. The ghost, however, phrases a faint hint of something more:

> thy paleness makes me glad;
> Thy beauty grows upon me, and I feel
> A greater love through all my senses steal.

The poem is one of tragic intuition, and is, typically, fascinated by death's physical aspect. Melancholy, music, and Melpomene herself are invoked in terms of 'syllables of woe' in 'tragic order', working at the heart of 'mystery'. There is meaning in the symbolism: through love a sweet acceptance of ultimate physical horror is made poetically explicit, and, in so far as we remember the plant, given something of a pantheistic resolution.

Hyperion is generally called Miltonic. The beginning shows some structural similarity to the beginning of *Paradise Lost*, though the pathetic Saturn has scarcely any valuable correspondence with Satan. Here both the old and the new orders have their emotional rights. Saturn's words can sometimes be alined with Wordsworth's *Immortality Ode* and Shelley's *Prometheus* in thoughts of a lost golden past. The old gods endure sufferings and an evil generally that corresponds to present humanity: the new ones seem to suggest an as yet unrealized future, such as you get after the liberation in *Prometheus*. Clearly Apollo is some such figure, and the new sea-king is given similar outline.

Hyperion himself is, at first sight, enigmatic. He does not, as sun-god, give place to Apollo. In neither version of the poem does he fall, and in both he is a dominating, if insecure, figure. If the fall of the old gods symbolizes the fall of man to his present blindness and nature to its corresponding state of supposed inanimacy, while the new gods mean both awakened man and awakened nature as Shelley describes them, then Hyperion's position becomes intelligible. *Hyperion* is a sun-poem as *Endymion* is a moon-poem. That which keeps alight, as it were, our sense of the sacred in nature, of original vitality, of electric mystery, and so forth, is, clearly, the sun. Hence we have metaphors of light to indicate truth, and images of fiery splendour continually assist poetic description of any high and unified consciousness, as of love or nature glorified. Similarly, the mystic fresh from communion with life-origins tends to see, or at least describe, objects as tipped with flame, borrowing associations from that element which holds to all men the tingling warmth he himself now recognizes in stone or tree-trunk. In this way Hyperion bridges the old and new. How can he then fall? Keats's poem bears his name, not Apollo's. I do not say Keats himself realized all this—his naming of the second version as *The Fall of Hyperion* suggests that he did not— but possibly his failure to complete either version may be traced to the poem's refusal to do what he wanted; that is, to Hyperion's refusal to fall.

Certainly a purely poetic and critical judgement supports this view, outstanding passages of impressionistic weight underlining my argument. Consider the opening:

> Deep in the shady sadness of a vale
> Far sunken from the healthy breath of morn,
> Far from the fiery noon, and eve's one star,
> Sat gray-hair'd Saturn, quiet as a stone,
> Still as the silence round about his lair;
> Forest on forest hung about his head
> Like cloud on cloud. No stir of air was there,
> Not so much life as on a summer's day
> Robs not one light seed from the feather'd grass,
> But where the dead leaf fell, there did it rest.
> A stream went voiceless by, still deadened more
> By reason of his fallen divinity
> Spreading a shade: the Naiad 'mid her reeds
> Press'd her cold finger closer to her lips.   (I. I)

The effect is one of deathly stillness, cut off from health, sun, and star; of life excessively limited to an opaque and limited naturalism felt in heavy forests like clouds weighing on the head (cp. 'and custom lie upon thee with a weight heavy as frost' . . . in Wordsworth's ode); above all, of stone and cold. In the rewritten version this sight almost drives the poet mad. Saturn is, as here, a 'frozen god' and the watching poet has to bear agonizedly the 'load of this eternal quietude' (1. 386–90). This is the load of dead nature, of warm life enclosed, doomed and tombed by a cold inanimacy, as in the poetic pattern of *The Eve of St. Agnes*. The 'vale' is therefore our normal human existence and the poet prays for death, though the poetry has, of course, as always, a poetic warmth and beauty, infused by the very desire its images negate. This interpretation is really forced by Moneta's words at the start of Canto II of the revised version:

> Mortal, that thou may'st understand aright,
> I humanize my saying to thine ear,
> Making comparison of earthly things;
> Or thou might'st better listen to the wind,
> Whose language is to thee a barren noise . . .
>
> (II. 1)

That is: 'The vision I show might be read from nature itself.' Her image is well chosen, since the wind is, to Keats, a 'barren noise': its appeal is alien to the repose of his poetry, which shows no feeling for its demonic or angelic energies such as you find in Wordsworth, Coleridge, Byron, and Shelley: compare the 'gusts' of *The Eve of St. Agnes* with the wind in *Dejection*. So Fate has 'pour'd a mortal oil' upon Saturn's head, a 'disanointing poison' (II. 97). To Keats nature's life is always a warm sanctity leading to ritualistic images, and here the reverse process, with *cold*, is indicated.

Moreover, there is an especially fine Hyperion passage illustrating admirably the technique already discussed of the Neptune description in *Endymion*. He alone of the Titan 'brood' still kept his majesty, he remained 'blazing Hyperion' who still sat 'on his orbed fire', and 'snuff'd' incense from man's world (i.e., very nearly, man's mind): yet he is troubled by vast death-horrors like man's but proportioned 'to a giant nerve' (I. 164–76). He is conceived physically, as a great power. 'Snuff'd' suggests something very physical and perhaps not too intelligent. Yet his giant glory is magnificent:

> His palace bright
> Bastion'd with pyramids of glowing gold,
> And touch'd with shade of bronzed obelisks,

> Glar'd a blood-red through all its thousand courts,
> Arches, and domes, and fiery galleries;
> And all its curtains of Aurorian clouds
> Flush'd angerly.   (I. 176)

This is his palace, the molten language again fusing the architectural and fiery-natural into one human and cosmic blaze. And this is himself:

> He enter'd, but he enter'd full of wrath;
> His flaming robes stream'd out beyond his heels,
> And gave a roar, as if of earthly fire,
> That scar'd away the meek ethereal Hours
> And made their dove-wings tremble. On he flared,
> From stately nave to nave, from vault to vault,
> Through bowers of fragrant and enwreathed light,
> And diamond-paved lustrous long arcades,
> Until he reach'd the great main cupola;
> There standing fierce beneath, he stamped his foot,
> And from the basements deep to the high towers
> Jarr'd his own golden region.   (I. 213)

Notice the fusion of light with both vegetable nature and architecture. Hyperion's anger concerns man's loss of piety towards him as central to those cosmic and natural significances that so continually give rise to ritualistic tonings in Keats's own poetry. When he desired the 'spicy wreaths of incense, breath'd aloft from sacred hills' he tasted instead 'savour of poisonous brass and metal sick' (I. 186–9): the savour of man's metallic, mechanical, mentalized existence,' and thence impiety. The conception of Hyperion is magnificent, and the human-natural fusion one of sublime poetic force, the sun becoming man without ceasing to be fire. This grandeur it is which the tragedy of Saturn's fall negates, though of course the poetry there is at work to re-realize significance in the very description of its loss, or it would not be poetry at all. Now Hyperion's grandeur is powerfully maintained. He impatiently rushes to his orient garage to get out his sun-chariot before its time:

> The planet orb of fire, whereon he rode
> Each day from east to west the heavens through,
> Spun round in sable curtaining of clouds;
> Not therefore veiled quite, blindfold, and hid,
> But ever and anon the glancing spheres,
> Circles, and arcs, and broad-belting colure,
> Glow'd through, and wrought upon the muffling dark
> Sweet-shaped lightnings from the nadir deep
> Up to the zenith . . .   (1. 269)

Here the circular-geometrical intuition finds natural place.
Indeed, all primary essences, of vegetable nature, light
and fire, architecture, the geometrical, a cosmic chariot,
the human and the divine, contribute to realization of
Hyperion. The orb raises its wings in salute, but it may
not disturb the 'sacred seasons' by starting too soon.
Coelus, a background deity (= sky) beyond all conflicts,
mothers the angry Hyperion in an important speech.
She calls him 'son of mysteries' and attributes to him all
creative glory. Though gods and men are both plunged
in evil,

> Yet do thou strive; as thou art capable,
> As thou can'st move about, an evident God;
> And can'st oppose to each malignant hour
> Ethereal presence . . .   (1. 337)

She is only 'winds and tides': i.e. the apparently inanimate
nature. He is to be in the 'van of circumstance'. She
sends him back to comfort the gods, to be an eternal comfort, a rainbow promise, as it were, to gods and men.
When he approaches their fallen state his own glory is
still 'undisgraced' (11. 344). He is *the sun as we know it*,
keeping alive man's faith in cosmic vitality. Yet his very
'brilliance' causes the fallen gods (or men) to see and know
their own misery more clearly (11. 369–70).

Hyperion cannot fall because in man's experience the
sun has never been dethroned. The symbolic projection is
so powerful—yet withal so concrete, even human (e.g. his
'numidian curl' at 11. 371)—that the vividly spiritualized

conception of Apollo is not of sufficient strength to over-throw his more purely physical and cosmic impact. The old problem of Milton's Satan is repeated; and with Apollo, in spite of a host of differences, taking the place of Milton's Christ. Both Satan and Hyperion incorporate power-thrusts that an idealized and spiritualized human-ism only very rarely masters, as in Coleridge's *Zapolya* and Nietzsche's *Zarathustra*. The problem is ultimate and ubiquitous. Keats's failure to finish the poem is therefore understandable.

In Book III of the first version the interest transfers to Apollo but only as 'father of all verse' (III. 13): the re-deemer who is, through poetry, to reveal and reinstate the vitality of man-nature. He is actually contrasted with the 'giant of the sun' (III. 29) and drawn as a very human poet, lonely and passionately ill at ease. In Clymene's intro-ductory speech his magic is associated with a 'living death' and 'joy and grief at once' (II. 281, 289), the bitter-sweet that is Keats's own continual experience. He is later (III. 7–21) introduced by an invocation to all that is most beautiful in nature including 'faint-lipp'd shells' and their 'vermilion labyrinths', the first phrase referring to the music through which the shell becomes a natural symbol of inanimate life. A shell is also used by Clymene as a musical instrument; and Keats has a separate short poem on receiving a shell-gift himself. Mnemosyne, an awe-inspiring person rather like Demogorgon, symbolizes that remembrance which Keats and other poets feel within highest intuition. Apollo is therefore nostalgic like 'one who once had wings' in Platonic phrase, now 'curs'd and thwarted' (III. 91–2). Stars, sun, and moon madden him with a baffling glory, just as Hyperion's enigmatic royalty succeeds in maddening the structure of our poem:

> Point me out the way
> To any one particular beauteous star,
> And I will flit into it with my lyre,
> And make its silvery splendour pant with bliss.
>
> (III. 99)

We may remember Shelley's 'panting' meteor. 'Where is power?' asks the poet, more pregnantly—in view of the whole poem's troubled pattern—than a hasty judgement might note. The verse keys up to an excruciating and almost Shelleyan intensity of fervour as Apollo changes before our eyes:

> Knowledge enormous makes a god of me . . .
>
> (III. 113)

The knowledge is poetic and Shakespearian, involving historic grandeurs in martial progress, legends and agonies, the continual interplay of creation and destruction, the inward mechanisms of history. Intoxicating elixirs render him now 'immortal'. The goddess holds up her hands, dominating, compelling, willing the new birth, splitting and distending the mind towards comprehension. It is a 'death' struggle, or rather a move from 'pale immortal death' to some new unspeakable life (III. 120–30). Apollo's final shriek preludes the full consciousness we are not shown.

The poet is clearly in some indecision, for in the revised version he practically admits the equation of Apollo with himself as poet, Moneta replacing Mnemosyne. The interest, however, is darker and mainly concerned with death. Of course, the opposition of Hyperion and Saturn concerned life and death, since many death-horrors can be associated with failure to recognize a breathing sun-kissed life in, say, earth and stone, or fiery excitement in a skull. But an initiation into the supreme mystery is here dramatized from a less pantheistic, more tragic, inward and spiritual, angle. · A dream-structure (the poem is now called a dream) is prepared. The poet stands in a wood, with fountains and flowers. It is an earthly paradise in the usual tradition. There are 'floral censers' and a typically Keatsian 'wreathed doorway'; also a feast on the moss. He eats and drinks, falls under the 'domineering potion' into a 'cloudy swoon', and next finds himself in a temple:

I look'd around upon the carved sides
Of an old sanctuary with roof august,
Builded so high, it seem'd that filmed clouds
Might spread beneath, as o'er the stars of heaven;
So old the place was, I remember'd none
The like upon the Earth: what I had seen
Of grey cathedrals, buttress'd walls, rent towers,
The superannuations of sunk realms,
Of Nature's rocks toil'd hard in waves and winds,
Seem'd but the faulture of decrepit things
To that eternal domed Monument.
(Revised Version, I. 61)

A new variation on our *Kubla Khan* dome-temple. Notice
that the poet has moved from a nature-paradise (Coleridge's 'fertile ground', 'incense-bearing' trees, and fountains) to a domed temple. This temple is, like Coleridge's
dome, eternity, here felt more darkly through associations
of ruins such as you find in Wordsworth's 'Druid' passage
and often in Shelley (cp. also *The Duchess of Malfi* and the
conclusion to Hardy's *Tess*). There are sacred and ritualistic objects: robes, golden toys, censer, holy jewelleries.
The architecture is given further cloudy description:

The embossed roof, the silent massy range
Of columns north and south, ending in mist
Of nothing, then to eastward, where black gates
Were shut against the sunrise evermore.   (I. 83)

Mr. Middleton Murry has well noticed the significant
facing west of this temple of tragic intuition. Hyperion's
fire forgotten, the poet is now to penetrate this place of
ghostly architecture and dim religious significance. From
the dark loom altar and shrine and a 'lofty sacrificial fire'
with 'Maian incense'.

Though the tragic tonings are different, the experience
of Apollo is repeated. Apollo has to 'die into life', and the
poet here suffers a 'palsied chill'; he, like Apollo, shrieks.
The 'cold' grows 'stifling': it is the death-horror. His foot
is 'iced'. But now, as his foot touches the lowest altar-stair
(we may compare Eliot's use of stairs in *Ash Wednesday*),

life pours in 'at the toes' (1. 121–34). Moneta, the new presiding goddess, is a 'Holy Power'. Mr. D. G. James has acutely observed that both Mnemosyne and Moneta appear as *maternal* figures, which is natural in this more Wordsworthian mode of religious solemnity. Moneta relates the poet's presence at this inner shrine directly to his poetic and human sympathies, his emotional reserves of *agapé* rather than *eros*. Only they 'usurp this height'

> . . . to whom the miseries of the world
> Are misery, and will not let them rest.   (1. 148)

It is, we may observe, a 'height', however darkly toned: it is Keats's variation on Shelley's skyey 'Temple of the Spirit' and Coleridge's dome. There follows a discussion of the comparative value of poetry and action like that in Yeats's *Ego Dominus Tuus*. The antithesis of poet and dreamer that succeeds is complex, and rendered additionally so by the high place anyway accorded sleep and dream in Keats's poetic system, which always plays on the border territory between sleeping and waking life. Moneta becomes a symbol of the tragic mystery. Her 'immortal' voice sounds with something of a 'mother's' softness. She removes her veil:

> Then saw I a wan face,
> Not pin'd by human sorrows, but bright-blanch'd
> By an immortal sickness which kills not;
> It works a constant change, which happy death
> Can put no end to; deathwards progressing
> To no death was that visage; it had past
> The lilly and the snow. . . .   (1. 256)

This Mr. Middleton Murry has already discussed. Here we may note further how it blends brightness and darkness, motion and changelessness, in a fashion peculiarly Keatsian: it is the synthesis, the resolving dimension of eternity given human, here maternal, presentment. The balance is, however, heavily weighted on the side of gloom. Moneta's eyes are strikingly described, visionless of 'external things', seeing inward into the depths of human personality. The blindness of Shirin in my own (un-published) novel, *The Shadow of God*, is directly analogous. The poet too sees *inside* her mind:

> . . . for the scenes
> Still swooning vivid through my globed brain,
> With an ,electral changing misery,
> Thou shalt with these dull mortal eyes behold,
> Free from all pain, if wonder pain thee not.
>
> (1. 244)

'Globed brain': the strong physical impact is maintained even in this scene of cloudy mystery and inward sight. Elsewhere (276) it is a 'hollow brain', holding suggestion of a skull. Throughout, the emphasis on the temple, its altar and steps, incense and sacrifice, load the incident with ritualistic solemnity. And henceforth the poet gains god-like sight:

> . . . there grew
> A power within me of enormous ken
> To see as a god sees, and *take the depth*
> *Of things* as nimbly as the outward eye
> Can size and shape pervade.   (1. 302)

'Enormous' echoes 'knowledge enormous makes a god of me' from the first *Hyperion*. Now our present passage is intended to prelude the main narrative: so we see how precisely the story of Saturn, Hyperion, and Apollo is presented as a symbolic interpretation of deepest issues; an attempt to see into the extra vertical dimension of experience, whether as depth or height—the difference is, very nearly, that of Keats and Shelley.

Next we may glance shortly at *Otho the Great*, itself an attempt at the glamorous dramatic poetry hinted by Apollo's vision, but which ranks, I think, slightly below the plays of Keats's contemporaries. It was written at an early age: but so were *The Borderers* and *Remorse*. It lacks, as a whole, subtlety of conception, metaphysical weight, and symbolic counter-checks. However, the story is overlaid with magnificent passages and rises to a remarkable projection of erotic anguish. The settings are especially rich

U

in feasting, music, and display, and the poetry large and broad in movement and happy in description of riches barbarically imagined. One is often reminded of *Antony and Cleopatra* and Coleridge's *Zapolya*. Many poetic units beat with a sweet and strong humanism of highest significance. Prince Ludolph is the 'younger sceptre to the realm', his youth spoken of as 'thy virgin crownet's golden buds' (II. i. 27–8). He speaks out 'large as a God' (II. i. 134). 'Large' is appropriate to the magnificent phrases. He and his lady are 'fair children, stars of a new age' (III. ii. 22), like Shakespeare's later young lovers and Coleridge's Andreas. They are to play with the earth as a 'little ball' (III. ii. 24). Ludolph speaks:

> Though heaven's choir
> Should in a vast circumference descend
> And sing for my delight, I'd stop my ears!
> Though bright Apollo's car stood burning here,
> And he put out an arm to bid me mount,
> His touch an immortality, not I!
> This earth, this palace, this room, Auranthe!
>
> (III. ii. 38)

Notice the geometrical intuition, and the use of 'car'.

His love threatened, he becomes a figure of tyrannic extravagance. At this moment power and its barbaric concomitant of pain-infliction are vivid, and a strong *physical* impact emphatic:

> Tremble! for, at my nod, the sharpen'd axe
> Will make thy bold tongue quiver to the roots . . .
>
> (III. ii. 86)

and

> O that that dull cowl
> Were some most sensitive portion of thy life,
> That I might give it to my hounds to tear!
> Thy girdle some fine zealous-pained nerve
> To girth my saddle! (III. ii. 92)

These are aspects, but important ones, of the joy felt in human physique elsewhere which finely notices Ludolph's 'yeasting youth', turbulent in passion, but soon again as 'crystal'; the description exactly reflecting Coleridge's of Andreas and Shakespeare's of his 'princely' boys in *Cymbeline*. Thus 'a young man's heart' is a world of new possibilities (III. ii. 178–82). Agony, however, wrings from his 'brow' a 'wrathful dew' (III. ii. 221). Perhaps the two directions of love-ecstasy and power, both physically, the one almost sadistically, toned, meet in Auranthe's fine apostrophe to the crown she expects:

> O, thou golden Crown,
> Orbing along the serene firmament
> Of a wide empire, like a glowing moon . . .

See the circular emphasis. The sceptre is a 'fair Hesperian tree', with wondrous fruit, all 'godlike' and 'magic': the metallic and vegetable intermix. So her common hand is to be 'imperial' (IV. i. 78–87). The phrases may be compared to Coleridge's and Wordsworth's more metaphoric, spiritualized, use of human sovereignty. Poetically the contact is close, though Keats is here avoiding, as does Marlowe, such extensions. Yet he is more fecund than Marlowe, with, typically, some fine imagery of 'autumn's sun' and 'ripening harvests' (IV. i. 166), a 'sheafed harvest of ripe bliss', and much Bacchanalian exuberance in terms of 'pulpy wine presses' (v. v. 117–25). The concluding scene, set in a brilliant interior, recalls *Lamia*. Ludolph has experienced, like Lycius and Troilus, the falsity of his love-paradise. The agony is again physically projected:

> She stings me through!—
> Even as the worm doth feed upon the nut,
> So she, a scorpion, preys upon my brain!
> I feel her gnawing here! Let her but vanish,
> Then, father, I will lead your legions forth,
> Compact in steeled squares, and speared files,
> And bid our trumpets speak a fell rebuke
> To nations drows'd in peace! (v. v. 155)

Exactly like Troilus, he feels warrior-strength, as, too, do Tennyson (in *Maud*) and Coleridge (in *Remorse*), as fresh air after spiritual torture. Throughout poetry these two, the love and power impulses, are subtly *balanced*: it is, pretty nearly, the opposition of Apollo and Hyperion. Their unity would be an ultimate strength. This play dramatizes a love-agony, a dissolving, too, of an especially *palatial* bliss, as in *Lamia*, Ludolph aspiring to some even 'wider-domed' magnificence, with hangings of rich clouds 'slung from the spheres', and 'gauzes of silver mist'—a beautiful fusion of cosmic nature and interior decoration (v. v. 31–9). But, in so far as we feel the whole as pointing towards a more comprehensive statement such as Coleridge's *Zapolya* (where the two elements are blended), we may conclude by Otho's noble sense of his own kingly gentleness and integrity:

> And thus a marble column do I build
> To prop my empire's dome.   (I. ii. 160)

For

> I know how the great *basement* of all power
> Is frankness, and a true tongue to the world . . .
> (I. ii. 175)

Which hints at what greater works Keats might have written had he lived.

III

The odes are richly mature expressions and condensations of the main essences hitherto observed. Their profundity is the more valuable in that it matures directly from Keats's early voluptuousness. Poetic sensuousness becomes a perfect medium for spiritual transmission.

The *Ode on a Grecian Urn* explores that eternity intrinsic to art, a smooth circularity and 'quietness' enclosing wild action and fierce desires of 'mad pursuit', 'struggle to escape', 'wild ecstasy', to make a miniature of human life, with its desires and conflicts. These are captured in a frozen activity: the youth always about to kiss, the maiden never fading, with nature sharing in this artistic immortality in enjoyment of eternal spring. The ode concentrates on and expands that recurring tendency in Keats to

image a poised form, a stillness suggesting motion, what
might be called a 'tiptoe' effect. So the urn pipes inward
and spiritual music in terms of a fusion of stillness and
motion. This somehow explores the 'depth of things', to
recall a phrase from *Hyperion*, since the essence of love and
indeed all action and life is desire, a projection not sharing
the negation of satisfaction, the 'cloyed' and 'sorrowful'
heart, the physical anguish. The main business of all art
is precisely such a union of time and space as you have
here: whether in using the spatial as rough material for
vital, and therefore temporal, significance, as in architecture or sculpture; or in building a time-sequence of words
or sounds into an architectural unity. We are again reminded of the river and dome in *Kubla Khan*, and indeed
the choice of an urn with its smooth surface and circular
form is not fortuitous: urns, like cars, are favourites of
Keats from the start. Temporal and nature suggestion
(in the various actions, 'leaf-fring'd legend', 'boughs',
'trodden weed') is subdued within the one still, dome-like
harmony, which here breathes a life 'above' all 'human
passion', corresponding to the sublimated icy-sunshine of
Coleridge's paradox-resolving palace. This blends into
the other fusion of man and nature so exquisitely realized
in all Keats's handling of Greek myth, here recurring in
'Tempe' and 'Arcady' delicately placed. Pagan piety
again crowns these with 'sacrifice', 'green altar', and the
heifer's 'silken flanks', ritual tonings being strong in all
the odes. When the 'little town' is pitied for its consequent emptiness, an inevitable disparity between art and
life is hinted; that difficulty in fitting the human form to
the circle in Dante which causes the child's mockery in
Shelley. The problems involved 'tease us out of thought'
like 'eternity': indeed they are problems expressly of
eternity. In *Endymion* (III. 1–43) 'majestic' powers, set,
as in *Kubla Khan*, above 'Fate', the 'abysm-birth' of
elements and 'feud' of 'nothing' and 'creation', are *'silent
as a consecrated urn'*. So, though it be a 'cold pastoral'—
the ode itself is far more philosophical, and in that sense

colder, than the others—it remains a 'friend to man', speaking, like all great art, like *Paradise Lost* or *Hamlet*, the same spirit-tones to generation after generation, a basic language of which individuals themselves are only transitory expressions. There is sweetness and bitterness in the conception. But to each generation it utters one assurance perhaps not to be grasped until the mind is teased *out* of thought into some wider comprehension: that the fusion of the spatial and temporal which conditions what we call 'beauty' is a penetration of essential being and therefore identical with 'truth'.

Elsewhere, the resolution is less philosophical. But before advancing to the more velvet textures of *Melancholy* and the *Nightingale* we may glance at the *Ode on Indolence*, whose geometrical propensities draw it close to the *Grecian Urn*. 'Drowsy' and 'blissful' summery indolence is set against values of love, ambition (=power), and (fusing these) poetry. This indolence is a compact symbolization of that stream of swoon and sleep that all but dominates Keats's work. It is here a happy satiety leading the sense beyond all but 'nothingness': observe the continuity of sense-fulfilment and unconsciousness. So 'drowsy noons' (a typically precise exploitation of vowels) and evenings of 'honey'd indolence' are welcomed. Sleep is 'embroidered with dim dreams', the soul a 'lawn' of flowers and shadows. The spiritual is naturalistically weighty. There is a 'budding warmth'. A psychological or spiritual growth is symbolized; and, as in our last ode, the setting is an 'urn'. Here its circularity is more emphatic and the allegorical figures pass and re-form to its slow revolving movement. A soft harmonious unity is induced by this as well as by the rich vowellings and unity-suggestion of the peaceful and unperturbed state of being it describes. Nature, human forms, and a circular art-form all interrelate. Passivity encloses images of passion, action, and, finally, poetry itself.

The *Ode on Melancholy* celebrates an acceptance of sorrow. All Lethean anodynes or poisons are rejected as means to alleviate the 'pale forehead' of agony; yet the 'wolf's-bane' and its 'poisonous wine', 'night-shade', the 'beetle', 'death-moth', and 'downy owl' weave a softly dark embroidery of word-music to tone with the melancholy that yet puts them aside, not allowing them entry to the sacred 'mysteries' of 'sorrow'. For their alleviation would come 'too drowsily' and 'drown' the 'wakeful anguish'. It is the Shakespearian thought, 'ripeness is all': death must not be *prematurely* sought. The argument is the more keen if we remember the positive good, to Keats, of drowsy potions, of sleep and death. Some organic value thus inheres in *conscious* suffering. Melancholy falls as a cloud both fertilizing and 'fostering' flowers and hiding greenery in a 'shroud': both aspects are necessary. Deep inward experience is neatly given appropriate naturalistic expression. So feed sorrow rather on nature's sweets—the rose, sea-shore rainbow, 'globed peonies'; hold your mistress's hand—she is, perhaps, a symbol of earthly destiny widely understood—when she is most cruel, feeding deep on her 'peerless eyes'. The intimate relation and organic interdependence of beauty to sorrow, as in the Indian Girl's song, is to be accepted. A lovely 'tiptoe' phrase follows of

> . . . Joy whose hand is ever at his lips
> Bidding adieu . . .

Pleasure becomes 'poison', is one with poison as poison so often is all but pleasure. A beyond-human realization is shadowed, and we end with one of Keats's finest temple-images. In the 'very temple of Delight' stands 'Melancholy', like Moneta, veiled, in her own 'sovran shrine', existing at the heart of pleasure. Yet only he whose sensuous richness can 'burst Joy's grape against his palate fine' will see her there; only he attain honour among her 'cloudy trophies' (cp. 'huge cloudy symbols of a high romance' elsewhere). A 'strenuous' voluptuousness— and how that one adjective spans a universe of important reservations and inclusions—almost becomes one with tragic insight. The poem moves from a dark, death-impregnated nature (Coleridge's caverns and 'sunless sea') and mythology through beautiful nature and human love to an architectural conclusion, following Coleridge's nature-lady-dome pattern, with 'temple of delight' to balance 'pleasure-dome'. All interweaves, and the move to temple-imagery is organic.

In his *Ode to a Nightingale* Keats has found a perfect poetic occasion for poetic release of all his baffling identities of joy with pain, darkness and beauty, nature and spiritual experience. It starts with the usual aching excess of happiness and frustration associated with 'drowsy numbness', 'hemlock', 'opiate', and 'Lethe', followed by an invocation to Bacchic delights in an earthy setting of pagan dance and mythology and Mediterranean sunshine, which in turn gives place, as did the Bacchus description in *Endymion*, to the melancholy of tragic realism. The troubles are those most insistent in Keats: fever, palsy, paleness, thinness, age, the only obvious omission being that of cold. Next poetry is chosen as the transporting medium. The progress from opiates through pagan ecstasies to a sense of tragic reality and thence to poetry as the final choice has a significant precision. Poetry is to waft him to the world of the nightingale's music. He is in a dark forest. Though the night is 'tender' and the queen moon shines with her starry realm, no light penetrates to these 'verdurous glooms and winding mossy ways': he is, as it were, utterly buried, inserted into, one with, the mazy forest-darkness. All summer's wine and murmurous music is, however, implicit, as a child in the womb, among the invisible scents of this dark, leafy luxuriance. Darkness and odours realize a fusion of mind with song that no visual image could quite accomplish. This forest setting, as so often in Shelley, replaces architectural symbols: we have no dome but that of the lighted, though obscured, heavens ('Queen-Moon', 'throne', 'starry Fays'), and the thick forest, which is at once roof and opacity. The 'winding mossy ways' may very distantly suggest the labyrinths of life in general, as with Coleridge. The divine reality is, however, here not visual, but rather in the nightingale's music; which, with the summer scents, shows an approach discarding emphasis on visual projection. Earthy naturalism is delicately countered by religious suggestions in the 'incense' of boughs and the 'requiem' and 'anthem' of the song. Moreover, the poet is 'embalmed': it is a kind of death. So next death itself is invoked as the final hope, called 'easeful', 'soft', and 'rich' at this supreme moment. Though he himself become a 'sod', that which makes him desire death is immortal. The bird is itself no death-symbol. Its voice persists, like that of the Grecian Urn, from generation to generation, expressing the undying life and darkly-sweet mystery of our universe: even if it, as a bird, dies, its instinctive music lives on. So Ruth, symbol of nostalgic and frustrated human individuality, listens to it one day, Keats the next: it is the same bird, as perhaps he the same person. The ultimate nature of human personality is involved, the darkest mysteries of its furthest adventures in question. The bird is therefore as a 'magic casement' in the 'forlorn', nostalgic, fairyland of the poet's consciousness, showing glimpse of 'perilous seas' beyond, yet 'charming' those seas of death as Ariel's music charms the 'wild waves' in *The Tempest*. And now the death is accomplished: the poet is 'tolled' back by his own mournful music to *self*-consciousness. The bird is gone, over darkened meadow, stream, hill-side, and is again deep 'buried' in a new glade. Characteristically, the ode ends on the question whether all this be 'vision' or 'waking dream'; does he 'wake or sleep'? But that cannot be answered until we know what sleep is, why it so nurtures Keats's early and mature work alike; and when we know that, we may know too what is death. For this poem blends burial with life, darkness with richest summer scents and song. It is rich with intoxicating draughts of a hitherto unknown liquor as knowledge of some compact yet unrecognized unity wrings out this passionate yet assured music. In his later work Keats writes as a priest-like celebrant of the mystery, unhurrying and unperturbed.

There is a fertility and ripeness in his poetry, whether in his nature impressionism or imaginative probings into human destiny, which gives his *Ode to Autumn* something of an inevitable place among his crowning works. It is notable for subtle, and new, consonant-use. The clustering *s*-sounds increase sense of an almost drowsy fertility reaching its climax in

> Thou watchest the last oozings, hours by hours.

There is the usual vowel play, especially where slumberous feeling is induced: 'drows'd with the fume of poppies'. But there is an opposite, countering, employ of short syllables, especially in the last stanza: 'wailful choir', 'light wind', 'hilly', 'twitter'. The ode moves from a certain sticky interplay of sibilants and rich vowels to a queer thin music where one can delicately feel a suggestion of fertility and ripeness on the edge of dissolution. Keats's general tendency from the sensuous to the sleepy and spiritual with no conflict is therefore repeated. The first stanza is heavily weighted with natural richness. The second begins to drowse with a remarkable instance of Keats's gift of fluid personification in the human embodiment of Autumn and a fine 'tiptoe' effect in his 'lifted' hair and hook sparing 'the next swath', wherein we can, if we like, feel a tragic pathos further continued in the remorseless god-like figure squeezing every drop of fertility from his own creation. You may, that is, feel a human reference, with suffering as a creative process. Reference of the seasons to human life is the subject of one of Keats's best sonnets, and elsewhere he considers a man who cannot face mortal destiny with acceptance as a 'ripe plum' spoiling its own bloom. Thought of death is unobtrusively present in the bare stubble and sunset of the last stanza. But the 'soft-dying day' has its own beauty. The gnats may 'mourn' in 'wailful choir', but they contribute to a music sweet as spring's. The issue is uncertain as the

wind that 'lives or dies' by turns. Now the last four lines
begin to swell with new promise in 'full-grown lambs'
bleating loud, crickets singing, the robin whistling; and
when the music thins again in the masterly reserve of the
final line, we may feel in the swallows preparing for their
departure a distant, yet distinct, reference to tragic destiny.
For, if the new lambs suggest a seasonal continuance
within the natural order, as symbols of rebirth, the swallows
'in the skies' may hint some other mysterious migration
(the very word 'twitter' has been applied to spirits) within
the dimension of eternity, though Keats here attempts
no precise definition. The ode is notable for its ability to
suggest to the deeps of a sensitive contemplation far more
than it says. The word 'soft', always a favourite, occurs
three times. The poem is itself soft-voiced: in place of
Keats's usual 'full-throated ease' it offers a breathless
placidity.

There is, however, one ode where a more positive
loveliness challenges both the luxurious glooms of
Melancholy and the *Nightingale* and the *sub specie
aeternitatis* insight of the *Grecian Urn* and *Autumn*. This
is the *Ode to Psyche*: the only one on which, he tells us,
Keats took 'even moderate pains'. He knows, and poetically enjoys, the picturesque sex horror of *Lamia* and *Otho
the Great* and the Circean death-in-love of *La Belle Dame
sans Merci*. But against such icy transmutation and
'palely loitering' reminiscence we may set the 'rosy sanctuary' and 'warm love', like that of Porphyry and Madeline, celebrated in *Psyche*. First we have the usual softness,
dreaminess, faintness, under a 'whisp'ring roof' of leaves,
developing to a luscious and colourful nature-description,
and then a lovely 'tiptoe' presentation of Cupid and
Psyche together:

> They lay calm-breathing on the bedded grass;
>   Their arms embraced, and their pinions too;
>   Their lips touch'd not, but had not bade adieu,
> As if disjointed by soft-handed slumber.

The sleep half-parting them is seen also as half-joining

them. The image treads the borderland of waking and sleep, of individual consciousness and love. The poet now hymns Psyche's praise:

> Fairer than Phoebe's sapphire-region'd star,
> Or Vesper, amorous glow-worm of the sky.

Heavenly bodies are never, to Keats, facile cosmic symbols: here one is close-defined by mythological personification and a realised setting, the other earth-related. They are felt as bodily, almost breathing, organisms. Now Psyche has no temple, no altar, like those. That is, the soul of human love has not received the imaginative and religious recognition accorded nature and the heavenly bodies. The implications concern pagan religion. But a modern statement might read: the revelations of *dark instinctive desire* have not been allowed to challenge the sense-world and intellectual schemes of our culture. Cupid and Psyche are shown *asleep*. Moreover Cupid is the God of Love, and we watch, not precisely human lovers, but the love-affair of *love itself*, what Patmore meant by the 'unknown Eros'. Our next stanzas celebrate the holiness not merely of love, but rather of that inmost physical-magical potentiality prompting all daylight wisdom:

> O brightest! though too late for antique vows,
> Too, too late for the fond believing lyre,
> When holy were the haunted forest boughs,
> Holy the air, the water, and the fire;
> Yet even in these days so far retir'd
> From happy pieties, thy lucent fans,
> Fluttering among the faint Olympians,
> I see, and sing, by my own eyes inspir'd.
> So let me be thy choir, and make a moan
> Upon the midnight hours;
> Thy voice, thy lute, thy pipe, thy incense sweet
> From swinged censer teeming;
> Thy shrine, thy grove, thy oracle, thy heat
> Of pale-mouth'd prophet dreaming.

Notice the precise formulation in terms of ancient belief of that association so pressing in Shelley and Keats of temples or domes with forests. This marks the culmination of Keats's ritual impressionisms. See how in expression of sacramental nature there is a sense of accomplishment, none of impatience; how the truth exposed or asserted yet finds room for all modern scepticism in the use of 'antique' and 'fond'. 'My own eyes' suggests a personal, inward, authority and assurance beyond sense-images, asserting the sacredness of instinct. 'Happy pieties' and 'lucent fans' accompany this vision more human, realistic and warm than those we have been discussing; yet complex dark associations are channelled in the usual fashion by 'haunted' and 'moan'. The celebration is to be not communal but personal:

> Yes, I will be thy priest and build a fane
> In some untrodden region of the mind,
> Where branched thoughts, new grown with pleasant pain,
> Instead of pines shall murmur in the wind.

The recurring 'temple' image becomes one with both the psychological and natural order. The fane is, we may suggest, the dome of man's consciousness, and yet more too. Certainly Keats is both celebrating the sacramental in nature, something found likewise in Shakespeare's last plays (e.g. 'chaliced flowers' in *Cymbeline*) and aiming to form creatively, as it were, a new structure of the mind. This is what all ritual intends, and hence the strongly ritualistic tone of most high poetry and drama and Keats's imagery in particular. But the process is both personal and natural. The temple is to be secluded, associated both with moss, as in *Hyperion* and the somewhat different hermit passages of Coleridge and Shelley, and sleeping Dryads, again emphasizing the sleep with which the vision started, and relating sleep to the unconscious life of nature. There is no facile optimism. The new structure is built with pain, yet that very pain is the pain of organic growth: hence 'branched thoughts, new grown with pleasant pain', the bitter-sweet of happy things and the velvet gloss of tragic things. The fane, like Coleridge's dome, is, indeed, poetry itself. Poetry is at once the transforming medium and the ritual, the 'rosy sanctuary' to be dressed by 'the wreathing trellis of a working brain', Fancy, the 'gardener', breeding ever-new flowers. Softly the ode steps to its conclusion where 'shadowy thought' welcomes the unknown wooer in darkness with a 'bright torch', a 'casement' not opening from fairyland on perilous seas but awaiting the entrance of a 'warm' love. 'I will be thy priest': the definition is exact. Keats's poetry is priest-like, with the selfless pomp and unperturbed assurance of a celebrant at a Christian Mass. His whole work moves to this point, challenging our limited sense not of the beautiful but of the sacred.

We may end with the Bright Star sonnet, like the *Ode to Psyche* a concentration of his life-work:

> Bright star, would I were steadfast as thou art—
>   Not in lone splendour hung aloft the night
> And watching, with eternal lids apart,
>   Like nature's patient, sleepless Eremite,
> The moving waters at their priestlike task
>   Of pure ablution round earth's human shores,
> Or gazing on the new soft-fallen mask
>   Of snow upon the mountains and the moors—
> No—yet still steadfast, still unchangeable,
>   Pillow'd upon my fair love's ripening breast,
> To feel for ever its soft fall and swell,
>   Awake for ever in a sweet unrest,
> Still, still to hear her tender-taken breath,
> And so live ever—or else swoon to death.

The star is felt as hung from a vast dome-like interior looking down, as other poetic domes, on water and earth. It symbolizes eternity, in so far as that suggests everlasting stillness and wakefulness, playing the part of a cosmic 'eremite' or hermit (remember the use of hermits in relation to love in *Romeo and Juliet*, *Pericles*, *The Ancient Mariner*, and *The Revolt of Islam*) whose office it is to 'watch', like the wakeful Beadsman praying for man's sins in *The Eve of St. Agnes*, while others live their various lives. And what it sees is the everlasting interplay of movement and stillness, liquid and solid. 'Priestlike' and 'ablution' may suggest human death, this carried over into the 'soft-fallen' mask of whiteness. The earth is as a human body, the mountains and moors delicately corresponding to the 'breast' of the poet's love later. What is this ablution? Partly perhaps the continual preparing, revitalizing, of dead earth buoyed up into ever-new and sacred existence by a divine force, water being a holier element to the imagination than rock or stone. The ritual 'task' is deliberate as Keats's poetry. Though cold and heavy with eternal *stillness* above nature, and possessing tonings of death, the octave remains as beautiful a cosmic realization as any in English: it is at once lustrous, physical, and sacred. Within this vastness is set the other changelessness of eternal human passion, with a rising warmth in 'ripening', and favourite words, 'pillowed' and 'soft'. 'Sweet unrest' repeats the sense so continual in Keats of such ultimate paradoxical interdependences. 'Awake', like the star: it is a wakeful sleeping, a living swoon, a life riding on death. The human passion is contrasted, yet one in nature, with the life of star and pulse of ocean: there is the same rhythmic balance in each. The culmination blends all under the conception of everlasting life or swooning death, which in Keats are converging concepts; and only in the consciousness that feels their convergence can the relation of lover and loved to star, ocean, and earth, of human personality to the cosmic vastness, be known. The deathly-sweet grandeur of the universe is balanced against a love that demands its right of full consummation in death: the circle is complete. The octave corresponds to the darker odes, such as the *Nightingale*; the sestet to *Psyche*; and the whole is a richer embodiment of that motion within stillness that builds the more intellectualized eternity of the *Grecian Urn*. It is probably Keats's greatest poem, and perhaps the most marvellous short poem in our language.

306 THE PRIEST-LIKE TASK: AN ESSAY ON KEATS

Keats's world is haunted by sense of the divine: from the start he offers that revelation of the sacred which Shelley reached in *Prometheus*.

His work may seem to be equalled at its best separate movements by only the best of Shakespeare and Pope. But reservations are necessary. He has left no single poetic art-form of a comprehensive social realism. *Otho the Great* holds magnificent Shakespearian promise, but nevertheless lacks the varied and complex tensions of greatest drama. Nor is it all a question of maturity: in *Venus and Adonis* you have a quarrel set going with the universe that argues some tough, revolutionary, indomitable human essence that relates equally to the iron puritanism of Milton and the prophetic enthusiasm of Shelley: both those running poetic risks, and getting the occasional nasty fall, that Keats with uncanny natural wisdom and exclusion avoids. *Isabella* is nearer Webster than Shakespeare, with the same relaxation of an enjoyed horror: horror, not terror. *Macbeth* and *The Ancient Mariner* have intensities closely related to sin, which Keats does not offer; though in *Otho the Great* the crucial *Troilus* experience certainly attains the required energy and impact. However, for many of the most important, because more socially active, Shakespearian essences, we find no poetic parallel in English outside Byron, whose stature has not been properly appreciated. Communal contemporary problems are, of course, involved; which in turn involves the *fact* of traditional Christianity. *Eloisa to Abelard* has a wider sweep than anything in Keats, dramatizing a conflict of erotic versus Christian sanctities of which the later poet comprehends only the one side. Even Keats's nature is limited to his favourite effects, and he is no master of the Shelleyan swiftness. Yet he does things that, after their fashion, not even Shakespeare can rival. If Byron is a lesser Shakespeare in his treatment of human action and its impulses, he remains lesser; and Shelley's Ariel-quality is implicit in much of Shakespeare. But has anyone, before or since, said anything like:

As when, upon a tranced summer-night,
Those green-rob'd senators of mighty woods,
Tall oaks, branch-charmed by the *earnest* stars,
Dream, and so dream all night without a stir . . .
                          (*Hyperion*, 1. 72)

Unless, indeed, the conception is implicit in *A Mid-summer Night's Dream*, as the work of Shelley in that of Ariel.

We must, also, remember Milton's *Nativity Ode*, where a closely similar feeling for pagan ritual and belief joined to a certain buoyancy of rhythm and intimacy of physical approach ('pillows his chin upon the orient wave') points to a more Keatsian development than his stern destiny allowed; just as the rich flavour of the physical impressionism in *Otho the Great* has kinship to the inmost germ-plasm of Shakespeare's power. Despite all limitations Keats touches the centres of both Shakespeare and Milton; and it would perhaps be churlish to deny that, granted a steadily expanding range of interest and experience, he might finally have out-distanced even his greatest predecessors.

X

V

SYMBOLIC ETERNITIES

DANTE relates his various human and theological interests to the circles of Hell, the spiral ascent of Purgatory, and the spheres of Paradise, circularity thus working in transcendence of ethic; while his poem's conclusion re-emphasizes the relation of the human form to a divine 'circling'. Keats's *Grecian Urn* is thus a precise miniature of Dante's poem.

Milton, too, resembles Keats in his rounded nature-perception and fondness for oak-trees, architectural woodland, moon and nightingale, urns and cars. His Messiah rides in a chariot, with which we may compare Beatrice's elaborate chariot-appearance. In Keats the Miltonic solidity attains warmth, but the affinities, most obvious from inspection of the *Nativity Ode*, are striking. In Milton labyrinthine rivers and serpent-symbolism assume importance, together with a labyrinthine technique in verse manipulation, blending into a sculptural and architectural impressionism. He has semi-artificial mountains and spheres. In such terms his subject-matter and technique converge, though natural vitalities suffer from a too forceful eternity-pressure in poetic handling.

Pope's *Windsor Forest* has 'sacred domes' and 'pompous turrets'. His *Temple of Fame* offers a finely *vitalized* architecture. From a 'thundering ocean' of sound rises a 'glorious pile', cloudcapped on an ice-rock shining like 'Parian marble'; a deathless structure 'not reared by mortal hands' and called a 'dome'. Here

> Heroes in animated marble frown,
> And legislators seem to think in stone.

It is strangely light:

> There might you see the length'ning spires ascend,
> The domes swell up, the wid'ning arches bend,

> The growing tow'rs like exhalations rise,
> And the huge columns heave into the skies.

Pope is re-expressing the significant dynamic within a static art. All interweaves with world-history and literary greatness, including Pindar on a 'car of silver' borne by swans. Keats's 'tiptoe' effects are present:

> The youths hang o'er their chariots as they run;
> The fiery steeds seem starting from the stone;
> The champions in distorted postures threat;
> And all appeared irregularly great.

Another noble passage offers a *growing*, flowering, architecture and sculpture (with, on a circle of columns, a 'pompous' and sky-'*invading*' 'dome'), and even involves us in the watcher's 'aching sight', capturing the whole physical drama like Byron's lines on St. Peter's. A Shelleyan 'structure', uncertain whether in earth or air, whirls in 'rapid motion' (like Shelley's revolving orbs), drawing to it all sounds, loud or soft, and this circularity blends into wave-circles of sound out-rippling. The poem's symbolisms are referred to 'eternal' issues. Most of Pope has little to offer, but one startling geometrical-mechanical image sticks out vividly from the first epistle of the *Essay on Man*, the more significant for its solitude:

> So Man, who here seems principal alone,
> Perhaps acts second to some *sphere* unknown,
> Touches some *wheel*, or verges to some goal;
> 'Tis but a part we see, and not a whole.

Pope, however, usually rejects the architectural and mechanical, preferring a more human concentration.

From Byron's human conflicts the symbols normal to his contemporaries often assert themselves. *Manfred* has 'caves of death' and *Sardanapalus* life as a 'labyrinth of mystery'. There is the fine torrent-turbulence in *Childe Harold* (iv. 69–72) where 'infant' waters are 'torn from the *womb* of mountains' and go off in 'many windings' over the plain, with the waterfall itself called 'an eternity' and its colourful Iris-rainbow above 'infernal cauldrons' like Hope above 'a death-bed'. *Childe Harold* has many domes: 'the dome of Thought, the palace of the Soul' at II. 6 being important. St. Peter's, Rome, is nobly addressed:

> But lo! the dome, the vast and wondrous dome . . . (IV, 153)

This, 'Christ's mighty shrine', surpassing St. Sophia, is the 'fit abode' for 'hopes of immortality'. Mystic resolutions are shadowed in the sense-baffling phrase 'musical in its immensities'. It outspaces 'nature's littleness'. Like Pope and Wordsworth in the *Ecclesiastical Sonnets* Byron considers the complex mind-process needed to *build* the one vastness from a series of particular sense-perceptions.

Tennyson's *Palace of Art*, Browning's *Abt Vogler*, O'Shaughnessy's *We are the Music-makers*, and the river-ending to Arnold's *Sohrab and Rustum* are all relevant. Much could be said of Mr. Eliot's use to-day of winding stairs, circular motion and *living* design:

> As a Chinese jar still
> Moves perpetually in its stillness   *(Burnt Norton)*

—also of the geometrical impressionism of Mr. Charles Williams's *Taliessin through Logres*, Miss Dallas Kenmare's sphere-symbol expressive of tranquillity induced by music, and Mr. Francis Berry's dome-conclusion to *Fall of a Tower*.

Yeats's *Sailing to Byzantium* contrasts the 'sensual music' of young love, trees and water-life, all existence, we are told, *within the birth-death enclosure*, with 'monuments of unageing intellect' and artistic wisdom. Having sailed the 'seas' to the 'holy city of Byzantium' he prays sages standing in 'God's holy fire' as in 'the gold mosaic of a wall' to gather him 'into the *artifice* of eternity'. The symbolism is deliberately metallic, almost brittle, and ends by imaging life beyond nature as golden birds (like the miracle-bird in *Zapolya*) singing of past, present, and future to amuse a Byzantine Emperor. This 'emperor' is all but 'God'. In the sister poem, *Byzantium*, Coleridgian reminders cluster:

> A starlit or a moonlit dome disdains
> All that man is,
> All mere complexities,
> The fury and the mire of human veins.

See how the 'haughty dome'—to quote Byron on St. Peter's—rises above man's labyrinthine and passionate confusions, as in *Kubla Khan*. Yeats also glimpses a semi-human shape like the hermaphrodite-seraphs in Coleridge and Shelley, at once 'shade', 'image', and 'man', referred to the unwinding of maze-paths, itself beyond *moisture* and *breath*, a 'superhuman' creature of 'death-in-life' and 'life-in-death'. There are more bird-miracles whose 'glory of changeless metal' is contrasted with 'complexities of mire and blood'. 'God's holy fire' of our other poem is here expanded into the Emperor's flames, whereby you can see how God = Emperor = Kubla Khan, Coleridge's monarch:

> At midnight on the Emperor's pavement flit
> Flames that no faggot feeds, nor steel has lit,
> Nor storm disturbs, flames begotten of flame,
> Where blood-begotten spirits come
> And all complexities of fury leave . . .

They die agonizingly 'into a dance'. The self-generating flames recall the definition of poetry in *Timon of Athens*. When 'spirit after spirit' is seen 'astraddle on the dolphins' mire and blood' we may compare (i) the seraph-forms above dead bodies in *The Ancient Mariner*, and (ii) Shelley's boys riding alligators in *The Witch of Atlas*. The Emperor's 'golden smithies' are said to 'break the flood': that is, annihilate sensual existence. 'Marbles of the dancing floor' now 'break bitter furies of complexity'. The universe is a 'dolphin-torn' and 'gong-tormented' sea. Gong-music suggests eternity-compulsion and relates to the 'great cathedral gong' earlier where its 'resonance' is set between a purified 'night-walker's song' and both 'unpurged images of day' and the Emperor's *drunken* soldiers.

In her fine study *A Servant of the Mightiest* (London, 1927) Mrs. Alfred Wingate describes Kubilai Khan's 'imperial palace' in Peking as a *circular* 'Temple of Heaven' wherein the Emperor as 'Son of Heaven', mediates between God and man (Ch. x). The description, in no sense derivative from Coleridge's poem, underlines my own interpretations.

A good dome-comment occurs in *The Wisdom of God* by Sergius Bulgakov (London, 1937):

> Anyone who has visited the church of St. Sophia in Constantinople and fallen under the spell of that which it reveals, will find himself permanently enriched by a new apprehension of the world in God, that is, of the Divine Sophia. This heavenly dome, which portrays heaven bending to earth to embrace it, gives expression in finite form to the infinite, to an all-embracing unity, to the stillness of eternity, in the form of a work of art which, though belonging to this world, is a miracle of harmony itself. The grace, lightness, simplicity, and wonderful symmetry of the structure account for the fact that the weight of the dome and even of the very walls seems to dissolve completely. An ocean of light pours in from above and dominates the whole space below—it enchants, convinces, as it seems to say: I am in the world and the world is in me. Here Plato is baptized into Christianity, for here, surely, we have that lofty realm of his to which souls ascend for the contemplation of ideas.

Later it is called a 'symbol of eternity', and a 'prophetic symbolism'. Domes are at once prophecy and poetry.

Nevertheless, most of Shakespeare lies outside our present study, his work being peculiarly non-vertical, with comparatively slight emphasis on the sculptural and plastic, though the sonnets provide relevant passages:

> Not marble nor the gilded monuments
> Of princes shall outlive this powerful rhyme . . .

Tomb-monuments occur occasionally in the plays. Such impressions gain in importance in his final period, corresponding to the concept 'eternity': as in the engraved imagery of *Cymbeline*, Prospero's 'cloud-capped towers' and 'solemn temples', and Hermione's *living* statue; and emphasis generally on sacred buildings and religious ritual. Pope, though normally avoiding architectures, concludes his satires with a 'Temple of Eternity' (*Epilogue* ii); and Byron's latest work resembles Shakespeare's in its tendency to plastic, though vital, eternities.

Byron's 'style', in the cruder sense, has not the surface lustre of Milton's or Pope's. It is adequate but undemonstrative. Though behind Shakespeare's in wealth of resource it resembles his in its malleability to the subject in hand. Both trust the main eternalizing to their own inseeing into and display of energies in the co-ordination of an art-form possessing, without claiming, eternal sanction; itself embodying the *interplay of action and structure* which all *Kubla Khan* mechanisms assert. Eternity, though often appearing as a necessary contrast, is properly itself inclusive and dynamic: of this the Shakespearian play is a living witness. The complicated rhythmic geometrics of seventeenth-century metaphysical poetry enweave colloquial realism and suggestion of the speaking voice with a subject-matter and philosophic adventure mainly concerned with the eternity dimension. What is technique in one poet becomes subject-matter in another, but all poetry works for the one fusion. All rhyme-schemes and stanza-forms, all projection of the evanescent intuition into the mould of imagery, indeed language itself, is an eternalizing process. Pope's refusal of the plastic is balanced by his harmonics of couplet-rhyme and lustrous phrase. You can see why the so-called 'romantics' have no surface 'style': that eternity-pressure forcing the Miltonic solidity which Shakespeare, Byron, and the *later* Pope manage only by a superb realization to incorporate without ostentation, is the central subject, through symbolism, of Wordsworth, Coleridge, Shelley, and Keats; though each of those, on occasion, himself shows dramatic mastery.

This rough assortment makes no claim to inclusiveness. In *The Christian Renaissance* I have published the relevant metaphysical speculations. Here I merely aim to show what such poets are writing about. Hitherto these precise and crowning symbolisms (domes corresponding directly to the Crown in the political order and throughout poetry) have been dismissed as fanciful ornamentation, with excessive attention given to the thought in unfair abstraction and the amazing results we have all witnessed whereby the sovereign wisdom of poetry becomes the monopoly of an erring intelligence. From such contradiction no advance is possible. True, these symbols *alone* are of little value either; but only in such reference do the various thought-directions themselves hold meaning. Each poem is a unique whole, with its own way of introducing us afresh to transcendental awareness. We have watched, moreover, various attempts to shape a new structure of the human personality in direct contact with the eternity-dimension. I make here no appeal whatsoever for belief in such higher dimensions of existence, but merely hope to clear the ground for intelligent reading and re-reading. It is the poets', or rather the poems', business to create the necessary experience. That is what poetry is for. But this it cannot do whilst we remain impervious to its method.

APPENDIX

SPIRITUALISM AND POETRY*

WE are at a stage of thought which urges us to reconsider the status of Spiritualism within our culture. The evidence of realities beyond the comprehension of our established schools is overpowering, but there is little awareness of the discrepancy, and nothing is being done to remove it. There are, it is true, some chairs of 'parapsychology'; and there are Professor Rhine's investigations. But the very name 'parapsychology' deflects attention from the real issues; and we can say, in general, that the so-called 'scientific' approach, and the unending demand for what is called 'scientific' evidence, is likely to be fruitless. At the best, it will have merely some ancillary, supporting, value; it cannot do more.

Meanwhile such institutions as the Marylebone Spiritualist Association and the College of Psychic Science in London, and centres elsewhere, in big and little towns, throughout England, Europe, Africa, and America, are busily engaged in positive activities which are, apart from all theory, of great, practical importance. They are in themselves miniature universities; and yet the link with our greater universities is missing.

Is there then no hope? Surely we cannot suppose that. After all, our foremost seats of learning are not merely scientific. Their scientific schools are comparatively new, and the central tradition looks back to theology and literature, to the Bible and the classics of the ancient world. Those are the roots of our culture; and the tradition is based on a mass of imponderables of which twentieth-century science knows nothing.

* Originally published in *Light*, March 1956

Religion in our time has become so highly organized, and its intellectual structure is so rigid, that it shows at present little likelihood of opening itself to the influx of any new acceptances. That may change, but it will not change quickly. My purpose here is to suggest that it is in the other great root of western culture, in poetry and literature, that our best hope lies.

If we attempt to align the revelations of Spiritualism with great literature, we find not merely a possibility of contact, but a remarkable kinship, almost an identity, of purpose. Now literature is today a highly respected element in our educational system. Never has the interest in the works of Shakespeare been so widespread and intense. But, even so, there remains, even here, a barrier; for our schools of learning remain at present very far from a just recognition of the more spiritualistic properties of the works they study. This is a battle which is today being fought in literary and academic circles; and though the issue is not in doubt, and indeed the greater part of the ground already gained, the natural inertia of academic studies makes progress slow.

From the ancient world down, from Homer and Aeschylus to Byron and Hardy, the business of great literature may be defined as the interweaving of human affairs with spiritualistic appearances, phantasms of the dead, portents, resurrections and visitations; or, if these are not present, with symbols of eternal suggestion or atmospheric effects which may be called 'numinous'. Literature reveals a spiritualized universe, and the close study of its implications, which is only beginning, introduces us directly to those realities which are the stock-in-trade of modern Spiritualism.

In *The Birth of Tragedy* Nietzsche defined the essence of the dramatic as the union of what he called the 'Dionysian' and the 'Apollonian'. By the 'Dionysian' he meant the creative energies, or energies deeper even than creation, the 'otherness' behind the veil of manifestation; and by the 'Apollonian' he meant the ideals of the created world, as man knows it. Drama wills to relate these to each other, and at its greatest it fuses them. In great drama the 'Dionysian' element must always be present; it is only in the lesser, more ephemeral, forms that the surfaces are shown as independent of the mysteries.

Let us inspect two examples. One of the most electrifying scenes in all drama is that in Aeschylus' *Agamemnon* where the captive prophetess Cassandra smells out, bit by bit, in a sequence of disjointed but fascinatingly dramatic speeches, the hideous past of the palace to which she has been brought, and next feels into, and prophesies, the impending disaster. This is an instance of what in spiritualistic circles is termed 'psychometry'. The academic student tends to read it as a matter of forgotten superstition; and yet you can take courses in psychometry today.

Again, are not the Ghost-scenes in *Hamlet* among the few most dramatic that have ever been composed? And is not their peculiar impact exactly related to their subject? I am not insisting merely that the great drama of the past preserves records of such beliefs, but rather that what we ourselves today instinctively recognize as the specifically dramatic involves inevitably the specifically spiritualistic. I have given two extreme instances; but wherever great drama exists, Nietzsche's theory will be found, in its degree, true.

Of course, it is not a question only of ghosts and clairvoyances; these have to be interwoven with a realistic reading of human affairs, and all the finest, Apollonian, ideals. We must have both. This is as true today as ever. John Cowper Powys' *A Glastonbury Romance*, probably the greatest imaginative work of our time, derives much of its extraordinary power from its awareness, on page after page, of the deeper and more mysterious forces emanating from nature, from legendary places, and from dimensions beyond human understanding; and yet it is also as realistic a work as was ever written. What might be called its 'uncanny' realism is precisely that just because it is shot through and supported by insight into those greater powers which entwine themselves with man's being, especially his sexual being, to condition and determine the human drama.

But indeed, you find it everywhere; throughout Elizabethan and Jacobean drama, in Milton and the Metaphysical poets, in Pope's *Essay on Man* and the Sylphs of his *Rape of the Lock*, in all the Romantics, in Byron's dramas pre-eminently,* in Tennyson and Browning, in the overwatching chorus of spirits in Hardy's *Dynasts*, in Yeats and Eliot.

All this is, surely, obvious enough. But there is more to say. The very nature of literary composition introduces us to the categories which we are discussing.

Literature, though itself a temporal art, may yet be felt as a blending of the arts of space and time. Painting, sculpture and architecture exist in space; music and poetry in time. But each kind always aspires towards the other. The spatial arts either suggest narrative, or at the least are alive with a significance on the brink of motion; and the temporal arts achieve 'form', or 'structure'. But poetry, though itself temporal, appears to be peculiarly adapted to include, and blend together, the other arts, fusing the visual with the aural, space with time, at every instant. One of its favourite devices is to create ultimate symbols which hold such opposing qualities in a mysterious identity, as in Wordsworth's description of the statue of Newton as

> The marble index of a mind for ever
> Voyaging through strange seas of Thought,
>   alone . . .

(The Prelude, III, 62)

Or in the still forms which yet suggest motion of the figures on Keats' Grecian Urn; or Byron's St. Peter's as 'all musical in its immensities' in *Childe Harold* (IV, 156);

* See my essay 'Shakespeare and Byron's Plays', the *Shakespeare-Jahrbuch*, 1959.

or Shelley's line 'the music of the living grass and air', in *Prometheus Unbound* (iv, iv, 257). From the general mass of the sense-confusing impressions which constitute poetic imagery or symbolism I have elsewhere selected for primary attention two main types of symbol, which I have called: (i) the action-pose, and (ii) musical buildings. These grow from a world of poetic reality which is simultaneously shape and motion, sound and colour. Often a particularly fine poetic stroke will be interpreted by one reader in terms of imagery, or sight, and by another in terms of word-music, or sound. Particular senses are provisional, and we are really being introduced to a super-sensuous, but not at all a non-sensuous, reality, or world; and it is a world which is, though as rich and concrete as any one could wish, yet also, like Coleridge's dome in *Kubla Khan*, a world made by *thought*; in it thought becomes concrete. Or, conversely, the paradox of man may be driven home with Byronic realism and finality in description of a skull as having once been 'the Dome of Thought, the Palace of the Soul' (*Childe Harold*, ii, 6).*

Now what appears to me to be so peculiarly interesting is this. The descriptions of higher planes given by spirit-entities speaking through trance-mediums correspond closely with those qualities which are the essence of poetic composition. I am thinking of certain descriptions by the spirit Ugandi through the mediumship of Mr. Frank Spencer of Manchester, and of others from various spirit-personalities received from Miss Dorothy Perkins of Exeter. The literature of spiritualism is rich in accounts— you find them in Mr. Shaw Desmond's *How You Live When You Die*—of a world where the intangible is concrete and thought creative; where architecture lives, flowers sing, music is colour, and all of them not merely passive experiences, but active powers; in short, the very world announced by art, and in particular by poetry. Spiritualism introduces us to a *poetic world*.

* For a more comprehensive treatment of the subject of this paragraph see my *Laureate of Peace* (1954; iii, 80–91).

Such accounts suggest that our poets have themselves
been, wittingly or not, describing the very same realities
as those of which the spirit personalities tell us. Browning
has a precise statement in his *Epistle containing the strange
medical experience of Karshish the Arab physician*, a poem
on Lazarus troubled, after return to earthly existence, by
recollection of his great adventure:

> He holds on firmly to some thread of life
> (It is the life to lead perforcedly)
> Which runs across some vast distracting orb
> Of glory on either side that meagre thread,
> Which, conscious of, he must not enter yet—
> The spiritual life around the earthly life.

Orbs, domes, urns, wheels: all serve to symbolize the
other dimension. And in spiritualistic accounts of that
dimension, poetic symbolism becomes actual. We find
some interesting correspondences in Mr. Anthony
Borgia's recent book *Life in the World Unseen* (1954),
which claims to have been dictated by the spirit of
Monsignor Robert Hugh Benson.

The descriptions include some rich accounts (i, 65–7;
ii, 107–8) of orchestral music, and as you read you are
vividly aware of the usual semi-identifications of thought,
structures, especially domed structures, music, and
colour. We have a perfect example, even for a straight
'literary' discussion, of what I have called 'musical buildings'. As for the 'action-pose', this too is represented.
When a visitor descends from one of the highest planes,
his appearance is, naturally, hard—I will not say to
'describe'—but hard for this superior being to impress on
the senses of those below; and his first appearance is done
entirely through his being visible for a short while in an
action-pose, with just the lifting of his arms: 'His movements were majestic as he raised his arms and sent forth
a blessing upon us all' (i, 97).

Mr. Borgia's book does not tell us how the messages
were received, and offers nothing to help us to assess their
authenticity. From a scientific, or scholarly, view, it is

inadequate. But how far does this matter? Whatever the evidence produced, should we be scientifically convinced? I shall not deny that one part of my own mind likes such evidence; but I would suggest that this is a comparatively unimportant part. What grips me in Mr. Borgia's book, which contains some fine descriptive writing, is not so very different from what grips me in Dante's *Paradiso*. I accept both on what may be called 'imaginative' grounds; and are there any other on which such accounts can ever be accepted? Does not the imagination, what Shelley in his *Defence of Poetry* called 'that imperial faculty whose throne is curtained within the invisible nature of man', necessarily condition our entrance to these mysteries? We may recall how, when the sceptical Robert de Baudricourt in Shaw's play tried to dismiss Joan's voices by saying that they came not from God but from her own imagination, she replied demurely: 'Yes, squire. That is how the messages of God come to us'. We are finally thrown back on ourselves; unless a bell is rung within the individual, no amount of proof is of any use; and when it is rung, proof is of secondary importance. As Nietzsche's Zarathustra puts it: 'None telleth me news: therefore I tell myself to myself' (*Thus Spake Zarathustra*, III, 56).

Is all our evidence then useless? Surely not. But it has a subsidiary and accumulative, rather than a forcing, value. It can work gradually to dissolve the barrier severing religion and science; it can touch the 'man in the street', and the Sunday press; and it can help us all in our moods of twentieth-century scepticism. But it is no final guide. Whenever the desire for 'proof' overrules the spirit of dispassionate, and open, enquiry, real investigation has stopped; we are, in effect, trying to bend nature to the confines of a thesis. If we ignore everything which is not 'scientifically' proved to be what modern science requires, we shall end up with nothing to study. And we shall soon become blind to the most obvious facts. Modern spiritualism, apart from all theory, produces results, and goes on, daily, producing them; but these results, instead of being analysed, documented, and correlated by trained experts, are utterly ignored, for the simple reason that they offend the scientific intelligence of our time. The Society for Psychical Research, which once studied the phenomena produced by Spiritualism, appears now in danger of studying little but psychical research. Such tendences are, of course, well-known, in all branches of learning. They did much to bring about the fall of Medieval Scholasticism; and you find them today in the study of literature, literary investigation only too easily becoming an art quite divorced from the content of the literature which it is supposed to investigate. Such studies end by merely studying themselves. Nor can we say that, according to Nietzsche's Zarathustra, this is a good thing to do, because the personal element, the imagination, Shelley's 'imperial faculty', Nietzsche's 'myself', is, I will not say absent, but ignored. Even the scientist has, in his non-scientific moments, a non-scientific self, an imaginative faculty; and on this he must surely draw when his science proves inadequate to the object.

We must, too, be on our guard against the purely provisional nature of the concepts used by the scientific investigator. They are, for the most part, concepts which explain nothing. Neither the paradoxical 'unconscious mind' nor the question-begging 'telepathy' *explain* anything; they are merely provisional terms used to designate certain aspects of the mystery. No concrete phenomenon can very well be explained, and certainly never explained away, by the use of an abstract term. If we try to do that, all our equations end with $x=x$. This we knew before; but we have advanced no farther in our understanding of 'x'.

When once the sovereignty of the imagination is recognized, there will be room for all our criticism in vassalage to that sovereignty; but until the drag and inertia of twentieth-century scepticism is shattered, no profitable research can be undertaken. As Pope says, writing of the absurd intellectual *pride* which clouds and befumes man's muddled consciousness:

If once right reason drives that cloud away,
Truth breaks upon us with resistless day.

(An Essay on Criticism, 211)

The truth cannot be proved, but the obstructions of false rationalism can be dispelled. Then whatever elements there may be of either truth or falsity in our phenomena may be expected to reveal themselves. They will need, more than ever, to be studied; but, given their chance, new powers may be expected to sweep in, like a great tide, refreshing our culture. Byron has a word to offer, in *Don Juan*:

> For me, I know nought; nothing I deny,
>   Admit, reject, contemn; and what know *you,*
> Except perhaps that you were born to die?
>   And both may after all turn out untrue.
> An age may come, Font of Eternity,
>   When nothing shall be either old or new.
> Death, so call'd, is a thing which makes men weep,
> And yet a third of life is pass'd in sleep.

(xiv, 3)

'Both', meaning both terminals of life as we know it, is here an important word. He thinks that

> 'Tis time that some new prophet should appear,
> Or old indulge man with a second sight.

(xv, 90)

That is what lies before us. It is the business of both Spiritualism and Poetry to assist our advance; together they might remove the obstructions at present barring our established schools from so many of the most fascinating mysteries which interpenetrate our life; and it is hard to see what other lines of action and enquiry could prove adequate to such a task.

v

INDEX